C000126594

Pope Pius I

Our Lady of Lourdes

The history of the miraculous sanctuary of our Lady of Lourdes

Pope Pius IX.

Our Lady of Lourdes
The history of the miraculous sanctuary of our Lady of Lourdes

ISBN/EAN: 9783741164057

Manufactured in Europe, USA, Canada, Australia, Japa

Cover: Foto ©Lupo / pixelio.de

Manufactured and distributed by brebook publishing software
(www.brebook.com)

Pope Pius IX.

Our Lady of Lourdes

OUR LADY OF LOURDES.

OUR LADY OF LOURDES.

THE HISTORY

OF THE

MIRACULOUS SANCTUARY OF OUR LADY OF LOURDES,

IN THE DEPARTMENT OF THE UPPER PYRENEES, FRANCE.

TRANSLATED BY THE

REV. F. IGNATIUS SISK, O. C.,

OF ST. BERNARD'S ABBEY, LEICESTERSHIRE,

FROM THE FRENCH OF

HENRY LASSERRE,

WITH HIS SPECIAL PERMISSION.

A WORK HONOURED THROUGH TWENTY-FIVE EDITIONS,

WITH A BRIEF OF APPROVAL ADDRESSED

TO THE AUTHOR

BY POPE PIUS IX.

LONDON:
THOMAS RICHARDSON AND SON;
DUBLIN AND DERBY.
MDCCCLXXII.

Dear Rev. Mother,

Please to accept the Dedication of this little effort to promote devotion towards the Most Blessed Mother of God. It is a Translation of a carefully authenticated History of Eighteen Apparitions of Our Lady, a few years ago, to a poor Shepherdess at Lourdes, in France. In issuing this Publication, I can think of no one, under whose name I should prefer it to appear, than that of yourself, for whom I have entertained so great a respect and affection during the forty years that I have been in the sacred ministry.

How dear and interesting to me are the recollections of so many of my spiritual children, who, within that period, have, like yourself, fervently corresponded with the highest of graces, viz., that of a vocation to the Religious State, which, through my advice, they have embraced.

Happy is the Community which possesses you, as their Mother and Superioress. Long may you be preserved so worthily to preside over them. The Spirit of Wisdom with which you are animated and your love of Regular Observance, cannot fail to draw down upon them the Blessing of God, and ensure their Religious Perfection and Happiness.

Recommending myself to your, and their pious prayers,

I remain, Dear Rev. Mother,

Yours ever affectionately in Christ,

BROTHER IGNATIUS SISK, O.C.

CONTENTS.

DILECTO FILIO HENRICO LASSERRE.

PIUS PP. IX.

Dilecte Fili, salutem et Apostolicam Benedictionem.

Gratulamur tibi, Dilecte Fili, quod, insigni auctus beneficio, votum tuum accuratissimo studio diligentiaque exsolveris; et novam clementissimæ Dei matris apparitionem ita testatam facere curaveris, ut e conflictu ipso humanæ malitiæ cum cœlesti misericordia claritas eventus firmior ac luculentior appareret.

Omnes certe in proposita a te rerum serie perspicere poterunt, religionem nostram sanctissimam vergere in veram populorum utilitatem; confluentes ad se omnes supernis juxta et terrenis cumulare beneficiis; aptissimam esse ordini servando, vi etiam submota; concitatos in turbis animorum motus, licet justos compescere; iisque rebus sedulo adlaborare Clerum, eumque adeo abesse a superstitione fovenda, ut imo segniorem se præbeat ac severiorem aliis omnibus in judicio edendo de

1

factis, quæ naturæ vires excedere videntur. Nec
minus aperte patebit, impietatem incassum in-
dixisse religione bellum, et frustra machinationes
hominum divinæ Providentiæ consiliis obstare;
quæ imo nequitia eorum et ausu sic uti consuevit,
ut majorem vide quærat operibus suis splendorem
et virtutem. Libentissime propterea excepimus
volumen tuum, cui titulus Notre Dame de Lourdes;
forefidentes, ut quæ per mira potentiæ ac benigni-
tatis suæ signa undique frequentissimos advenas
accersit; scripto etiam tuo uti velit ad propagan-
dam latius fovendamque in se pietatem hominum
ac fiduciam, ut de plenitudine gratiæ esse omnes
accipere possint. Hujus, quem ominamur, exi-
tus labori tuo auspicem accipe Benedictionem
Apostolicam, quam tibi grati animi nostri et pa-
ternæ benevolentiæ testem peramanter imperti-
mus.

Datum Romæ apud St. Petrum die 4 Septem-
bris, 1869, Pontificatus Nostri Anno XXIV.

Pius PP. IX.

TRANSLATION OF THE BRIEF OF
HIS HOLINESS PIUS IX.,

TO THE AUTHOR OF OUR LADY OF LOURDES,

HIS WELL-BELOVED SON HENRY LASSERRE.

———

Well - Beloved Son, Health and Apostolic Benediction.

Receive our congratulations, very dear son, since honoured by a singular benefit, you have succeeded in accomplishing your work with the most accurate research and diligence, and have endeavoured so to establish and demonstrate the new apparition of the most clement Mother of God, that from the conflict itself of human malice with the Divine mercy, the truth of the event should appear stronger and clearer.

In the exposition you have given of every detail, all will be able to see, how our holy religion redounds to the advantage of the people; how it fills those who have recourse to it, not only with spiritual and heavenly goods, but also with such as are temporal and earthly; that it is most adapted to promote order in the absence of material force; that, in the minds of the multitude, who are disturbed, it appeases emotions, however great; that

the clergy zealously strive for such results, and are
so far from favouring superstition, that they show
themselves slower and more severe than all others
in passing a judgment on facts that seem to be
beyond the powers of nature.

Nor less clearly will it be made known, that
impiety declares war in vain against religion, and
that the wicked uselessly attempt to frustrate the
designs of Divine Providence, which ever is wont
so to use their wickedness and audacity, as to acquire thence a greater splendour and power in His
works.

Therefore, we most willingly accept your volume,
the title of which is "Our Lady of Lourdes."
We have a Faith, that she who, by the wonderful signs of her power and goodness, draws to herself multitudes of pilgrims from every side, wills
to make use of your composition, in order to pro-
pagate still further, and to nourish towards herself
the filial piety and confidence of men, that, out of
the fulness of her grace, all may partake. As a
pledge of this success for your labour, which we
foretell, accept our Apostolic Benediction, which
we address to you very affectionately, in testimony
of our gratitude and our paternal regard.

Given at Rome, at St. Peter's, 4th September,
1869, the twenty-fourth year of our Pontificate.

PREFACE.

In consequence of a signal grace, an account of which will be found in the pages of this volume, I promised, several years ago, to write a history of the extraordinary events which have occasioned the pilgrimage to Lourdes. If I have committed a grave fault in delaying so long the performance of my promise, I have, at least, made it an absolute matter of conscience, to study, with scrupulous care, the subject I desired to treat.

Amidst the unceasing concourse of visitors, pilgrims, men and women, and whole populations, who come this day from every side, to kneel before a desert grotto, entirely ignored till ten years since, and which the voice of a child has all at once caused to be considered as a divine sanctuary; on beholding the vast edifice which popular faith is erecting on this spot, and which will cost about two million (francs), I have felt the need, not only of investigating the proofs of the supernatural fact, but also to examine in what manner, through logical links in theory or ideas, the belief of it was universally spread.

How has this been produced? How has such an event been accomplished in the nineteenth century? How has the testimony of a little ignorant girl, upon a fact so extraordinary, upon apparitions, which no one around her perceived, been able to find credit and engender such prodigious results?

There are persons who reply to such questions, with a peremptory word, and the word, "superstition" is very convenient for the purpose. As for myself, I am not so precipitate; and my desire has been to satisfy myself as to a phenomenon so completely out of the ordinary course of things, and so worthy of attention in every point of view in which it can be considered. Whether the miracle is true or false; whether the cause of this vast concourse of populations be due to a divine action or a human error, such a study is not less highly interesting. I observe, nevertheless, that the votaries of free inquiry are very cautious not to make it. They prefer to cut the matter short by denying everything. It is a method at once the easiest and the most discreet.

I understand, in a way different from them, the anxious toil of investigating truth. If, to deny everything at once, appears to them the simplest course, to affirm everything at once would seem to me hazardous.

I have seen savants toiling up the steep paths of the mountain, in order to discover the reason why a certain insect is found in summer on the summits, and during winter only in the plains. That is all very well and commendable. But it also appears to me, that great movements among men, that great causes which stir up agitation among great masses, deserve, perhaps, as much to engage and occupy the human mind. History, religion, science, philosophy, medicine, the analysis of the various intricacies of human nature, have an equal claim to interest our attention in this curious study.

This study, it has been my purpose to endeavour fully to pursue. Thus, I have been satisfied neither with official documents, nor letters, nor legal proceedings of courts, nor written attestations. But I have wished, as much as possible, to know everything, to see everything by myself, to make everything be renewed before my own eyes by the remembrance and the narrative of those who have been eyewitnesses. I have made long journeys across France in order to interrogate all those who had taken a part, whether as principals or as witnesses, in the events which I had to describe, to check their statements by one another, and to arrive thus at a complete and luminous knowledge of the truth.

In my inquiries upon the subject of this Divine History, I have desired, in a word, to follow and to persevere in adopting as much as possible, the excellent method which M. Thiers has employed with such success in the long labour and the searching investigations which preceded his Chef d'Œuvre on the Consulate and Empire.

I possess the confidence to hope, that, by the help of God, my efforts have not been altogether vain.

Having ascertained the truth, I have described it with as much freedom as if, like the Duke De St. Simon, I had closed my door and published a history destined to appear only once in a century. My desire has been to state everything as long as the witnesses were still living; my desire has been to give their names and their residences, in order that it might be possible to ask them and to repeat, in order to test my own labours, the inquiry which I have myself made. I have wished that every reader might be able to examine by himself, my assertions, and render homage to truth if I have been sincere ; that he might put me to confusion and dishonour if I were guilty of untruth.

The thorough and solid inquiry to which I have devoted myself, the documents which I have con-

sulted, the numerous testimonies which I have
heard, have given me the opportunity of entering
into circumstantial details which the brief account
at first published, could not touch upon, and to
rectify some mistakes which had found their way
into the chronology of the facts. I have re-estab-
lished, with extreme care, the exact order of the
events. This was necessary, in order to understand well their logical connection, and penetrate
their intimate essence.

To study facts, not only in their exterior surface,
but in the delicacies of their physiognomy and
their hidden life ; to search out, with a constant
vigilant attention, the link often remote, often
immediately unperceived, which unites them ; to
understand and clearly express their cause, their
origin, their generation ; to discover and behold
in operation, mid the depths which we endeavour
to fathom, the eternal laws and the marvellous
harmonies of the miraculous order ; such is the
object I have had the resolution to propose under-
taking.

With such a thought, no circumstance was a
matter of indifference or could be neglected. The
smallest detail might contain a light and admit of
one seizing the hand of God, so to speak, in the
very act.

Hence my inquiries ; hence the form, very different from the usual style of official histories, which my narrative has of itself assumed; hence, as well in the account of the apparitions as in that of the miraculous cures, those portraits, those dialogues, those descriptions of landscapes, those circumstances of hour and place, those verifyings of the time they occurred; hence those countless details which have cost me so much trouble to un-ravel, but which have given me, in proportion as I piously collected them together, the unspeakable joy of seeing by myself, of tasting and feeling, in all the charms of a discovery, scarcely suspected beforehand, the profound harmony of the works that come from God.

This joy, I am endeavouring to impart to my readers, to my friends, to those who are curious in the secrets of above. Some of these details hap-pen, sometimes with such a marvellous appropri-ateness, that the reader, accustomed to the dis-cordances of the world, might suspect the Painter to have taken some self-satisfaction in His Picture. But God is an Artist who has no need of any one inventing for Him. The supernatural works which He deigns to accomplish here below, are perfect of themselves. To copy them faithfully, would be to meet with the Ideal. But who could copy them in this manner? Who could behold them in all their beauty and harmony? Who has not but an imperfect sight? Who can penetrate all the secrets of those humble and great things? Nobody, alas! almost everything escapes from us, and we can only get a glimpse of it. I have ventured to utter what I have desired to do. The reader alone will see what I have done.

OUR LADY OF LOURDES.

BOOK I.

I.

The little town of Lourdes is situated in the department of the Hautes-Pyrénées, at the opening of the seven valleys of the Laveran, between the last undulations of the small hills that terminate the plain of Tarbes and the first abrupt steeps that commence the Grande Montagne. The houses, seated irregularly upon an uneven plot of ground, are grouped almost in disorder, at the base of an enormous rock, isolated entirely, and upon which is perched, like an eagle's nest, a formidable fortress. At the foot of this rock, on the opposite side of the town, beneath the shade of ash and poplar trees, the Gave flows tumultuously, dashing its frothy waters against a barrier of pebbles, and causing the sonorous wheels of three or four mills to be turned that are on its banks. The noise of the mill-stones, and the murmuring of the wind mid the branches of the trees, mingle with the roar of its fugitive billows.

This Gave is formed by different torrents from the upper valleys, which proceed themselves from perpetual glaciers and spotless snows, which cover

up, in the depths of the chain, the barren sides
of the Haute Montagne.   The chief of these
streams comes from the Cascade of Gavarnie,
which falls, as every one knows, from one of those
rare peaks which no human footstep has hitherto
been able to tread.

Leaving on its right, the town, the castle, and,
saving one which is on its left, all the mills of
Lourdes, the Gave, urged on its course, precipi-
tately rushes towards the city of Pau, which it will
pass with great rapidity in order to cast itself into
the Adour, and thence into the great ocean.

In the environs of Lourdes, the landscape which
lines the Gave, is sometimes wild and rough, sometimes charming.   Verdant meadows, cultivated
fields, thick woods, steep rocks, descend by turns
into its waters.   There are smiling and fertile
grounds, beautiful prospects, the high road to
Pau, furrowed out at all times by conveyances,
horsemen, and pedestrians; here, are wild mountains with their terrible solitude.

The fortress of Lourdes, almost impregnable
before the invention of artillery, was formerly the
key of the Pyrénées.

Tradition relates that Charlemagne, during a
war with the infidels, was unable to succeed in
getting possession of it.   At the moment when he
was about to raise the siege, an eagle, passing
over above the highest tower of the fortress which
was besieged, let fall upon it a magnificent fish,
which it had just caught in a neighbouring lake.

Was this because on this very day the laws of
the Church imposed abstinence ?   Was it because
the fish was a Christian symbol still popular at

that period ? Nevertheless, it is a fact that the
Saracen Chief Mirat, who occupied the castle, saw
in it a prodigy, and became converted to the true
faith. It required nothing less than the miracle
of the conversion of Mirat, and his baptism, to
cause this castle to be restored to the dominion of
Christianity. The Saracen, says the Chronicle,
also stipulated that "becoming a knight of our
Lady, the Mother of God, he understood, both for
himself and his descendants, that his earldom,
free from all feudal fiefs, should never be held but
from herself."

The actual arms of the town render testimony
to this extraordinary fact of the eagle and the fish.
Lourdes bears gules with three golden towers,
masoned in sable, upon a rock of argent; the
tower in the middle being higher than the two
others, and surmounted by a spread eagle sable,
formed of gold, and holding in his beak a trout
argent.

During all the period of the middle ages, the
Castle of Lourdes was a centre of alarm for
all the surrounding country. Sometimes in the
name of the English, sometimes in the name
of the Counts de Bigorre, it was occupied by a
species of captains of brigands, who, in reality,
depended upon no authority but themselves, and
who ransomed the inhabitants of the plain for
forty or fifty leagues of the surrounding country.
They had, it is related, the incredible audacity to
lay their hands on property and person even up to
the gates of Montpellier ; then they returned, like
true birds of prey, to their inaccessible nest.

In the eighteenth century, the Castle of

Lourdes became a state prison. It was the Bastille of the Pyrenees. The Revolution opened the doors for three or four prisoners who had been sent by the arbitrary orders of despotism, and peopled it in revenge with several hundred criminals, who were criminals of a far different stamp. A contemporary author has extracted from the registers of entries in the gaol book the heinous crimes of these villains. By the side of the name of each prisoner, " behold," says he, " how the qualification of each crime was formularized : *' unpatriotic'*—*' having refused the kiss of peace to Citizen N. before the altar of the country'*— *' a caviller'*—*' a drunkard'*—*' icy towards the Revolution'*—*' a hypocritical character, reserved in his opinions'*—*' a lying character like a tooth drawer'*—*' a pacific Harpagon, indifferent to the Revolution,'* &c.[*]

II.

The town, nevertheless has continued the key of the Pyrenees, but in an entirely different point of view from heretofore. Lourdes is the cross way to the hot baths. Whether we have to go to Baréges, Saint-Sauveur, Canteret, Bagnères de Bigorre, whether we want to go from Cantaret or Pau to Luchon, we must always pass by Lourdes. At all periods, the countless diligences which were employed for the service of the waters during the summer season had to stop at the Hotel de la

[*] Bascle de Lagrèze Conseiller à la Cour Impériale de Pau.— Chronique de la Ville de Lourdes.

Poste. Travellers were ordinarily allowed time to dine, visit the castle, and admire the scenery, before departing.

For a century or two this little town has thus been constantly traversed by bathers and tourists who came from all corners of Europe. From thence a certain degree of civilization has resulted.

In 1858, the epoch at which this history com-mences, the journals from Paris were received at Lourdes. The *Revue des Deux Mondes* counted there several subscribers. As everywhere else, the wineshops and coffee houses kept for their customers three copies of the *Siecle*, one for the day, another for the evening, and a third for the preceding evening. The citizens and the clergy divided among them the *Journal des Debats*, *La Presse*, *Le Moniteur*, *l'Univers*, and *l'Union*.

Lourdes had a club, a printing office, and a journal. The sub-prefect resided at Argelès; but the inconvenience which the inhabitants of Lourdes felt at being deprived of this functionary was alleviated by the satisfaction of possessing a *Tribunal de Première Instance*, that is to say, three judges, a president, a *procureur impérial*, and a substitute. Other satellites of inferior degree gravitated round this enlightened centre, viz., a justice of the peace, a commissáry of police, six ushers, seven gendarmes, of whom one was a Brigadier. In the interior of the town there was a hospital and a prison, and as we shall have occasion to verify it, circumstances presented themselves when certain free-thinkers, fed with the sound and humanising doctrines of the *Siecle*,

2

pretended that criminals should be sent to the
hospital, and the sick to the prison.

But it possessed only a few of these mighty rea-
soners; there were to be found at the bar of Lourdes,
in the medical body, men of the deepest knowledge and the highest distinction—men of as remarkable talent, and impartial observers, as are
ever to be met with in cities of the utmost importance.

Races which dwell in mountainous districts are
generally gifted with good and solid practical
sense. Such populations, being slightly mixed
with foreign blood, are excellent. There are few
parts of France where the schools are so much
frequented as at Lourdes. There is not a boy in it
who has not gone for several years to lay teachers
or the Christian Brothers; there is not a little
girl who does not equally follow up a complete
course of popular education at the school of the
Sisters of Nevers. Better instructed than the
working classes usually are in the greater part of
our towns, the inhabitants of Lourdes retain at
the same time that simplicity which is peculiar to
a country life. They possess hot blood, and a
southern head; but they have an upright heart,
and are perfectly moral. They are honest, religious, and averse to innovations.

Certain local institutions, reaching back to an
immemorial date, contribute to maintain such a
happy condition of things. The people of these
districts, long before the pretended discoveries of
modern progress, had understood and practised,
under the shadow of the Church, ideas of joint
liability and prudence which have given rise to

our benefit societies. Such societies exist at
Lourdes, and have been in operation for centuries;
they date from the middle ages; they have passed
through the Revolution victoriously, and philan-
thropists would have adopted them long since, as
they were in high repute, had they not drawn
their vitality from a principle of religion, and were
they not called, as in the fifteenth century, "confraternities."

"Almost all the people," says M. de Lagrèze,
"enter into these associations, which are as philosophic as pious. The labourers, whom the name of
Confréres unites together, place their work under
a heavenly patronage, and make an interchange of
mutual benefit and Christian charity. The common chest receives the weekly offering of the
workman, full of strength and health, to restore it
one day to the workman suffering from sickness
and misery, to the workman, when dead, whose
funeral expenses the association defrays, and
whom it accompanies to his last resting place.
Every confraternity, with the exception of two,
which divides the high altar between them,
has a private chapel, from which it takes its
name, and which it keeps up by a collection
on Sunday. The Confraternity of Notre Dame-
des-Grace is composed of husbandmen; that
of Notre-Dame-Mont-Carmel is composed of
workmen in the slate quarries; that of Notre-
Dame-de-Monsarrat, of masons; that of St. Anne,
of carpenters; that of St. Luke, of tailors and
dress-makers; that of the Ascension, of quarry
men; that of the Holy Sacrament, of church-
wardens; that of St. John and St. James, of all

those who have received either of these names in baptism."

The women equally have a part in similar religious associations. One of them, "the Congregation of the Children of Mary," has a special character. It is also, but in the order of things spiritual, a benefit society. To enter into this Congregation, which is well understood to be a lay society, it is necessary to be possessed of well-tried virtue. Children think of it a long time before they are young girls. The Congregationists engage themselves never to put themselves into a position of evil, by frequenting worldly feasts where a religious spirit is soon lost, not to follow eccentric fashions, to be exact at the meetings of the society and instructions on Sundays. It is an honour to be admitted into it; it is a disgrace to be excluded from it. The good this association has done, the morality which it has maintained in the country, the good mothers it has prepared, is incalculable. Thus, in a great number of dioceses, many confraternities have been founded on the model of this mother congregation.

The country has a particular devotion to the Blessed Virgin. The sanctuaries which have been consecrated to her are numerous in the Pyrenees, from Pietat or Garaison to Bétharram. All the altars in the church at Lourdes are dedicated to the Mother of God.

III.

Such was Lourdes ten years ago. The railroad did not as yet pass through it, and there was not even a question of its ever doing so. A route, much more direct, appeared to be marked out beforehand, as the line for the Pyrenees.

The entire city and fortress are situated, as we have said above, on the right bank of the Gave, which, after having dashed itself, on coming from the south, against the enormous rock which serves as a pedestal to the castle of the fortress, makes a bend, and hastily takes a direction to the west.

An old bridge, built up the stream, at some distance from the first houses of the town, opens a communication with the country, the meadows, the forest and mountains on the left bank.

On this last bank, a little below the bridge, and fronting the castle, a current of water, detached from the Gave, produces a rapid canal. This canal rejoins the Gave at the distance of three thousand feet down the river, after having passed along, for a short distance, the Massabielle rocks, the base of which it waters.

The lengthened island which is formed by the Gave and this current is a spacious and verdant meadow. In the country it is called the Ile de Chalet, or more briefly, the Chalet.

The mill of Savy, which is the only one on the left bank, is built over both banks of the canal, and serves as a bridge between the meadow and the mainland. This mill, as well as the Chalet, belongs to an inhabitant of Lourdes, of the name of M. De Laffitte.

Now in 1858 there was scarcely in the environs of the little busy town which we have described, any spot more solitary and more of a desert than these Rocks of Massabielle, at the part where the Gave and the canal of the mill met together.

A short distance above this confluence, on the water side, the rugged rock was pierced at its base by three irregular excavations, somewhat fantastically placed on one another, and communicating with one another as the holes of an enormous sponge.

The singularity of these excavations renders them rather difficult of description. The first and the greatest was on the level of the soil. It had something of the appearance of a shopkeeper's sort of shapeless and lofty oven, which would be cut in two, and which, in place of forming an entire arch, would not make more than a semi-arch.

The entry, in the form of a crooked circle, was about twelve feet in height at its most elevated point. The breadth of the grotto, nearly equal to its depth, was from thirty-six to forty-five feet.

On going within the entry, the rock continued gradually to lower, in the manner of the ceiling of a granary when viewed from below, and went on contracting itself on both sides.

Above, a little on the right of the spectator, two other openings placed upon one another presented themselves, which were as it were the appendages and hangers on of this first cavity.

As seen from the outside, the chief of these two openings had, under an oval form, the height and breadth of a window in a house, or a niche in a church. It darted itself from bottom to top in the rock, then, having reached a depth of about six feet, it twists like a fork, descending on one side into the interior of the grotto below, and remounting on the other side, returning on itself as far as the exterior of the rock, where its orifice formed that second upper opening of which we have already spoken, and which had no importance, save inasmuch as it contributed to light up, perfectly and in every way, all that supplementary cavity.

A sweet briar, or a wild rose-tree, thrust into the bend of the rock, extended its long stems along the base of the orifice in the form of a niche.

At the foot of this little system of excavations, very simple to the eye, but very complicated for whoever wishes to attempt to give a description of it, across a chaos of enormous stones that had fallen from the Montagne, the rapid mill canal ran its course, in order, at six or seven paces further, to rejoin the Gave.

The grotto was thus immediately in front of the lower point of the Isle of Chalet, formed as we have said, by the Gave and the canal.

These excavations were called the Grotto of Massabielle, from the name of the rocks on which it depended. "Massabielle," in the patois of the country, signifies " old rocks."

Down the stream, on the banks of the Gave, extended an uncultivated and steep eminence,

belonging, as all the rest, to the commune of
Lourdes, and where the swineherds of the country
came sometimes to conduct their flocks.

When a storm arose these poor people sheltered
themselves in the grotto, as also some fishermen
who came to cast at that spot their nets into the
Gave.

As in all excavations of this kind, the rock was
dry at ordinary times, and slightly moist during
the period of rain. This rare humidity, and this
imperceptible running in the rainy seasons, could
only be remarked on one side, that is, on the
right on entering. This side is precisely that
from which the rain usually comes, brought by the
westerly winds; and it happened naturally—for
the rock, which was very slender, was full of clefts
at that spot—as happens to the walls of houses
which are similarly exposed, and are built of very
inferior mortar.

The left side and the bottom, being unsuscepti-
ble of these effects, were constantly dry as the
flooring of a room. The accidental humidity of
the west caused even to be more manifest the dry-
ness of the north, of the east, and the south of the
grotto.

Above the triple cavity arose, almost perpen-
dicularly, the enormous mass of the rocks of
Massabielle, tapestried, in many places, with ivy
and box, heath and moss. Entangled brambles,
hazel trees, briars, some trees, the branches of
which the wind often broke, had forced their roots
into the crevices of the rock, wherever the soil, falling from the mountains or brought by the winds, had
lodged. The Eternal Sower, He Whose invisible

hand fills with stars the immensities of space, He
Who has drawn out of nothing the land on which
we tread, the plants and animals, the Creator of
so many millions of men who have peopled the
earth, and so many milliards of angels who in-
habit heaven, the God whose riches are beyond
bounds, and power without limits, understands
that no atom is lost in the vast regions of His
workmanship. And behold the reason why He
leaves nothing barren that can produce ; behold
why, throughout the whole extent of our globe,
innumerable animalculæ float in the air, covering
vegetation wherever it appears, had it only room
for a tuft of grass, or for the existence of a blade
of moss. In the same way, O Divine Sower, Your
graces like an invisible collection of fertile grains,
float round our souls, like the mounting of a good
soil. And if we are so barren, it is because we
present ourselves to you, sometimes with hearts
more sterile than the rock, sometimes with paths
that are worn down, which the feet of passers-by
trample on without ceasing, sometimes with
bushes of thorns, where weeds occupy all the
space and stifle the good seed.

IV.

It was necessary to describe the country where
the different scenes were to take place which we
had to relate. It is not of less importance to
indicate previously what light, that is to say, what
profound moral truth enlightens the commencement of this history, in which, as we shall see,

the hand of God has appeared visibly. These reflections will delay but for a moment our entry on the narrative.

It is, it seems to me, a trite remark that everything is a contrast on this earth, where the wicked and the good are mixed together, as well as the rich and the poor, and where the cottage of the poor is sometimes separated only by a simple wall from the residence of a rich personage. On one side are found all the pleasures of an easy life, agreeably arranged in the middle of the most delicate pursuit of every comfort and elegancy of life; on the other, the horrors of misery, cold, hunger, disease, the sorrowful accompaniments of human sufferings. Around the first are adulations, assiduous visits, noisy friendships; around the others, indifference, solitude, and abandonment. Whether it fears the importunity of its formal or tacit applications, whether it fears, like a reproach, the spectacle of this frightful destitution, the world shuns the poor and organizes itself aloof from him. The rich, forming themselves into an exclusive circle, which their pride calls "good society," consider as having but a secondary existence, and unworthy of their attention, all that is exterior to them, all that does not belong to the high class called "gens comme il faut." When they employ a workman, even when they are good or help the needy, they treat him as a protegé, as an inferior; they show not to him that simple and intimate mode of dealing which they would exhibit towards one of their own. With the exception of some rare Christians, none concerns himself with the poor man as with a

brother, as with an equal. With the exception of
the saints, alas! but thinly sown in the times in
which we live, to whom would occur the idea of
showing him the respect which we have for a
superior? In the world, properly called, in the
vast world, the poor is absolutely abandoned.
Overwhelmed under the burden of labour, exhausted with wants, disdained and forsaken, does
it not seem that he is cursed by the Creator of
the earth? Well, it is precisely quite the re-
verse; he is the beloved of the Universal Father.
Whilst the world has been cursed by the infallible
word of Christ, it is the poor, the suffering, the
humble, the lowly, who are for God the "good
society," the chosen society in which His heart is
well pleased. "You are My friends," says He,
in His Gospel; He does more, He identifies
Himself with them, only opening heaven to the
rich inasmuch as they shall have been the bene-
factors of the needy: "What you have done to
the least of My little ones, you have done it unto
Me."

Thus, when the Son of God came on earth, He
willed to be poor, to live and die in the midst of
the poor, to be Himself a poor man. It is from
them He took His apostles, His principal disciples, the first-born of His Church. In the history, already long, of His Church, it is on the
poor that He has generally poured out His spiritual graces. At all times, and with few exceptions, apparitions, visions, particular revelations,
have been the privilege of these poor and little
ones, which the world despises.

For nearly two thousand years the words of the

Apostle have been verified : "the foolish things of the world hath God chosen, that He may confound the wise; and the weak things of the world hath God chosen, that He may confound the strong."[*]

The narrative which we have undertaken will furnish perhaps some proofs of this high truth.

V.

The 11th of February inaugurated, in 1858, the week of profane rejoicings which, according to an immemorial usage, precede the austerities of Lent. It was the day of Jeudi-gras. The weather was cold, a little sheltered, but very calm. In the depths of the sky the clouds kept themselves immoveable. No breeze drove them against one another, and the atmosphere possessed an entire tranquillity. Occasionally a few drops of water fell from above.

On this very day, after the particular privileges of its proper offices, the Diocese of Tarbes celebrated the festival of the illustrious shepherdess of France, St. Genevieve.

It had already struck eleven o'clock at the church of Lourdes.

Whilst almost everywhere preparations were being made for joyful meetings and festivities, a family of poor people, who lived as lodgers in a wretched house in the Rue des Petits-Fosses, had not even wood to cook their sorry dinner.

The father, still a young man, followed the trade of a miller, and he had for some time

* 1 Cor. i. 27.

worked as a farmer at the little mill situated on
the north of the town, upon one of the streams
that cast themselves into the Gave. But this
employment requires money in hand, people being
accustomed to get their corn ground on credit,
and the poor miller for this reason had been
obliged to give up the farm of the little mill,
where his labour, far from enabling him to live at
his ease, had contributed to throw him into
greater want. In the expectation of better days
he worked, not indeed at home, for he had nothing
in the world, not even a little garden, but in
different directions, among some of his neighbours, who gave him employment from time to
time by the day.

His name was Francis Soubirous, and he was
married to a very worthy woman, Louisa Casterot,
who was a good Christian, and who kept up his
spirits.

They had four children; two girls, of whom
the eldest was about fourteen years, and two boys
much younger, the last was about three or four
years old.

Their eldest daughter, a poor miserable object,
had only lived with them for fifteen days. It is
this little girl that has to sustain an important
part in our narrative, and we have studied with
care all the particulars and details of her life.

After her birth, her mother, who was unwell at
that period, had not the power to suckle her, and
had placed her out to nurse in a neighbouring
village, at Bartrés, where the child remained until
it was weaned.

Louisa Soubirous had become a mother a second

time, and two children to look to at once would
have detained her at her lodging, and hindered
her from going out during the day and into the
fields, which she could easily do with only one to
nurse.   It was for that reason that the parents
left their eldest child at Bartrés.   They paid for
her keep, sometimes in money and sometimes in
kind, a pension of five francs a month.

When the little girl had attained the age for
being useful, and there was a question for restoring it to its paternal roof, the good peasants who
had nursed it perceived that they were attached to
her, and considered her almost as one of their
children.   From this moment they took charge of
her for nothing, employing her to take care of the
sheep.   She grew up thus in the midst of this
adopted family, passing all her days in solitude,
in the desert hills where her humble flock was
feeding.

As to prayers, she knew none whatever except
her Rosary.   Whether it was that her nursing
mother had recommended it to her, or whether
rather it was an artless want of this innocent
soul, everywhere and at all times did she recite
this prayer of the simple.   Then she amused herself quite alone with those toys of nature, which a
maternal Providence furnishes for the children of
the poor, who are more easy to satisfy in this as
in all other things than the children of the rich—
she played with the stones, which she heaped up
into small infantine buildings, with the plants
and flowers, which she collected here and there,
with the water of the streams into which she cast
and followed with her eye immense fleets of blades

of grass; she played with that one which she preferred out of the flock which was confided to her care: "Of all my lambs," said she, one day, "there is one which I love the best."—"And which is it?" people asked her. "That which I love is the smallest." And she took a delight in caressing it, and sporting with it.

She was herself among children like this poor lamb which she loved, weak and little. Though she was now fourteen years old she did not look more than eleven or twelve. Without being, however, sickly, she was subject to the oppressiveness of an asthma which several times caused her to suffer much. She took this trial in patience, and she accepted physical pain with that tranquil resignation which seems so difficult to the rich, and which the poor appear to find so natural.

In this innocent and solitary school the poor shepherdess learnt perhaps what the world is ignorant of, that simplicity which is pleasing to God. Far removed from all danger of impure contact, entertaining herself with the Blessed Virgin Mary, passing her time and her hours in crowning her with her prayers while using her rosary, she preserved perfect openness of character, that baptismal purity which the breath of the world tarnishes so quickly, even among the best.

Such was the soul of this child, limpid and peaceful as those unknown lakes that are lost in the high mountains where are exhibited in silence all the splendours of heaven. "Blessed are the clean of heart," says the Gospel, "for they shall see God."

These great gifts are hidden gifts, and the

humility which possesses them is often ignorant of them itself. This little girl was now fourteen years of age, and if all those who approached her by accident felt themselves drawn to her and secretly charmed, she was unconscious of it. She considered herself as the last and the most backward child of her age. She knew not how to read or to write. Still more, she was altogether a stranger to the French language, and only knew her poor Pyrenean patois. She had never learnt her catechism. On this her ignorance was extreme. The *Our Father*, the *Hail Mary*, the *Apostles' Creed*, the *Glory be to the Father*, recited as she said her Rosary, constituted all her knowledge of religion.

After such details it is useless to add that she had never made her first Communion. It was precisely to prepare her for it, and send her to the Catechism, that the Soubirous had withdrawn her from this out-of-the-way village, which was inhabited by her nursing parents, and to bring her home to Lourdes, notwithstanding their excessive poverty.

She had returned a fortnight to her paternal lodging. Being taken up with her asthma, and her weak state, her mother bestowed particular care upon her. Whilst the other children of the Soubirous went barefooted with their sabots, she herself had stockings in hers; whilst her sister and her brothers ran about freely outside, she had almost continually to make herself useful inside.

The child, accustomed to the open air, would have preferred to have got out.

Then this very day was the Jeudi-Gras, eleven

o'clock had struck, and these poor people had no wood to prepare their dinner.

"Go and gather some on the banks of the Gave, or on the common," said the mother to Mary, her second daughter.

The same as in many other parts, the poor had, in the commune of Lourdes, a small right of gathering out of the dried up branches which the wind caused to fall from the trees, and out of the stray bits of dry wood which the torrent deposited and left among the pebbles on the bank.

Mary put on her sabots.

The, eldest, she of whom we have spoken, the little shepherdess of Bartrès, beheld her with an eye of envy.

"Let me go with her," said she at last to her mother. "I will bring back also a little bundle of wood."

"No," replied Louisa Soubrious; "you are coughing, and you will get ill."

Another girl of a neighbouring house, Jeanne Abadiè, about fifteen years of age, had entered in the meanwhile, and showed herself disposed to go and gather wood. They all joined their entreaties together, and the mother allowed herself to yield her consent.

The child at this moment, as is customary with the peasants of the South, had her head fastened up with a handkerchief, tied up in a knot on one side.

This did not appear enough for the mother.

"Take your capulet," said she to her.

The capulet is a very graceful garment: it is peculiar to the people of the Pyrenees; it forms a
3

head-dress and a mantle at the same time; it is a sort of a small capuche, made of thick woollen cloth, sometimes white, like the fleece of sheep, sometimes of bright red, which covers the head and falls behind on the shoulders, reaching a little below the waist. When it is very cold or windy the women throw it back in front and fold their neck and arms in it; when this garment seems too hot for them, they lap it up in a square, and carry it on their head as a sort of square cap.

The capulet of the little shepherdess of Bartrés was white.

VI.

The three children left the town, and, crossing the bridge, soon arrived at the left bank of the Gave. They passed by the mill of M. de Laffitte, entered the island of Chalet, looking everywhere for bits of wood in order to make up their little fagot.

They went by degrees down the meadow as they followed the course of the Gave. The weak child whom the mother had hesitated to allow to go out, walked a little behind; less fortunate than her two companions she had found nothing as yet, and her apron was empty, whilst that of her sister and Jeanne began to be stocked with little branches and chips.

Clad in a black dress quite worn out and mended, her delicate countenance wrapped up in the white capulet, which covered her head, and fell back over her shoulders, her feet fastened up within her rough sabots, she had an innocent and

rustic grace which charmed the heart more than
the eye.

She was small for her age. Though her infantine features were a little burnt up by the sun,
they had lost nothing of their native delicacy.
Her hair, black and fine, scarcely appeared under
her handkerchief. Her forehead, also uncovered,
exhibited an incomparable purity of outline.
Under her well arched eyebrows, her brown eyes,
milder in her than blue eyes, possessed a deep
and tranquil beauty, of which no evil passion had
ever troubled its magnificent limpid surface. It
was the simple eye of which the Gospel speaks.
The mouth, marvellously expressive, made the
beholder divine in the soul an habitual emotion of
goodness and compassion for every kind of suffering.

The physiognomy, meek and intelligent, was
pleasing : and the effect of the whole carried with
it an extraordinary attraction, which made itself
felt in the most elevated parts of the soul. What
was this attraction? I was going to say, What
was this ascendancy, this secret authority, in this
poor child, so ignorant and clad in rags? It was
the greatest and the rarest thing in the world:
the majesty of innocence.

We have not as yet uttered her name. She had
as her patron a great Doctor of the Church, he
whose genius was more particularly sheltered
under the protection of the Mother of God, the
author of the *Memorare*, "Remember, O most
pious Virgin Mary," the admirable St. Bernard.
However, according to a custom, which has its
advantage, this great name given to this humble

peasant girl, has taken an infantile and country tournure. The little girl bore a pretty name, as graceful as herself; she was called Bernadette.

She followed her sister and her companion along the mill meadow, and sought without success, amongst the grass, for some pieces of wood to light the fire of the house.

Such must have been Ruth or Noemi when they went to glean in the fields of Booz.

VII.

The three children, walking in this way, had reached the bottom of the Isle of Châlet, immediately in front of the triple excavation which exhibited to view the grotto of Massabielle, which we have attempted to describe a little above. They were only separated from it by the course of the water of the mill, usually very rapid, that watered the foot of the rocks.

Now, on this very day, the mill belonging to Savy was undergoing some repair, and they had, as much as possible, closed up the current of the water; and the canal was, if not altogether dry, very easy to get across; there was only a slender stream of water.

Some branches of dry wood which had fallen from the different bushes that extended into the sinuosities of the rock, tapestried this deserted place, which the accidental drying up of the canal rendered at this moment more accessible than usual.

Overjoyed at this piece of good fortune, diligent and active as Martha in the Gospel, Jeanne and Marie quickly took off their sabots and crossed the stream.

"The water is very cold," said they, when they reached the opposite bank, and were putting on again their sabots.

It was in the month of February, and these torrents from the Montagne, recently fallen from the eternal snows in which their source is formed, are generally of a glacial temperature.

Bernadette, less alert or less ardent, otherwise a very puny object, was already on this side of the little channel of the water. It was altogether an embarrassment to cross this feeble current. She had stockings on, whilst Marie and Jeanne had bare feet with sabots, and she had to pull her shoes off.

In presence of the exclamation of her companions she dreaded the cold of the water.

"Throw two or three large stones into the middle of the stream," said she to them, "in order that I may be able to get over with dry feet."

The two wood gleaners had already occupied themselves with arranging their little fagot. They did not wish to lose any time in putting themselves to any trouble.

"Do as we did," replied Jeanne, "cross with your bare feet."

Bernadette submitted, and leaning her back against a portion of the rock that was there, began to undo her shoes.

It was about midday. The *Angelus* had to be

rung at that moment in all the steeples of the
Pyrennean villages.

VIII.

She was in the act of taking off her first stock-
ing, when she heard around her something like
the noise of a blast of wind arising in the meadow
with an unknown character of an irresistible
power.

She thought it was a sudden hurricane, and she
instinctively went back. To her great surprise,
the poplars which border the Gave were completely motionless. Not even the slightest breeze
had agitated their peaceable branches.

"I must have been mistaken," said she to herself.

And, thinking still about this noise, she did
not know what to suppose it.

She sat down again to take off her shoes.

At this moment the impetuous rolling of this
unknown wind made itself heard again.

Bernadette lifted her head, looked in front of
her, and immediately uttered, or endeavoured to
utter, a loud scream, which was stifled in her
throat. She shivered in all her members.
Astounded, dazzled, and overwhelmed to a certain
degree by what she saw before her, she sunk down
on herself; she bent, so to speak, her whole body,
and fell on her two knees.

A spectacle truly unheard of had just struck
her sight. The description of the child, the
countless questions which a thousand investigat-

ing and shrewd minds have put to her since this epoch, the precise and minute particulars into which so many persons of intelligence on the watch have forced her to descend, allow of our tracing with a sure hand every detail of the general physiognomy, the astonishing portrait of the wonderful being which appeared at this moment to the eyes of Bernadette, who was terrified and ravished.

IX.

Above the grotto before which Marie and Jeanne, busy and stooping towards the earth, were collecting together the dry wood; in that rustic niche formed by the rock, there stood upright, in the midst of a superhuman brightness, a lady of incomparable splendour.

The unspeakable glimmering which hovered about her did not disturb nor hurt the eyes like the brightness of the sun. Quite on the contrary, the aureole, bright as a pencil of rays, and peaceful as a deep shadow, invincibly attracted the view, which seemed to be bathed in it, and repose in it with delight. It was, like the morning star, the light in the coolness of the day. There was nothing vague otherwise, or vapoury in the apparition itself. It had none of the fugitive outlines of a fantastic vision; it was a living reality, a human body, which the eye judged to be palpable as the flesh of us all, and which only differed from that of an ordinary person by its aureole, its divine beauty.

It was of a middle stature. It seemed to be
quite young, and had the graces of twenty years of
age; but without losing anything of its tender
delicacy, that splendour, fugitive in time, had in
it a character that was eternal. Still more, in its
features, amid lines that were divine, were
blended in a manner, without disturbing its harmony, the successive and isolated beauties of the
four seasons of human life. The innocent frankness of a child, the absolute purity of a Virgin,
the tender gravity of the highest of maternities, a
wisdom superior to that of all accumulated ages,
were summed up and melted together, without
injuring one another, in this marvellous countenance of a young person. To what are we to com-
pare it in this decayed world, where the rays of
the beautiful are scattered, broken, and tarnished,
and where they can never appear to us without
some impure mixture? Every image, every com-
parison, would be a lowering of this inexpressible
type. No majesty in the universe, no distinction
in this world, no simplicity here below, can give
an idea of it, nor help us better to understand it.
It is not with the lamps of the earth that we can
cause to be seen, and, so to speak, lighten up the
constellations of the heavens.

The regularity even, and the ideal purity of
these features, in which there is nothing to shock
us, carries them beyond the reach of description.
We must nevertheless state that the oval bend of
the countenance possessed an exquisite grace, that
the eyes were blue, and had a sweetness that
seemed as if they could melt the heart of any one
who was beheld by her. The lips breathed a

goodness and a meekness that were divine. The forehead appeared to contain a wisdom that was supreme, that is, a knowledge of all things, joined to an unlimited virtue.

The garments being of an unknown material, and woven doubtless in the mysterious workshop where the lily of the valley is clothed, were white as the spotless snow on the mountains, and more magnificent in their simplicity than the brilliant costume of Solomon in his glory. The robe, long and trailing, the robe with chaste folds, allowed her feet to come out, which rested on the rock, and trod lightly the branch of the sweet briar. Upon each of her feet, of a virginal nudity, bloomed the mystical rose of a golden colour.

Before, a girdle, blue as the sky, and tied in a knot half round the body, hung in two long bands that touched almost the top of the feet. Behind, enveloping in its folds the shoulders and the upper part of the arms, a white veil, fixed round the head, descended even to the bottom of the robe.

Neither ring, nor necklace, nor diadem, nor jewels; none of those ornaments with which human vanity at all times is adorned. A Rosary, the beads of which were as white as drops of milk, the chain of which was as yellow as the gold of the harvest, hung in her hands, that were fervently joined together. The beads of the rosary slided one after the other through her fingers. Notwithstanding, the lips of this Queen of Virgins remained motionless. Instead of reciting the Rosary, she heard perhaps in her own heart the eternal echo of the Angelical Salutation and the

immense murmuring of the invocations that came
from the earth. Each bead that she touched was
without doubt a shower of heavenly graces, which
fell upon souls as pearls of dew into the chalice of
flowers.

She observed silence; but later her own words
and the miraculous facts which we shall have to
describe will necessarily attest that she was the
Immaculate Virgin, the most august and most
holy Mary, Mother of God.

X.

The child, in the first moment of stupefaction,
had instinctively placed her hand upon her
rosary; and holding it in her fingers, she wished
to make the sign of the cross, and lift her hand to
her forehead. But her terror was such that she
had not the strength to raise her arm; it fell
down powerless on her bended knees.

Nolite timere—" Fear not," said Jesus to His
disciples, when He came to them walking upon
the waves of the Sea of Tiberias.

The look, the smile of the incomparable Virgin
seemed to say the same thing to the little
frightened shepherdess.

With a grave and gentle gesture, which had the
air of an all-powerful benediction for earth and
heaven, she made herself, as if to encourage the
child, the sign of the Cross. And the hand of
Bernadette, raising itself by degrees, as if invisibly carried by her who is called the Help of

Christians, made the sign of the cross at the same time.

Ego sum, nolite timere—"It is I Myself, fear not," said Jesus to His disciples.

The child had no longer any fear. Dazzled, charmed, doubting herself nevertheless at moments, and rubbing her eyes with her hands, her looks constantly attracted by this celestial apparition, not knowing what to think, humbly recited her rosary—" I believe in God"—" Hail Mary, full of grace."

As she was going to finish it by saying, "Glory be to the Father, to the Son, and to the Holy Ghost, world without end," the luminous Virgin all at once disappeared, without doubt returning to the eternal heaven where the Holy Trinity dwells.

Bernadette experienced, as it were, the feeling of some one who descends again, or who falls down again. She looked round her. The Gave ran as usual, roaring against the pebble stones and the broken rocks; but this noise seemed to her harsher than before, the waters appeared to her more sombre, the scenery more dull, the light of the sun less bright. Before her lay the rocks of Massabielle, beneath which her companions were gleaning bits of wood. Above the grotto, the niche in which the branch of sweet briar reposed was still open; but nothing unusual appeared in it, there was no trace left there of the divine vision—it was no longer the gate of heaven.

XI.

The scene which we have just related lasted about a quarter of an hour; not that Bernadette had had the consciousness of the time, but it could be measured by this circumstance, that she could say the five decades of her rosary.   .

Completely returned to herself, Bernadette finished taking off her shoes, crossed the little current of water, and rejoined her companions. Absorbed by the thought of what she had just seen, she was no longer timid for the coldness of the water. All the infantine strength of the humble little girl was concentrated to ruminate in her heart the remembrance of this unheard of apparition.

Jeanne and Marie had seen her fall on her knees, and give herself to prayer; but that is not unusual, thanks be to God, among the children of the Montagne, and being occupied in their task they had paid no attention to it.

Bernadette was surprised at the perfect calm of her sister and Jeanne, who had terminated just at that moment their little labour, and who, entering under the grotto, had begun to play as if nothing extraordinary had taken place.

"Have you seen nothing then?" said the child to them.

They remarked then that she appeared agitated and affected.

"No," replied they. "And thou, hast thou seen anything?"

Did the child who had seen dread a profanation,

if she told them what filled her soul ? Did she
desire to enjoy it in silence ? Was she reserved
through a sort of fearful timidity ? Or is it, notwithstanding, a feeling of obeying that instinctive
wont of humble souls to hide as a treasure the
particular graces with which God favours them ?

" If you have seen nothing," said she, " I have
nothing to say to you."

The little fagots were made up. The three
children resumed their path to Lourdes. But
Bernadette had been unable to dissemble · her
trouble. As they went along, Marie and Jeanne
tormented her to know what she had seen. The
little shepherdess yielded to their entreaties, and
to their promise to keep the secret.

" I have seen," said she, " something dressed
in white."

And she described to them, in her own language,
her marvellous vision.

" Behold what I have seen," said she in conclusion; " but I beg of you, say nothing about it."

Mary and Jeanne doubted not. The soul, in
its purity and its first innocence, is naturally a
believer, and doubt is not the evil of artless
infancy. Moreover, the earnest and sincere tone
of voice of Bernadette, still overpowered, had an
irresistible influence. Mary and Jeanne doubted
not, but they were frightened. The children of
the poor are always timid. This is easy to
explain ; suffering comes to them from every side.

" It is perhaps something to do us harm," said
they. " Let us not go back any more, Bernadette."

Scarcely had they reached the house, when the

confidants of the little shepherdess were no longer able to keep their secret. Marie related every thing to her mother.

" These are childish tricks," said she ; " let your sister then tell me ?" replied she, asking Bernadette.

This one began again her description.

The mother Soubirous shrugged her shoulders.

" Thou art deceived. It is nothing at all. Thou hast thought to have seen something, but thou hast seen nothing. These are fancies, child's play."

Bernadette persisted in her story.

" At all events," replied the mother, " thou must not go there again, I forbid it."

This prohibition struck Bernadette to the heart ; for since the apparition had vanished, her greatest desire was to see it again.

Nevertheless, she resigned herself to it and made no reply.

XII.

Two days, Friday and Saturday, passed over. This extraordinary event was continually coming into the mind of Bernadette, and it formed the constant subject of her conversations with Marie, with Jeanne and other children. Bernadette had still in the midst of her soul, and in all its sweetness, the remembrance of the heavenly vision. A passion, if we can employ such a profane word to designate a feeling so pure, had sprung up in the innocent heart of the little girl ; an ardent desire to see again the incomparable Lady. This name of "Lady" was that which she gave her in her rustic language. Nevertheless, when she was asked if this apparition resembled any of the ladies whom she saw, whether in the street or in the church, or any one of those who were celebrated in the country for their striking beauty, she shook her head and sweetly smiled.

"Nothing of all that gives an idea of it," said she. "She possesses a beauty that cannot be expressed."

She desired then to see her again. The other children were divided between fear and curiosity.

XIII.

On Sunday the sun rose full of rays and the weather was magnificent. There are often in the Pyrennean valleys some days in spring, that are warm and pleasant, that have as it were lost their way in the season of winter.

On returning from Mass Bernadette begged her sister Marie, Jeanne, and two or three other children to press her mother to take off her prohibition and allow them to return to the Rocks of Massabielle.

"Perhaps there is something wrong," said the children.

Bernadette replied that she did not think so, that she had seen so good a countenance.

"At all events," replied the little girls, who, better instructed than the poor shepherdess of Bartrès, knew a little of the catechism; "at all events, we must throw some holy water upon it."

If it is the devil he will go away. You will say to
it : 'If you come on the part of God approach ; if
you come from the devil, get away from me.'"

It was not, at all events, the formula precisely
prescribed by the exorcism ; but in reality, these
little theologians at Lourdes reasoned in this
affair with as much justice and prudence as could
have been done by a Doctor of Sorbonne.

It was then decided, in this infantine council,
that they should carry some holy water with them.
A certain degree of apprehension had likewise
come upon Bernadette herself, in consequence of
these little discourses.

There remained only the obtaining permission.

The children all together asked it after dinner.
The mother Soubirous wished at first to adhere to
her prohibition, alleging that the Gave went along
and bathed the Rocks of Massabielle, that there
might be some danger, that the hour of Vespers
was at hand, that they should not expose themselves to stay away, that these were childish fancies, &c. But we know to what an extent of
pressure and irresistible entreaty a legion of children will go. All promised to be very prudent and
expeditious, and be well behaved, and the mother
finished by giving in to them.

The little group went to church, and prayed
there for a short time. One of the companions of
Bernadette had brought a half-pint bottle ; they
filled it with holy water.

When they reached the grotto, nothing manifested itself at first.

"Let us pray," said Bernadette, "and say our
rosary."

All at once the countenance of Bernadette appeared to be transformed, and was so in effect; an extraordinary emotion was exhibited in her features; her looks, more brilliant, seemed to aspire to a light that was divine.

With her feet placed upon the rock, clad as at the first time, the marvellous apparition came and manifested itself to her eyes.

"Look," said she, "there it is."

Alas! the sight of the other children was not miraculously divested, like hers, of the veil of flesh which hinders us from seeing spiritualized bodies. The little girls only perceived the desert rock and the branches of sweet briar, which descended, whilst forming a thousand arabesque shapes, to the foot of the mysterious niche where Bernadette contemplated an unknown being.

Nevertheless, the countenance of Bernadette was such that there were no means of doubting. One of the children placed the bottle of holy water in the hands of her who saw.

Then Bernadette, remembering what she had promised, arose, and shaking quickly and with several repetitions the little bottle, sprinkled the wonderful lady, who quite graciously remained at some paces before her, in the interior of the niche.

"If you come on the part of God, approach," said Bernadette.

At these words, at these gestures of the child, the Virgin bowed several times and advanced almost to the end of the rock. She seemed to smile at the precautions of Bernadette, and at her weapons of war, and at the sacred name of God her countenance lighted up.

4

"If you come on the part of God, approach," said Bernadette.

But, seeing her so beautiful, so resplendent with glory, so adorned with heavenly goodness, she felt her heart fail her at the moment of adding, "If you come on the part of the devil, begone." These words, which had been dictated to her, seemed monstrous to her in the presence of the incomparable being, and they fled for ever from her thoughts, without even mounting to her lips.

She prostrated again, and continued to recite her rosary, which the Blessed Virgin seemed to hear, in causing herself her own to pass through her fingers.

At the end of this prayer the apparition vanished.

XIV.

In resuming the road to Lourdes, Bernadette was full of joy. She ruminated in the depth of her soul on these most extraordinary events. Her companions conceived a vague terror. The transformation of the countenance of Bernadette had shown them the reality of a supernatural apparition. Now all that surpasses nature, alarms it. "Depart from us, O Lord, for fear lest we die," said the Jews in the Old Testament.

"We are afraid, Bernadette. Let us not go back there. What you have seen may do us harm;" said her timid companions to the young girl who saw.

As they had promised, the children returned for

Vespers. As they came out of church the beauty of the weather attracted on the way a portion of the population, going, and coming, and chatting in the last rays of the sun, so soft during these splendid days of winter. The story of the little girls circulated up and down among the different companies of pedestrians. And it is thus that the report of these strange occurrences commenced to spread about the town. The rumour, which at first only agitated a humble society of children, increased like a wave which mounts and penetrates from one to another in popular circles. The quarry men, who are very numerous in this country, the sempstresses, the workmen, the peasants, the servant maids, the housekeepers, the poor people held discussions together; some were for believing in it, some for disputing it, others for laughing at it, several for exaggerating it and amplifying the account of this pretended fact of the apparition. Save one or two exceptions, the townspeople did not take even the trouble to dwell upon these fancies of children.

Strange occurrence! The father and mother, though they fully believed in the sincerity of Bernadette, considered the apparition as an illusion. "She is a child," said they. "She thought she saw it; but she has seen nothing. They are the imaginations of a little girl."

Nevertheless, the extraordinary precision of the statements of Bernadette engaged their attention. Sometimes, struck by the peculiar manner of speaking of their daughter, they felt themselves shaken in their incredulity. Though they fully

desired that she should not go any more to the
grotto, they no longer dared to forbid her.

She nevertheless did not return there till
Thursday.

XV.

During these first days of the week, several persons among the people called on the Soubirous
and interrogated Bernadette. The answers of the
girl were frank and precise. She might be under
an illusion; but it sufficed to see her and hear her
to be satisfied of her good faith. Her perfect simplicity, her innocent age, the irresistible accent of
her words, carried with it in her whole manner,
a most astonishing authority, which inspired
confidence, and for the greater part of the time,
secured conviction. All those who saw her came
away from their interview completely satisfied as
to her veracity, and persuaded that an extraordinary fact had transpired at the rocks of Massabielle.

The declaration of a little ignorant girl could
not however be enough to establish a fact so entirely out of the ordinary course of things; other
proofs were required besides the word of a child.

What, besides, was this apparition, supposing
it to be real? Was it a spirit of light or an angel
of the abyss? Was it some soul in a state of
suffering, wandering and asking for prayers? or
was it such or such a person, not long since dead
in the odour of sanctity, and manifesting itself in
its glory?—Faith and superstition started each of
these hypotheses.

The mournful ceremonies of Ash Wednesday contributed to dispose towards one or other of these solutions, a young girl and a lady of Lourdes. Did they see, in the dazzling whiteness of the dress of the apparition, some idea of the winding sheet or appearance of a phantom? We know not. The young lady's name was Antoinette Peyret, and she was one of the Congregation of Mary; the other was Madame Millet.

"It is without doubt some soul from purgatory who is asking for Masses," thought they, and they went to visit Bernadette.

"Ask that lady who she is and what she wishes," said they to her. "Let her explain herself to you, or better still, as you cannot understand her well, let her put it into writing."

Bernadette, who felt herself, by an interior motion, strongly impelled to return to the grotto, obtained leave again from her parents; and the following morning, Thursday, the 18th February, towards six o'clock, at dawn of day, after having heard Mass at the Church at half past five o'clock, she took, with Antoinette Peyret and Madame Millet, the way to the grotto.

XVI.

The repairs of the mill belonging to Monsieur De Laffitte were finished, and the canal which had caused it to be set in motion had been restored to its free course, so that it was impossible to pass as before by the island of Châlet in order to reach the end of the journey. It was necessary to go up

by the flank of the Espélugues, by taking a very
toilsome road which led to the forest of Lourdes,
then come down again by a very dangerous way to
the grotto, in the midst of rocks and hillocks,
rapid and sandy, of the Massabielle.

With these unexpected difficulties before them,
the two companions of Bernadette were a little
frightened. She herself, on the contrary, having
come to this spot, experienced a fluttering, a hurry
as it were to arrive. It seemed to her that some
invisible being raised her up and gave her an unaccustomed energy. She who was usually so
weak, felt herself at once quite strong. Her step
became so quick at the ascent of the side of the
rocks, that Antoinette and Madame Millet, both
in the prime of life, could with difficulty follow
her. Her asthma which hindered all quickness
in walking, appeared to have momentarily disappeared. When she got to the top, she was
neither panting for breath nor fatigued. Whilst
her two companions were dripping with perspira-
tion, her face was calm and composed. She came
down the rocks, which she traversed nevertheless
for the first time, with the same care and activity,
having ever the consciousness of an invisible support that guided her and sustained her. Over
those declivities almost at the peak, in the midst of
those rolling stones, above the abyss, her step was
as firm and safe as if she had walked on the broad
and level soil of a high road;—Madame Millet
and Antoinette did not attempt to follow her at
this impossible pace. They came down with the
slowness and precautions necessitated by so perilous a path.

Bernadette arrived consequently at the grotto a few minutes before them. She fell upon her knees, began to say her Rosary, while looking at the niche, still empty, which was tapestried by the branches of the sweet briar.

All at once she utters a cry. The well-known brightness of the aureole shore at the bottom of the excavation; a voice makes itself heard and calls her. The marvellous apparition displayed itself once more standing upright at some paces distant from her. The admirable Virgin inclined her countenance all illuminated with an eternal serenity towards the child; and with a gesture of her hand, she beckoned to her to approach.

At this moment, after a thousand painful efforts, the two companions of Bernadette, Antoinette and Madame Millet arrived. They perceived the features of the child, transformed by an ecstasy.

She herself hears and sees them.

" She is there," said she. " She is making me a sign to advance."

" Ask her if she is displeased that we should be here with you. Otherwise we shall go away."

Bernadette cast her eyes on the Virgin, invisible to all but herself, listened a moment, and returned to her companions.

" You may remain;" answers she.

The two ladies went on their knees by the side of the child, and lighted a blessed taper which they had brought with them.

It was doubtless the first time, since the creation of the world, that such a glimmer had shone in this wild spot. This simple act, which seemed to inaugurate a sanctuary, had in itself a mysterious solemnity. Supposing that the apparition was divine, this sign of visible adoration, this little humble flame lit up by two humble women of the country would not again be extinguished, and would go on increasing through a long series of ages. The breath of incredulity will vainly exhaust itself in efforts, the storm of persecution will raise itself in vain; this flame, fed by the faith of the people, would continue to mount, erect and inextinguishable, to the throne of God. While these rustic hands, without doubt unconsciously to themselves, lighted it up also in all simplicity, and for the first time, in this unknown grotto where a child was praying, the break of day, at first growing white, had successively assumed a hue of gold and then one of purple, and the sun, which soon would, across and in spite of the clouds, inundate the earth with his light, began to dawn from behind the summit of the mountains.

Bernadette, ravished in ecstasy, contemplated the beauty without spot. *Thou art all fair, my beloved, and a spot is not in thee.*

Her companions call to her again.

Advance to her, since she summons you and makes you a sign. Approach. Ask her who she is? Wherefore she is come here? Is it a soul from Purgatory who implores our prayers, who wishes to have masses said for her?......Beg of her to write what she desires, on this paper. We are disposed to do everything she wishes, all that is necessary for her repose.

The girl who saw took the paper ink and pen which they gave her, and went forward to the apparition, the maternal look of which encouraged her on seeing her approach.

Nevertheless, at every step that the child took, the apparition gradually retired into the interior of the excavation. Bernadette lost sight of it for an instant, and penetrated under the vault of the grotto below. There, still above her but much nearer, in the opening of the niche, she again beheld the Holy Virgin surrounded with rays.

Bernadette, holding in her hand the objects which had been given her, stood up on her feet to reach, with her little arms and her low stature, to the height where the Supernatural Being stood above.

Her two companions also stepped forward to try to hear the conversation which she was going to hold. But Bernadette, without returning, and as if obeying herself, a gesture of the apparition, made them a sign with her hand not to approach.

Quite confused, they withdrew a little aside.

" My lady," says the child, " if you have anything to communicate to me, would you have the goodness to write who you are and what you desire ?"

The Divine Virgin smiled at this simple request. Her lips opened and she spoke.

" What I have to tell you," replied she, " I have no need to write. Do me only the favour to come here during fifteen days."

" I promise you to do so," said Bernadette.

The Blessed Virgin smiled again, and made a sign she was satisfied, showing also her full confidence in the word of that poor peasant girl of fourteen years of age.

She knew that the little shepherd girl of Bartrès
was like those very pure children whose fair heads
Jesus loved to caress, when saying, "The kingdom of heaven is for such as resemble them."
At the word of Bernadette she replies, by a solemn
engagement,

"And I," said she, "promise you to make you
happy, not in this world, but in the next."

To the child who consented for a few days, she
gave an assurance, in compensation, for eternity.

Bernadette, without losing sight of the apparition, returned to her companions.

She remarked that, while all the while following
her with her eyes, the Blessed Virgin rested for a
considerable time and with tenderness her countenance upon Antoinette Peyret, that of the two
who was not married, and who formed a portion
of the Congregation of the Children of Mary.

She repeated to them what had just passed.

"She is looking at you at this moment," said
the girl who ran to Antoinette.

This young person was quite taken up with this
speech, and since that epoch, she lives on that
remembrance.

"Ask her," said they, "if it would annoy her,
for us, during the fifteen days, to come and accompany you here every day?"

Bernadette addressed herself to the apparition.

"They can return with you," answers the Holy
Virgin, "they and others also. I desire to see
people come here."

In saying these words, she disappeared, leaving
that brilliant brightness with which she was en-
compassed, and which vanished by degrees.

On this occasion, as on others, the child re-marked a detail which seemed, as it were, the law of the aureole with which the Holy Virgin was surrounded.

"When the vision takes place," said she, in her own language, "I behold the light at first and then the 'Lady;' when the vision ceases, it is the 'Lady' who disappears first, and the light after-wards."

BOOK II.

I.

On her return to Lourdes, Bernadette was
obliged to speak to her parents of the promise
which she had just made to the mysterious lady,
and of the fifteen consecutive days during which
she had bound herself to return to the grotto.
On their side Antoinette and Madame Millet related what had passed, the marvellous transformation of the child during the ecstasy, the words of
the apparition, the invitation to return for fifteen
days. The report of these strange events was
propagated immediately on all sides, and being
carried abroad very rapidly by the popular feeling,
caused, in one way or other, a most profound
agitation throughout the country. This Thursday, the 18th February, 1858, was precisely the
market day at Lourdes. There was as usual a
great number of people, so that, that very evening, the news of the visions, true or false, of Bernadette, spread themselves on the mountains and
in the valleys at Bagnères, at Tarbes, at Canteret,
at Saint-Pè, at Nay, in all directions of the department, and in the nearest towns of the Béarn. The
following morning, a hundred persons were already

stationed at the grotto at the moment that Bernadette arrived there. The next morning there were
five hundred. On Sunday morning there were
several thousand.

What did they see however ? What did they
hear under these wild rocks ? Nothing, absolutely nothing, except a poor child at prayer, who
said she saw and heard. The more slight the
cause in appearance, the more unaccountable
humanly was the effect.

It must have been, the believers pretended,
either that a reflection from on high was really
visible over this child, or that the breath of God,
which moves hearts as He pleases, had passed
over these multitudes. *Spiritus ubi vult spirat.*

An electric current, an irresistible power from
which no one could keep her, seemed to have excited this population at the word of an ignorant
shepherdess. In the timber-yards, in the work-
shops, in the interior of families, in societies,
among the laity and among the clergy, among the
poor and the rich, at the club, in the coffee-
houses, in the public-houses, in the squares, in
the streets, night and morning, in private and
public, nothing was talked of but this. Whether
anyone sympathised or was hostile, or whether
they were neither one nor the other, but only
curious or anxious about the truth, there was
nobody in the country whose minds at this moment were not ardently, I was going to say solely,
engrossed with these events.

The popular instinct did not wait till the apparition had told its name, to recognize it. " It is

without doubt the Blessed Virgin," said they, on all sides amongst the multitude.

Before the authority, so very small in itself, of a little girl of thirteen or fourteen years of age, pretending to see and hear what no one around her could see or hear, the philosophers of the country, fed with the powerful prose of the Journals, had a capital opportunity of inveighing against superstition.

" This child is not even of age to take an oath ; she would be listened to with difficulty in a court, giving her deposition on an insignificant fact ; and we are desired to believe her when it is a question as to an impossible event, an apparition....Is it not clear that it is a comedy, got up for some money-making by her family or by the priest-party ? Two clear-sighted eyes are enough to see through this miserable intrigue. The first comer amongst us would not require ten minutes to do so."

Some of those who held this language wanted to see Bernadette, interrogate her, and be present at her ecstasies. The answers of the child were simple, natural, without any contradiction, made in an accent of truth which it was impossible to mistake, which carried into the most prejudiced minds a conviction of her entire sincerity. As to ecstasies, those who have seen at Paris the great actresses of our time, declared that art could not attain to such a perfection. The comedy theme did not hold more than twenty-four hours before the evidence.

The Savants, those who had at first allowed the

philosophers to decide the question, took up the work at this moment.

"We know perfectly well that state," declared they. "Nothing is more natural. This little girl is sincere, quite sincere in her replies ; she is under a delusion ; she thinks she sees, and she does not see, she thinks she hears, and she does not hear. As to her ecstasies, which are equally sincere with her, they are the result neither of comedy nor of art, which would be powerless in producing such effects, but they proceed from medicine. The daughter of Soubirous is subject to a disease ; it is Catalepsy. A derangement of the brain complicated by a muscular and nervous affection, such is the entire explanation of the phenomena about which there is such a popular noise. Nothing is more simple."

The little weekly Journal of the locality, *The Lavedan*, an advanced Journal that appeared habitually late, postponed its publication for a day or two in order to speak of this event, and in an article as hostile as it knew how to make, summed up the high considerations of philosophy and medicine that had been worked up by the free thinkers of the place. From this moment, that is to say, from Friday evening or Saturday, the comedy theme had already been given up in presence of the clearness of the facts, and the free thinking gentlemen no longer returned to it, as can be ascertained through all the journals of that period.

In conformity with the universal tradition of the grand critic in matters of religion, the good Editor of the *Lavedan* began by calumniating a

little and insinuating that Bernadette and her
companions were thieves.

"Three children of low degree went to collect
some branches from the trees, the remains of a
wood which was cut down near the gates of the
town.   These girls, *seeing themselves surprised by
the proprietor*, fled with all their might into the
grotto which is near to the road of the Forest of
Lourdes."*

It is always in this style that free thought has
written history.   After this loyal act which manifested clearly his good will and his admirable sense
of justice, the editor of the *Lavedan* gave, without
any very gross errors, a description of the facts
themselves that happened at the Rocks of Massabielle.   They were too notorious, and had too
many witnesses to be denied.

"We shall not relate," added he, "the thousand
versions that have been given of this subject; we
shall only say that the young girl goes every
morning to pray at the entry of the grotto, having
a taper in her hand, escorted by more than five
hundred persons.   There she is seen to pass from
the greatest recollection to a gentle smile, and fall
back again into a completely extatic state; tears
drop from her motionless eyes, that remain continually fixed on the spot where the grotto stands,
in which she thinks she sees the Holy Virgin.
We shall keep our readers duly informed of this

* *The Lavedan* of the 18th February, 1858.   In spite of the
date, this number did not appear really till the evening of the
nineteenth or the twentieth, as the facts themselves, in the text
prove, and further announced an extract from a judgment pos-
terior to the date of the Journal.

occurrence, which every day gains fresh adepts."

Of comedy, of jugglery, not a word. It was felt that on this side everything fell to pieces at the first interview with the child, at the first glance given to Bernadette in ecstasy, to her tears, which at times inundated her cheeks. The excellent editor, to succeed better in making it believed that she was ill, affected to pity her. He only spoke of her as describing her with a kind sort of compassion. "Poor visionary." "Everything," said he, "from her first words, causes us to suppose that this young girl is attacked with catalepsy."

"Delusion and catalepsy," were the two great words among the savants at Lourdes. "Know well," repeated they frequently, "that there is nothing supernatural to which science has not done full justice. Science explains everything, science alone is certain. It compares, it judges, it only looks at facts. The supernatural was good during ages in which the world was buried in superstition, in which men knew not how to observe it, but now we defy it to show itself; we are at this point. See the stupidity of the people! Because a little girl is unwell; because in her state of fever, she has her crotchets and fancies, all these weak-minded people cry out a miracle. Human stupidity must surpass all bounds, to see an apparition in what appears not, and a voice in what nobody hears. Let the pretended apparition stop the sun like Josue, let it strike the rock like Moses, and let it cause the water to spring forth; let it cure the incurable, let it in some manner command nature; then we

5

shall believe. But who does not know that such things never happen, and have never happened."

Such were, in these and similar terms, the discourses that were interchanged from morning till night, among the sagacious intellects that represented at Lourdes medicine and philosophy.

·The greater part of these thinkers had seen Bernadette often enough to attest that she was playing no comedy. That sufficed for their spirit of inquiry. From the fact that she was evidently in good faith, they concluded that she must be either weak in her mind, or a Cataleptic. The possibility of any other explanation was not admitted by their strong minds. When it was proposed to them to study the fact, to see the child again, going or returning from the grotto, to follow in all their details these surprising phenomena, they shrugged their shoulders, laughed philosophically and said, " We know all that by heart. These cries are known. Before a month this child will be completely mad and probably paralyzed."

Some, nevertheless, did not reason altogether in the same way.

" Such phenomena are rare," said one of the most distinguished physicians in the town, Monsieur Dr. Dozous, " and for my part, I shall not fail on this occasion to examine them with care. The partisans of the supernatural throw them too often in the face of medicine for me not to be curious; since they are brought forward today within reach, I will study them attentively, and fathom to the bottom *de visu* and by experience, this celebrated question."

M. Dufo, the advocate, and several members of

the bar; M. Pougat, president of the tribunal; a great number of others resolved to devote themselves, during the fifteen days already announced, to the most scrupulous inquiries, and to attend as much as possible in the first places. In proportion as the matter assumed more considerable proportions, the number of observers augmented.

Some physicians, some suicidal Socrates, some local philosophers calling themselves Voltairians to make believe that they had read Voltaire, hardened themselves, solely against their own curiosity, and made it a point of honour not to figure in the stupid crowd that every day went on increasing. As it happens almost always, these fanatics of free inquiry had for principle never to inquire at all. For them no fact was worthy of attention, that disturbed the inflexible dogmas which they had learnt in the credo of their Journal. From the height of their infallible wisdom, at the door of their shop, in front of their coffeehouse, at the windows of the club, these spirits of the first water beheld with sublime contempt, the countless hosts of human beings, which I know not what vortex was carrying away to the grotto.

III.

The clergy, naturally, were strongly impressed by these facts; but with tact and good sense, they had assumed, from the commencement, an attitude of the most reserved and prudent kind.

The clergy, surprised as all the rest of the world by the remarkable event, which had forcibly gained possession of public attention, took considerable pains over it, that they might understand its character.   Where, in the expansion of their ideas, local Voltairianism could only see one possible solution, the clergy saw several others.   The fact might be natural ; and in this case, be produced by a very clever comedy, or by some very strange malady: but it might be very supernatural ; and then, the enquiry would be if this supernatural was diabolic or divine.—God has His miracles, and the devil has his wonders.—The clergy knew all these things, and they resolved to study with extreme care the smallest circumstances of the event, which was then in process of manifestation.   They had moreover, from the first moment, received with great distrust the report of a fact so surprising.   Nevertheless, it might be divine, and they did not intend to pronounce upon it hastily.

The child whose name had suddenly become so celebrated throughout the country, was completely unknown to the priests of the town.   During the fifteen days after her return to Lourdes, to be with her parents, she went to the catechism, but the ecclesiastic entrusted this year with the instruction of the children, M. L'Abbè Pomian, had not observed her.   He had however once or twice asked her a question, but without knowing her name, and without paying any attention to her person, lost as she was in the crowd of children, unknown still as those habitually are, who are the last comers.   When all the populations were now flocking to the grotto, towards the third of the fifteen days required by the mysterious apparition,

M. L'Abbé Pomian, desiring to know this extraordinary child, of whom everybody was speaking, called her by her name at the catechism, as he had the custom of doing, whenever he wished to interrogate anyone. At the name of Bernadette Soubirous, a little girl, mean-looking and poorly clad, humbly got up. The ecclesiastic did not remark in her anything, but her simplicity, and likewise her extreme ignorance of everything connected with religion.

The parish had at its head at this moment, a priest whose character it is important to describe.

M. L'Abbé Peyramale, who was about fifty years of age at that time, had been for two years the Curate-Dean of the town and canton of Lourdes. He was a man naturally rough, impetuous perhaps in his love of good, but softened by grace, in whom could be perceived at times, the primitive tree, the rustic but solidly good tree, on whom the delicate and powerful hand of God had ingrafted the Christian and the priest. This innate impulsiveness entirely subdued as to what concerned himself, had become pure zeal for the house of God.

In the pulpit, his language, always apostolic, was sometimes harsh ; he inveighed against everything that was evil, and any abuse, any moral disorder, from whatever quarter it came, did not find him indifferent or weak. Often the society of the town, scourged in some one of its vices or its irregularities by the earnest discourses of its pastor, had raised a loud cry. He had not been dismayed, and had finished by always being by the help of God, victorious in the combat.

These men of duty are troublesome; and the world rarely forgives the independence and sincerity of their language. Nevertheless they pardoned him; for when they saw him walk through the town with his cassock darned and patched, his thick shoes mended and his old three-cornered hat disfigured, they knew that the money for his wardrobe had been employed in succouring the unfortunate. This priest so austere in his manners, so severe in his doctrines, had an inexpressibly kind heart, and he spent his patrimony in doing good, as unostentatiously as he was able. But his humility could not succeed in hiding as he would have wished his life of devotedness; the gratitude of the poor had spoken; a private life is besides very quickly seen through in small towns, and he had become the object of general veneration. One had only to behold the fashion with which his parishioners took off their hat when he passed in the street. One had only to witness the familiar, affectionate and pleasing manner, with which the poor people, seated on the step of their door, saluted him, "Good day, Monsieur Le Curé," and it could be guessed that a sacred bond, that of good well performed, united the shepherd to his sheep. The free-thinkers said of him: " He is not always convenient, but he is charitable and does not look after money. He is the best of men, notwithstanding his cassock."

Full of disinterestedness and kindness of heart in private life, never supposing then any evil, and letting himself even sometimes be deceived by people who took advantage of his generosity, he was, as a priest, prudent to mistrust in everything that belonged to the functions of his ministry, and to the eternal interests of religion. The man might sometimes be taken in, the priest never. There are graces belonging to a state of life.

This eminent priest united to a heart of an apostle, a good sense, together with a rare firmness, and a character which nothing in the world could shake when there was a question about the truth. Events were not long before they brought to light these first-rate qualities. In placing him at Lourdes at this epoch Providence had had His designs.

Controlling in this his impatient nature, M. l'Abbe Peyramale, before permitting his clergy to take any step and shew themselves at the grotto, before he permitted himself to do so, resolved to wait till the events had assumed a character clearly determined, till the proofs had exhibited themselves in one sense or other, and till ecclesiastical authority had pronounced.

He commissioned some laymen of intelligence and reliance to go to the rocks of Massabielle every time that Bernadette and the multitude went there, and to keep him well-informed, day by day and hour by hour, of all that might pass there; but at the same time that he took these measures to be perfectly made acquainted with everything, he took them also in order not to compromise in any way the clergy in the matter, the true nature of which was doubtful.

"Let them go on," said he to the impatient; "if on one side we are rigorously forced to examine with extreme caution the facts which are now transpiring; on the other, the most common prudence forbids us to mix up our persons with the crowd which is going to the grotto singing these cantiques. Let us refrain from appearing in it, and let us not expose ourselves either to consecrate by our presence an imposture or an illusion, or to combat, by a premature decision, by a hostile attitude, a work coming perhaps from God. As to our going there as simple spectators, it is not possible, in the costume which we wear. The population, seeing a priest in the middle of it, would form itself around it, in order that it might march at their head and intone their prayers. Now, if it yielded to the public pressure or to its own inconsiderate enthusiasm, and later should discover that these apparitions were a delusion and a deceit, who can tell to what point religion would be compromised in the persons of the clergy? If he resisted, on the contrary, and later the work of God became manifest, would not that resistance have the same unfavourable consequences?

"Let us abstain, then, since we could not but compromise God, whether in the works which He designs to accomplish, or in the holy ministry which He has deigned to confide to us."

Some in their ardour insisted on going.

"No," replied he, with firmness; "we should have only to interfere when there was a likelihood of some manifest heresy arising from it, or some superstition or disorder. Then our duty would be clearly marked out by the facts themselves. By the evil fruits we should judge of the evil tree, and we should run at the first symptom of evil to preserve our flock.

"But as yet nothing of this has been exhibited; quite on the contrary, the crowd, in the most profound recollection, limits itself to praying to the Holy Virgin, and the piety of the faithful appears to increase.

"Let us know how then to wait, while we devote ourselves apart to a necessary examen, the supreme decision which episcopal wisdom will have delivered on these facts.

"If these facts are from God, they have no need of us, and the Almighty will know well, without our poor assistance, how to surmount every obstacle, and turn things at His will to His designs.

"If this work, on the contrary, is not from God, He will fix the moment at which we ought to interfere to combat in His name.

"In a word, let us leave things to Providence."

Such were the profound reasons, the considerations of high wisdom, which decided, under these circumstances, M. the Curé Peyramale formally to inderdict all the priests placed under his jurisdiction from appearing at the Grotto of Massabiele, and to abstain himself from going there.

Monseigneur Laurence, the Bishop of Tarbes, approved of this prudent reserve, and extended even to all the ecclesiastics of the diocese the prohibition to be mixed up in any way with the events at Lourdes. When a priest, whether in the tribunal of penance or elsewhere, was interrogated as to the pilgrimage to the grotto, the answer was already given beforehand.

"We do not go there ourselves, and we cannot in consequence ourselves pronounce on facts which we do not sufficiently know. But it is evidently lawful for any of the faithful to go there, if convenient, and to examine into facts hitherto out of all ecclesiastical decision. Whether you go or not, we do not undertake either to advise or forbid your doing so; nor to authorize you to go there, nor to interdict it."

Such an attitude of strict neutrality was, it must be said, very difficult to maintain; for every priest was obliged to fight against, on this occasion, not only popular pressure, but also against his own wishes, assuredly very legitimate, to be personally present at extraordinary things that were on the point of being accomplished.

This line of conduct, however disagreeable it might be to keep it up, was notwithstanding adhered to. In the midst of these populations, raised up all at once like an ocean by an unknown breath of wind, and urged on to the mysterious rock where the supernatural apparition held a conversation with a child, the whole entire clergy, without a single exception, abstained from appearing. God, who invisibly directed all things, gave to His priests the strength not to give way to this unheard of current, and to remain immoveable in the midst of this prodigious movement. This immense reserve of the clergy necessarily showed that the hand and action of man had no place in these events, and that we must look for their cause elsewhere, or, to speak more justly, in a higher place.

IV.

This, however, did not suffice. Truth has need of another crucible. It was necessary that, being without a support, it should resist by itself and alone the great human powers chained together against it. It must brave these persecutors, furious enemies, adversaries skilful in preparing their snares. When truth passes through this trial, the weak tremble and are afraid that the work of God may be overthrown. *Quid timetis, modicæ fidei?* Those men who threaten it now are its supports in the future.

Those violent adversaries attest to the eyes of the world that such a work, that such a belief, has not been established clandestinely and in the shade, but fully in the face of enemies interested in seeing everything and controverting everything; they attest to the eyes of the world that its foundations are solid, since so many united efforts have not been able to shake them at the moment at which they arose in their original weakness; they attest that these bases are pure, since, examining everything by the exaggerated humour of malice and hatred, they have not been able to detect any vice or defect. Enemies are unsuspected witnesses, who depose, in spite of themselves, before posterity, in favour even of what they have been willing to hinder or destroy. Then, if the apparitions of the grotto were a starting point for a work of God, it was necessary, besides the reserve of the clergy, that there should be hostility from the powerful of the world.

God had equally provided that there should be.
While the ecclesiastical authority, personified in
the clergy, kept the wise reserve counselled by the
Curè of Lourdes, the civil authority was taking
notice, also itself, of the extraordinary movement
which was in the act of taking place in the town
and neighbourhood, and which reaching nearer
and nearer the whole department, had already
passed over the limits of the coast of Béarn.

Though it was true there had not been any disorder, these pilgrimages, these assembled crowds,
this child in an ecstasy, made this shady world
uneasy.

In the name of liberty of conscience were there
no means of stopping these people from praying,
and, above all, of praying where it seemed best to
themselves?   Such was the problem which official
liberalism began to attempt to solve.

In different degrees, M. Dutour, the Procureur-
Imperial, M. Duprat, Justice of Peace, the Mayor,
the Substitute, the Commissary of Police, and
many others besides, took or gave the alarm. A
miracle in the midst of the nineteenth century,
exhibiting itself all at once without demanding
permission and without procuring authorization,
appeared to some an intolerable outrage to civilization, an attack on the safety of the state, and it
was important for the honour of our enlightened
age to bring good order to it. The greater part of
these gentlemen had no belief besides in the possibility of these supernatural manifestations, and
they could not consent to see in it anything else
but an imposture or some disease. At all events
many were opposed instinctively, to every occur-

rence whatever which could directly or indirectly increase the influence of religion, against which they had either blind prejudices or avowed hatred.

Without repeating the reflections we have just made, it is truly remarkable to see how the supernatural, every time it is presented to the world, constantly meets, under different names and aspects, the same oppositions, the same indifference, the same loyalties. With different shades, the Herods, the Caiphases, the Pilates, the Joseph of Arimatheas, the Peters, the Thomases, the Holy Women, the open enemies, the cowardly, the weak, the devout, the sceptics, the timid, the heroes, belong to all periods.

The supernatural never escapes especially the hostility of a portion more or less of the official world. Only this hostility sometimes comes from the master and sometimes from the servant.

The most intelligent of the little legion of functionaries at Lourdes at this period was certainly Monsieur Jacomet, though M. Jacomet was hierarchically the lowest of all, since he only filled the humble employment of commissary of police. He was young, very shrewd under certain circumstances, and gifted with an ability of speech very seldom found among his compeers. Nobody understood rogues better than he. He was wonderfully apt in detecting their tricks, and on this point astonishing anecdotes were related of him. He understood much less upright people. At his ease in complicated affairs, this man was upset when he had to do with simplicity. The truth disconcerted him, and seemed to be suspected by him; disinterestedness excited his mistrust;

frankness put his mind in a torture, eager to discover everywhere duplicity and subterfuge. On
account of this monomania, sanctity had appeared
to him without doubt the most monstrous of impostures, and had found him implacable. Such
cross ways are often met with among men in that
profession, addicted by their employment ever to
find out guilt and circumvent crime. Such men
acquire at length a disposition of mind eminently
restless and suspicious, which inspires them with
marks of genius when they have to deal with
rogues, and enormous foolishness when they have
to deal with upright people with candid minds.
Though young M. Jacomet had contracted this fantastic malady of old agents of police, he was then
like those horses in the Pyrenees whose feet are
firm on the crooked and stony paths of the mountain, and who fall down all the two hundred steps
on the broad and level roads ; like those night
birds who only see in the darkness, and who in
full day knock against the trees and walls.

Satisfied with his own person, he was discon-
tented with his position, to which by his intelligence he was superior. Hence a certain restless
pride and an ardent desire to distinguish himself.
He had more than influence, he had an ascendency over his chiefs; and he affected to be on
equal terms with the procureur imperial and all
the other functionaries; he meddled with everything ; he domineered almost over everybody, and
managed, almost entirely it may be said, the affairs
of the town. For all that concerned the Canton
of Lourdes, the prefect of the department, M. the

Baron Massy saw only through the eyes of Jacomet.

Such was the Commissary of police, such was the important personage at Lourdes when the apparitions at the grotto of Massabielle took place.

V.

It was the third day of the Fifteen, the 21st of February, the first Sunday of Lent.

Before sunrise, an immense crowd, several thousand persons had already assembled, before and all round the grotto, on the banks of the Gave and in the meadow. She arrived, wrapped up in her white capulet, followed by some one of her own family, her mother or her sister. Her parents had assisted on the eve and before the eve at her ecstasies ; they had seen her transformed, and now they believed.

The child traversed quite simply, without assurance or embarrassment, the crowd which made way respectfully before her in opening for her a passage, and without appearing to notice the universal attention, she went, as if she was accomplishing an ordinary thing, down on her knees, and prayed underneath the niche, round which winded the branch of sweet briar.

A few instants after, her face was seen to brighten up and become radiant. The blood, however, was not carried up to her face; on the contrary, she became slightly pale, as if nature bent somewhat in presence of the apparition that manifested itself before it. All her features mounted up and

entered as it were into a superior region, as if
into a place of glory, expressing sentiments and
things that belong not to here below.   The
mouth, which was a little open, was admirably
beautiful, and seemed to breathe of heaven.   The
eyes, fixed and happy, contemplated an invisible
beauty, which no other face perceived, but which all
felt was present, which all, so to speak, beheld by
reflection on the countenance of the child.   This
poor little peasant girl, whose usual condition was
so mean, appeared no longer to belong to the
earth.

She was an angel of innocence, leaving the
world for a moment behind her and falling down
in adoration at the moment at which the eternal
gates were just opening, and at which she was
beholding Paradise.

All those who have seen Bernadette in an
ecstasy, speak of this spectacle as of a thing which
is altogether without analogy on the earth.   Their
impression after ten years is as lively as on the
first day.

A remarkable thing!   Although her attention
was entirely absorbed by the contemplation of the
Holy Virgin full of grace, she was also conscious
of what was passing about her.

At a certain moment her taper went out; she
stretched out her hand in order that the nearest
person might light it again.

Some one having wished, with a stick, to touch
the sweet briar, she quickly made a sign to let it
alone, and her face showed signs of fear.   "I was
afraid," said she, simply, "that they might touch
the Lady, and do her some harm."

One of the observers, whose name we have assigned, M. the Doctor Dozous, was at her side.

"It is neither," thought he, "catalepsy, with its stiffness of position, nor an ecstasy unconscious of illusions; it is an extraordinary fact, of an order altogether unknown to medicine."

He took the arm of the child, and felt her pulse. She seemed to pay no attention to it. The pulse, perfectly calm, was as regular as in its ordinary state.

"There is then no sickly excitement," said the learned doctor to himself, more and more embarrassed.

At this moment the girl who saw went some paces on her knees in advance into the grotto. The apparition had changed its place, and it was now through the interior opening that Bernadette could perceive it.

The look of the Holy Virgin appeared in an instant to travel over the whole earth, and she directed it all, filled with sorrow, towards Bernadette, who was on her knees.

"What is the matter? What must I do?" said the child to herself.

"Pray for sinners," replied the Mother of the human race.

On beholding sorrow thus veiling, like a cloud, the everlasting serenity of the Blessed Virgin, the heart of the poor shepherdess all at once experienced a cruel suffering. An unutterable sadness spread itself over her features. From her eyes, continually quite open and fixed on the apparition, two tears rolled down her cheeks, and stopped there without falling.

6

A ray of joy returned again to enlighten her countenance; for the Holy Virgin had without doubt turned herself her look towards hope, and contemplated, in the Heart of the Father, the inexhaustible source of infinite mercy descending upon the world, in the name of Jesus, and by the hands of the Church.

It was at that instant that the apparition vanished. The Queen of Heaven had just entered into her kingdom.

The aureole, as usual, continued still a few seconds, then insensibly faded away, like an electric light which melts away and disappears in the atmosphere.

The features of Bernadette by degrees descended to their wonted expression. It seemed as if she passed from the region of the sun to that of the shade, and the vulgarity of earth retook possession of that countenance which an instant before was transformed. It was then only a humble shepherdess, a little peasant girl whom there was nothing in appearance to distinguish from other children.

Around her pressed a crowd that was breathless, anxious, impressed, and recollected. We shall have an occasion elsewhere to describe their attitude.

VI.

During all the forenoon, after Mass, and until the hour for Vespers, nothing was talked of at Lourdes but these strange events, to which various interpretations were assigned. For those who had seen Bernadette in an ecstasy a proof was given in a manner which they pretended was irresistible. Some described their thoughts by somewhat happy comparisons. "In our valleys the sun shows himself late, hidden as he is on the east by the peak and the mountain of the Ger. But long before perceiving him, we can remark to the west the reflection of his rays on the slopes of the mountains of Bastsurguères, which become splendid while we are in the shade, and then, we do not see the sun directly but only his presence behind the enormous masses of the Ger. Bastsurguères sees the sun, say we; and if we were at the top of Bastsurguères we should see him also. Well, then, it is the same when we cast our eyes on Bernadette illumined by the invisible apparition; the certainty is the same, the evidence alike. The countenance of the child who saw the apparition appeared all at once so bright, so transfigured so shining, so impregnated with divine rays, that this marvellous reflection which we beheld gave us a full assurance of the luminous centre that we saw not. And if we had not, to hide it from us, a whole mountain of faults, miseries, material distractions, and sensual darkness, if we were possessed of the eminent innocence of this child, of that everlasting purity which no human being has approached, we too should see, no longer by reflection, but directly, what Bernadette in her rapture beheld, what shed its rays over her extatic features."

Such reasons, excellent perhaps in themselves, and conclusive for those who had been witnesses of this unheard of spectacle, could not be enough for those who had seen nothing. Providence, supposing it was really concerned in this affair, should, it seems, confirm its action by proofs, if not better, (since no one could resist these when he was able to try them by experiment,) at least more material, more sustained, and in some manner more palpable. Perhaps this was the profound design of God, and He did not convoke together such multitudes but to have, at the hour He willed, innumerable and irresistible witnesses.

At the end of Vespers, Bernadette came out of the church along with a large body of the faithful. She was, as may be imagined, the object of general attention. The poor child, embarrassed by such a concourse, replied to them in a simple manner, and tried to get through the crowd, in order to return home.

At this moment, a man invested with the costume of the public force, a Sergent de ville, an officer of police, approached her and touched her on the shoulder.

" In the name of the law," said he.

" What do you want with me ?" said the child.

" I have an order to arrest you, and take you off."

" And where ?"

" To the commissary of police. Follow me."

VII.

A threatening murmur went through the crowd. Many of those who were there had seen in the morning the humble child transfigured by a divine ecstasy, illuminated by rays from on high. In their eyes this little blessed child of God possessed a something that was sacred. So, when they saw the agent of the public force lay his hand upon her, they trembled with indignation, and wished to interfere. But a priest, who came out of the church at that moment, made a sign to the crowd to be calm. "Let authority act," said he.

By a marvellous coincidence, as we often meet with in the history of supernatural events, when we give ourselves the trouble or rather the joy of searching into them, the universal Church had chanted on that day, the first Sunday of Lent, the immortal words destined to console and comfort the innocent and the weak in the midst of persecutions : " God has given His angels charge over thee, that they may guard thee in thy ways. They will bear thee up in their hands, for fear lest thou dash thy foot and become hurt against the rocks in thy path. Hope in Him, He will protect thee under the shadow of His wings....... His almighty power will encompass thee in some manner as with an invincible buckler.......Go in all confidence. Thou shalt crush under thy feet the asp and the serpent ; the lion and the dragon shall be overpowered by thee......Because he hath hoped in me, says the Lord, I will deliver him. I will protect him, because he hath confessed My

name. He shall call upon me, and I will hear
him. I *will be with him in his tribulation.*"

The Gospel of the day related how the Saviour
of men, the eternal type of the just on earth, had,
at the beginning of His divine mission, to undergo
temptation ; and it gave all the details of His illustrious contest, and His victory over the evil spirit
in the solitude of the desert. *Ductus est Jesus in
desertum, ut tentaretur a diabolo...*

Such were the texts, so consoling for innocent
and persecuted weakness, which the Church had
caused to be heard ; such were the great records
which she had evoked, and the memory of which
she had celebrated ; on this day, on which, at the
bottom of an obscure mountain town, an agent of
the public force came to seize, in the name of the
law, a little ignorant child, and conduct her before
the most skilful and crafty of the representatives
of authority.

The multitude affected and agitated had followed Bernadette, when carried away by the official agent. The Commissariat of Police was not
far off. The Sergeant entered with the child, and
leaving her alone in the corridor, came back to
close the door with lock and bolt.

A moment after, Bernadette found herself in
the presence of M. Jacomet.

VIII.

The intelligent individual who was going to examine Bernadette, felt himself assured of an easy triumph, and he was beforehand highly delighted.

He was one of those who reject with obstinacy the explanations of the learned men of a country. He neither believed in catalepsy, nor in hallucination, nor in the different illusions of an extatic disease. The precision of the statements which were attributed to the child, the remarks made by Dr. Dozous and several other witnesses of the scenes at the grotto seemed to him to be irreconcilable with such an hypothesis. As to the fact of the apparitions, he did not believe in the possibility of ultramontane visions, and his police genius, very clever in spying out rogues under an illegal act, could not perhaps go so far as to discover God, beneath a supernatural fact. So, convinced in himself that there could not be any but false apparitions, he had resolved to find out, by scheme or by force, the root of the error, and so render to the free-thinkers in power or elsewhere the signal service of detecting a supernatural manifestation, a popular belief in the flagrant guilt of an imposture. He had here an admirable occasion for striking a rude blow at the pretended authority of all visions in the past, above all, if he could succeed in discovering and showing that the clergy, who were holding back so carefully in this affair, directed or secretly promoted it.

In the supposition that God went for nothing

in this event, and that men were all in all in it, the reasoning of Jacomet was excellent.

But in the contrary supposition that God was all in all in it, and men nothing, the unfortunate Commissary of police was then taking a most fatal step.

In these dispositions of mind, M. Jacomet had, from the first days, carefully caused all the proceedings of Bernadette to be watched, in order to see if he could not intercept some mysterious communication between the child who saw the apparition and such and such a member of the clergy, whether at Lourdes or in the environs. He had even carried his zeal for his functions to such an extent, as even to place in the church one of his creatures to have an eye on the confessional. But the children for catechism went to confession in their turns every fifteen days or month, and the turn for Bernadette had not during these days come round. All these conscientious efforts had not brought with them a discovery of any complicity in the acts of knavery attributed to Bernadette. He concluded from them that she acted probably alone, without however giving up altogether his suspicions, for a true police officer always suspects, even without proofs. It is this that constitutes their particular type and their peculiar genius.

When Bernadette entered, he cast upon her for an instant his sharp and penetrating eyes, which he had the marvellous art of impregnating with an air of ease and self-possession. He, who habitually carried a high tone with all the world, showed himself excessively polite to the poor daughter of the Miller Soubirous; he was mild and insinuating. He made her sit down, and adopted, to interrogate her, the benevolent manner of a true friend.*

"It appears that you see a lady at the grotto of Massabielle, my good little child, tell me all about it."

Just as he had said these words, the door of the room was a little opened, and someone entered it. It was M. Estrade, the receiver of the indirect taxes, one of the most important men at Lourdes, and one of the most intelligent. This functionary occupied a portion of the house where M. Jacomet resided; and becoming aware, by the noise of the crowd, of the arrival of Bernadette at the office of the Commissary, he had had the very natural curiosity to assist at the examination. He shared besides, on the subject of apparitions, the ideas of Jacomet, and he believed, like him, that it was a piece of knavery by the child. He shrugged his shoulders when any other explanation was offered him. He judged these things to be so absurd that he had not even condescended to go to the grotto and see the strange things which were related about it. This philosopher sat himself

---

* We cannot evidently after ten years have passed over the memory of the witnesses in this history, guarantee the exact words of this dialogue and some others found in the course of this work. We give the sense and general substance of them, always endeavouring—thanks to the innumerable pieces which we have in our hands, printed documents or manuscripts, different statements written down at the time, official correspondence, private letters, &c.—to reproduce as much as possible the very form, the first original and life.

down a little apart, after having made a sign not
to interrupt the proceeding. All this occurred
without Bernadette seeming to pay it any great
attention.

The scene and the dialogue of the two speakers
thus obtained a witness.*

* This faithful witness, whom we went ourselves to examine at
Bordeaux, where he exercises his functions at this moment, was
very willing to collect together for us his memorandums, which
he had besides put down at the very time the events occurred,—
and gave us in a manner the means of completing and checking
the narrative of Bernadette.

As to the report of the Commissary of Police at the end of
the conversation, we have in vain called for this precious document at the Prefecture of the Hautes Pyrénées. It has been
impossible for us to get any information about it. The Prefecture has besides cut short every application on our part, by telling us that the bundle of papers relative to this affair had disappeared, whether through some disorder or by an accident, or
whether because it had been withdrawn by hands interested in
destroying it. We have equally applied to the imperial court
at Pau, for the reports which M. Dutour, then Procureur Impérial at Lourdes, sent in on this affair to the Procureur General.—M. the Procureur-General has objected to us an absolute
principle, and refused to communicate these pieces to us. We
had believed, before this refusal, made however with perfect
politeness, that the bar was not and could not but be the guardian of such documents, and that it was its duty to communicate them to whoever claimed the use of them for the purpose of
history.

The minister of worship to whom we have made repeated and
useless applications, has acted like the bar with less politeness.
What instinctive terror have these high personages for the
truth, that they strive thus, but happily in vain, to hide it under
a bushel ?

Therefore, if any error has crept, in the sight of these acts

In answer to the question of Monsieur Jacomet, the child cast on the police officer her beautiful innocent look, and proceeded to state in her own language, that is in the patois of the country, and with a degree of personal timidity which was some addition to her accent of truth, the extraordinary events in which she had been engaged for several days.

M. Jacomet listened to her with lively attention, continuing to affect a perfect ease and kindness of manner. From time to time he set down some notes on a paper he had before him.

The child remarked it, but was not put out by it.

When she had finished her statement, the Commissary, more fair-spoken and assiduous, put her no end of questions, as if his enthusiastic piety was interested beyond measure in such divine marvels. He drew up all his interrogatories one after another, without any order, in short and rapid phrases, in order not to give to the child time to reflect.

To these different questions Bernadette answered

of the administration, into our narrative, the official world will have to take the blame to itself, since it has allowed us to lose or refused us the knowledge of these different documents. Happily the pieces without number which we had elsewhere, and the investigations which we have made, have been able to supplement them entirely. We have had a little more trouble, that is all.

If, nevertheless, in spite of our efforts, our account exhibits some inaccuracies, we are ready to correct them on the production of the official documents. We doubt if any recourse may be had to them.

without any difficulty, without a shadow of hesitation, with the tranquil assurance of someone
who may be interrogated respecting the aspect of
a country or a picture which is under their eyes.
Sometimes, in order to make herself better understood, she added some imitative gesture, or mimic
expression, as it were to supply the deficiency of
her words.

The rapid pen of M. Jacomet had noted down,
however, in regular order, all the answers given
him.

It was then, having in a manner endeavoured
to fatigue and bewilder the mind of the child in
the infinite minutiæ of the details, it was then
that the formidable agent of police adopted, without transition, a threatening and terrible physiognomy, and harshly changed his language.

" Thou art a liar," exclaimed he, violently, and
as if seized with a sudden fit of anger. " Thou
art deceiving the whole world, and if thou dost
not confess to me at once the truth, I will have
thee taken up by the Gendarmes."

Poor Bernadette was so stupified at the sight of
this sudden and terrible metamorphosis, as if,
thinking she held in her hands an inoffensive
branch of a tree, she felt it all at once twist, move,
and appear between her fingers the icy rings of a
serpent. She was stupified with horror ; but contrary to the profound calculation of Jacomet, she
was not disturbed. She continued calm, as if an
invisible hand had sustained her soul before this
unforeseen shock.

The Commissary stood upon his legs and looked
at the door, as if to say that he had only to make

a sign to call the Gendarmes and send the visionary to prison.

"Monsieur," said Bernadette, with a peaceful and gentle firmness, which, in this poor little peasant girl, contained an incomparable and simple greatness—"Monsieur, you may cause me to be taken by the Gendarmes, but I cannot say anything else but what I have said. It is the truth."

"That is what we are going to see," said the Commissary, sitting himself down, and judging by a glance of his practised eye that the threat was absolutely powerless over that extraordinary child.

M. Estrades, who was a mute and impartial witness of the scene, was divided between the prodigious astonishment with which the accent of conviction of Bernadette inspired him, and the admiration with which he was struck, in spite of himself, at the skilful strategy of Jacomet, the whole bearing of which he understood, in proportion as it displayed itself before him.

The contest assumed a character altogether unexpected between this double force of finesse, and infantine weakness without any other protection than its simplicity.

Jacomet, notwithstanding, armed with the notes which he had just been putting down for three quarters of an hour, set himself about to begin again his examination, but in quite another order and with a thousand captious forms, always proceeding, according to his method, by harsh and hasty questions, and requiring immediate answers. He doubted not but that he should be able to entangle, at least in some points of detail, the little girl in a contradiction of herself. That being done,

the imposture was demonstrated and he became
master of the situation. But he exhausted in vain
all the dexterity of his mind in framing a maze of
questions for that subtle manœuvre. The child
did not contradict herself in anything, not even in
that imperceptible point, in that very small iota of
which the Gospel speaks. To the same questions,
whatever were the terms in which they were put,
she always replied, if not in the same words, at
least by stating the same things, and in the same
colour. M. Jacomet, however, was obstinate, and
was only for fatiguing more and more the intelligence which he wished to find at fault. He turned
over and over again in every sense the narrative of
the apparitions, without being able to touch it.
He was like an animal who wanted to bite a
diamond.

"Very well," said he, to Bernadette, "I am
going to draw an official report, and I will read it
for you."

He wrote rapidly two or three pages on consulting his notes. He had purposely introduced into
certain details some variations of little importance,
as for example, the form of the dress, the length
òr the position of the veil of the Holy Virgin. It
was a fresh snare. It was as useless as all the
others. While he read and spoke from time
to time, "It is so and so, is it not?" Bernadette replied humbly, but with a firmness, as
simple and gentle, as it was unshaken—"No, I
did not say so, but this, she did this."

And she restored the inaccurate detail to its
primitive truth and colour. The greater part of
the time Jacomet disputed with her.

"But you have said this? I even wrote it down at the moment! You have said so and so in this manner, to several persons in the town?" &c.

Bernadette answered:

"I have not spoken so; I could not do so, because it is not the truth."

Strange, the modest and invincible self-possession of this child! M. Estrade observed her with increased astonishment. Personally, Bernadette was and appeared to be extremely timid; her attitude was humble, even a little confused before every one she did not know; and yet, nevertheless, upon everything that related to the reality of the apparition, she showed a force of soul and an energy of persistence quite uncommon.

When it was question of rendering homage to what she had seen, she replied without emotion, and with an imperturbable equanimity. Still, it was easy then to discern the virginal purity of a soul which would have preferred to hide itself from the look of all. It could be manifestly seen that it was only out of respect for the interior truth of which she was the messenger among men, through love for "the Lady who appeared at the grotto," that she triumphed over her habitual timidity. It required nothing less than the feeling of her duty to surmount in her the intimate bent of her natural character, which was timorous in all other things, and an enemy to noise and display.

The Commissary began again to threaten her.

"If you continue to go to the grotto, I will have you put in prison, and you shall not go away

from here except you promise me that you will not
return there any more."

"I have promised the vision to go there," said
the child; "and then, when the moment arrives,
I am impelled by something that comes on me
and calls me."

The examination, it could be seen, was approaching an end. It had lasted a long time, and
had not been kept up less than a good hour.
Outside the multitude waited, not without some
restless impatience, the exit of the child whom
they had seen that same morning, transfigured in
the light of a divine ecstasy. From the room
where the scene was passing, which we have just
described, were confusedly heard the cries, the
discourses, the questionings, and a thousand different noises which constitute the tumult of a
crowd. Rumour seemed to increase and become
menacing. At a certain moment, there was a
particular movement in the crowd, as if in the
midst of it there had arrived a new comer who was
strongly expected and desired.

Almost immediately repeated knocks resounded
at the door of the house.

The Commissary appeared to be unmoved at
them.

The knocking became more violent. He who
rapped shook the door, at the same time endeavouring to break it open. Jacomet growing angry,
got up and went to open it himself.

"No one enters here," said he, in a passion.
"What do you want?"

"I want my daughter," replied the miller,
Soubirous, forcing himself in and following the

Commissary into the apartment where Bernadette was.

The sight of the peaceful countenance of his daughter calmed the anxious agitation of her father, and he was no longer but a poor man somewhat trembling before the personage, who, in spite of his inferior position was, through his activity and intelligence, the most important and the most dreaded in that little county.

Francis Soubirous had taken off his Bearnese cap, and was moving it about in his hands. Jacomet, whom nothing escaped, saw through the fear of the miller.

He resumed his air of easy politeness and condescension. He tapped him familiarly on the shoulder.

" Father Soubirous," said he to him, "take care, take care, take care ! Your daughter is about to compromise herself seriously, she is going straight on the road that will carry her to a prison. I will not, however, send her there this time, but upon the condition that you forbid her returning to that grotto, where she is playing a comedy. At the very next offence I shall be inflexible, and, besides, you know that Mons. the Procureur Impérial does not trifle with any one."

" Since you desire it, M. Jacomet," replied the poor affrighted father, " I will forbid her doing so, and her mother also ; and as she has always obeyed us, she certainly will not go."

" At all events, if she goes there, if this scandal continues, I will not only make her answer for it, but you," said the terrible Commissary, again, in

7

a threatening attitude, and making them a sign to go away.

Immediately Bernadette and her father came out, the crowd uttered shouts of satisfaction, Then, the child returning home, the multitude dispersed itself over the town.

The Commissary of police and the receiver remaining alone, communicated to one another their impressions of this strange examination.

"What unshaken firmness in her depositions!" exclaimed M. Estrade, struck with profound astonishment.

"What an invincible obstinacy in her lies!" replied Jacomet, amazed that he had been conquered.

"What an appearance of truth!" continued the receiver. "Nothing in her language or manner that once belied itself. It is evident that she believed that she saw."

"What subtility of intelligence!" replied the Commissary. "She never contradicted herself in spite of all my efforts. She has her fabulous history at her fingers' ends."

The Commissary and M. Estrade continued, both, however, in their incredulity relative to the fact itself of the apparition. But a shade already separated their two denials, and that shade was an abyss. One supposed Bernadette crafty in her lie, the other judged her full of good faith but under an illusion.

"She is clever," said the first.

"She is sincere," said the second.

IX.

Although he had been powerless against the answers, simple, precise, and uncontradictory of Bernadette, M. Jacomet had gained, at the end of this long contest, a decisive advantage. He had greatly frightened the father of the girl who saw the vision, and he understood that, in this quarter, for the moment at least, he was master of the position.

Francis Soubirous was a very brave man, but he was not a hero. Before official authority he was timid, as the lower orders and the poorer people usually are, for whom the smallest mischief is an immense disaster, on account of their misery, and who feel all their powerlessness in presence of what is arbitrary or an act of persecution. He believed, it is true, in the reality of the apparition, but, not understanding what it was, nor measuring its importance, experiencing even a certain terror on the subject of these extraordinary events, he saw no great inconvenience in opposing the return of Bernadette to the grotto. He had, perhaps, a vague fear of displeasing the invisible "Lady," who manifested herself to his child; but the dread of irritating a man of flesh and blood, of engaging in a contest with so formidable a personage as the Commissary, came the nearest home to him, and acted more powerfully on his mind.

"You see that all the gentlemen of the country are against you," said he to Bernadette, "and that if you return to the grotto, M. Jacomet, who can do everything, will put you and me in prison. Do not go back there any more."

"Father," said Bernadette, "when I go there, it is not altogether I myself. At a certain moment there is something in me which calls me, and which draws me there."

"Whatever it be," replied the father, "I formally forbid you to go there for the future. You would not disobey me certainly for the first time in your life."

The poor child, embarrassed thus between her promise made to the apparition, and the express prohibition of paternal authority, replied : "I will do then all I possibly can to hinder myself from going there, and resist the attraction which calls me there."

Thus sorrowfully was passed the evening of this same Sunday, which had risen in the glorious and happy splendour of her ecstasy.

X.

The following morning, the 22nd February, at the usual hour for the apparitions, the crowd which awaited the girl who saw them, on the banks of the Gave, did not see her coming. Her parents had at sunrise sent her to school, and Bernadette, not knowing anything but to obey, had gone there, her heart overflowing with tears.

The Sisters, whom their duties of charity and instruction, and perhaps also the recommendation of M. the Curè of Lourdes, had kept at the hospital or school, had never seen the ecstasies of Bernadette, and had no faith in the Apparitions. Upon these matters besides, if the people show themselves sometimes to be over credulous, it happens that, by a phenomenon which surprises at first, but which is incontestable, Ecclesiastics and Religious of both sexes are very sceptical and hard to make believe, and that, while quite admitting in theory the possibility of such divine manifestations, they exact, with a severity often excessive, that they should be proved ten times over. The Sisters joined then their formal prohibition to that of her parents, saying to Bernadette that all these visions had nothing real in them; that her brain was deranged, or that she had told an untruth. One of them, suspecting an imposture in a matter so grave and sacred, assumed a very harsh manner towards her, treating all these matters as nothing but trickery and knavery.

"Good for nothing girl," said she to her, "you are playing there a shameful carnival during the holy time of Lent."

Other persons, who saw her during recreation, accused her of trying to pass for a saint, and amuse herself with a sacrilegious jest. The mockery, of course, of the children in the School was added to the bitter reproaches and humiliations of which she had to drink.

It was the will of God to try Bernadette. Having, on the previous days, inundated her with consolations, He intended, in His wisdom, to leave her for a certain time in absolute abandonment, exposed to railleries and insults, to be left alone and unaided, to the hostility of all those by whom she was surrounded.

The unhappy little girl suffered cruelly, not only from exterior contradictions, but much more from interior anguishes in her soul.

This infantine shepherdess, who had never known before, during her short life, any other but physical pains, was entering on a higher path, and she began to feel other tortures and other lacerations. On the one side, she did not wish to disobey either the authority of her father, or that of the religious; and on the other, she could not endure the thought of failing in the promise which she had made to the divine Apparition at the Grotto. In this young soul, hitherto so peaceful, a cruel contest had sprung up. It seemed to her that she was invincibly oscillating between two equally mortal abysses. To go to the Grotto, was to commit a sin against her father; not to go there was to commit a sin against the Vision that had come from above. In both cases it was, in her eyes, evidently a sin against God. And yet, by the force of events, it was absolutely necessary to do one or the other; there was no alternative, and it was impossible to avoid making this fatal choice. It is true, what is impossible for man is possible for God.

The morning was passed in these anguishes, so much the more painful and cutting, as they occurred in a soul quite fresh, at that age, which is habitually calm and pure, at which impressions are so lively; a habit of human suffering had not yet formed as it were a callousness around the delicate fibres of her heart.

Towards midday the children returned for a short time to their homes to take their meals.

Bernadette, with a heart broken between the two irreconcileable characters of her position; from which there was no way out, walked sorrowfully towards her home. The church clock at Lourdes had just rung the Angelus at midday.

At this moment a strange power seized hold of her all at once, acting, not on her mind, but on her body, as if it had the power of putting an invisible arm upon her, and pressed her out of the path she was following, to lead her invincibly into the direction from the road which was to the right. This impulse was for her, it seemed, what would be, for a leaf lying on the ground, a mighty blast of wind. She could no more hinder herself from going than if she had been suddenly placed on the top of one of the steepest declivities. All her physical being felt itself powerfully drawn towards the grotto, to which this road led. She must go to it, she must run to it.

And, nevertheless, the movement which took possession of her was neither rough nor violent. It was irresistible, but had nothing in it to hurt or pain her; quite the contrary, it was a supreme power with supreme gentleness. The all-powerful hand showed itself maternal and gentle, as if it feared to do any injury to that weak child.

Providence, which governs all things, then resolved an insoluble problem. The child, in submission to her father, was not going to the Grotto, whither her heart alone bounded; and behold, hurried along by the angel of the Lord, she arrives there notwithstanding, according to her promise to the Holy Virgin, without, in spite of it, her will having disobeyed paternal authority.

Such phenomena have been more than once accomplished in the life of certain souls, whose profound purity has pleased the heart of God. St. Philip Neri, Saint Ida of Louvain, Saint Joseph of Cupertino, Saint Rosa of Lima, have experienced similar or analogous things.

That humble heart, wounded and desolate, now brightened up with hope in proportion as her steps approached the Grotto.

"There," said the child to herself, "I shall see again the beloved Apparition; there I shall be consoled for everything; there I shall contemplate that countenance so beautiful, the sight of which ravished me with joy. To these cruel pains is succeeding a joy without bounds, for the 'Lady' herself will not abandon me."

She knew not, in her inexperience, that the Spirit of God breathes where He wills.

XI.

A little before her arrival at the Grotto, the mysterious power which had seized hold of the child appeared but to be interrupted, and at least to diminish.

Bernadette walked less rapidly, and with a fatigue to which she was not habituated; for it was exactly at that spot that, on other days, an invisible power seemed both to draw her to the Grotto, and support her while she was going. She experienced, on this very day, neither this secret attraction, nor this mysterious support. She had been *pressed* towards the grotto, she had not been *drawn* there. The power which had seized her had marked out the path of duty, and showed that before all things she must obey and keep her promise to the Apparition, but the child had not, as at other times, heard the interior Voice, and felt the all-powerful attraction. Whoever has the experience for analysing such things, will feel the truth of these distinctions more easy to comprehend than to express. :

Although a very great multitude, which, during all the morning had so vainly expected Bernadette, had dispersed, yet there was at this moment before the Rocks of Massabielle a considerable crowd. Some had come to pray there, others through simple curiosity. Many, having seen Bernadette afar off walking in that direction, had run and arrived at the same time with her.

The child, as usual, went humbly on her knees, and began to say her Rosary while beholding the opening which was tapestried with moss and wild branches, in which the heavenly Vision had already six times deigned to appear to her eyes.

The crowd, attentive, curious, recollected, breathless, awaiting at every moment to behold the countenance of the child radiate, and mark by its splendour that the superhuman Being was standing before her.

A very long time was passed in this manner.

Bernadette prayed with fervour, but no divine reflection was lit up in her immoveable features. The marvellous Vision was not exhibited to her sight, and the child implored without being heard the realisation of her hopes. Heaven seemed to abandon her as well as the earth, and to remain as deaf to her prayers and her tears as the marble rocks before which her knees were bent.

Of all the trials to which she had been subjected since the day before, this one was the most cruel, and it was the extremity of bitterness to her.

"Why have you disappeared?" thought the child, "and why do you forsake me?"

The marvellous Being herself seemed in fact to cast her off, and by ceasing to manifest herself, to give a reason to those who contradict the truth of her Apparitions, and leave the field free to her enemies.

The disconcerted crowd interrogated Bernadette. A thousand questions were put to her by those who surrounded her.

"To-day," answered the child, with her eyes red with tears, the "Lady" has not appeared to me. I have seen nothing."

"You should now comprehend, my poor little girl, that it was an illusion, and that there never was anything in it; it was all your fancies," said some of them.

"In fact," added others, "why, if the Lady has appeared yesterday, could she not appear to-day?"

"On other days, I saw her as I see you," said the child; "and we spoke to each other, she and I. But to-day she is not there, and I do not know why."

"Bah," replied a sceptic, "the Commissary of Police has done his work, and you will see that all is over. By the king's command

"On th' part of th' King, 'It is forbid to God
To work a miracle in this abode.'"

The believers who were there were grieved at heart, and knew not what to say.

As to Bernadette, sure in herself, and sure as to the past, a doubt never for a moment crossed her mind. But she was in profound grief, and as she returned to her paternal lodging she shed tears and prayed.

She attributed the absence of the Apparition to some dissatisfaction. "I must have committed some fault," asked she of herself. But her conscience did not reply by any reproach. Her feeling towards the divine Vision which she burned to contemplate still redoubled, notwithstanding, with ardour. She sought in her simple soul what she should do to see it again, and she did not know how to act. She felt herself powerless, to evoke that spotless beauty which had appeared to her, and she wept, with her heart lifted above, not knowing what to do but to weep, that is to pray.

At the bottom, at the very bottom of her aching soul, a secret hope always remained, and some rays of joy, piercing here and there those dark clouds, passed at moments over her heart, and fortified her faith in the divine Apparition, which she always loved, and in which she believed, though she no longer saw it. And yet, without doubt, the poor ignorant child knew not, and could not know, the sense of the words which were chanted at that moment in the Epistle for Mass. "In which you shall greatly rejoice, now if need be for a little time to be made sorrowful in divers temptations; that the trial of your faith, much more precious than gold (which is tried

by the fire), may be found unto praise, and glory,
and honour, at the appearing of Jesus Christ:
*Whom, having not seen you love; in Whom also
now, though you see Him not, you believe; and
believing, shall rejoice with an unspeakable and
glorified joy.*"*

She no more had any presentiment of the event
which was on the eve of being accomplished, and
this humble peasant girl, could not know, nor
apply to the Rock of Massabielle those words
which the priests of the whole universe pronounced
on this same day at the Gospel of the Mass:
Super hanc petram ædificabo Ecclesiam meam,
"Upon this rock I will build My Church." She
did not foresee, that soon, that is to say, the
following day of these hours full of tears, she
would herself announce prophetically and demand,
in the name of the Apparition, the erection of a
church on these desert rocks.

All these things were hid in the unfathomable
obscurity of the future.

"Whence do you come?" said her father to
her, at the moment she came back.

She related what had just passed.

"And you say," replied her parents, "that a
power carried you in spite of yourself."

"Yes," answered Bernadette.

"This is true," thought they, "for this child
has never told a lie."

The father Soubirous reflected a good deal.
He seemed to have in him some inward contest.

---

* I. Peter, i. 6-9, and used in the Mass of 22nd February.

At last he lifted up his head and appeared to adopt a definitive decision.

"Well," said he, "since it is so, since a superior power has drawn you with it, I no longer forbid you to go to the Grotto, and I leave you free."

Joy, a pure and lively joy, descended upon the countenance of Bernadette. Neither the miller nor his wife had offered as an objection the non-appearance of the Apparition that day. Perhaps, in the intimate recesses of their heart, they saw the cause of it, in the resistance which through dread of official authority, they had made to orders that were supernatural.

XII.

What we have just described took place after midday, and the report of it quickly was spread throughout the town. The abrupt cessation of supernatural Apparitions gave room to the most opposite comments. Some pretended to make an argument from them that was unanswerable against all preceding visions ; others, on the contrary, drew from them a proof still more in favour of the sincerity of the child.

That irresistible power which had carried away Bernadette in spite of herself, made the philosophic shoulders of the locality shrug themselves, and furnished a subject of endless propositions for distinguished Savants, who explained it all by means of a certain disturbance of the nervous system.

The Commissary, seeing that his injunctions

had been violated, and learning, besides, that
Francis Soubirous had withdrawn the prohibition he had given his daughter, sent for them
both to come before him, as well as the mother,
and renewed his threats. He used new means to
intimidate them ; but, notwithstanding the terror
which he occasioned them, he no longer found, to
his great surprise, in Francis Soubirous, the docility or the pusillanimity he had seen the day
before.

"Monsieur Jacomet," said the poor man,
"Bernadette has never told me a lie, and if the
good God, the Holy Virgin, or some saint, calls
her, we cannot oppose it. Put yourself in our
place, Monsieur the Commissary, the good God
would punish us."

"Besides, you say yourself that the Vision has
no longer taken place," argued Jacomet, addressing himself to the child. "You have nothing
more to do there."

"I have promised to go there every day for fifteen days," replied Bernadette.

"All these things are tales!" exclaimed the
exasperated Commissary ; "I will put you all in
prison if this girl continues to collect multitudes
together with her grimaces."

"My God," said Bernadette, "I go there quite
by myself to pray ; I call nobody to go with me,
and if such a crowd comes after me or before me,
it is not my fault. It is because they say it was
the Holy Virgin, but for myself I do not know
who it is."

Accustomed to quibbles, to the twists and sub-
terfuges of the world of rogues, the officer of

police was disconcerted at such profound simplicity. His craft, his marvellous skill, his captious
questions, his threats, all the shrewd or terrible
artifices of his profession, had hitherto broken
down in opposition to what had seemed to him
altogether at first, in opposition to what still
seemed to him weakness itself.

" Really," exclaimed he, stamping with his foot,
" here is a stupid affair !" And letting the Soubirous return home, he ran to see the Procureur
Imperial.

M. Dutour, in spite of his horror of superstition,
could not find in the arsenal of our codes any text
that enabled him to treat the girl who saw the
Apparition as a criminal. She called no persons
together ; she derived no profit in money from all
these things ; she went to pray upon land that
was common, open to everybody, and where no
law forbade her from going down upon her knees ;
she did not attempt to hold with the Apparition
any discourse subversive of or opposed to the
government ; the populations did not give themselves up to any disorder. There was evidently
no cause to proceed with severity.

As to prosecuting Bernadette for the crime of
" false intelligence," it was established experimen-
tally that she never contradicted herself; and beyond a contradiction in her words, which was
perfectly cleared up, it was difficult to prove that
she lied, without attacking directly the principle
itself of supernatural Apparitions, a principle at
all times admitted by the Catholic Church. Now
without the consent of the high authorities in the
Magistracy and the State, a simple Procureur

Imperial could not take on himself to engage in such a conflict.

In order that she might be liable to be prosecuted, it required at least that Bernadette should some day or other contradict herself; that either her parents should get some gain by what was going on, or that the crowd should involve itself in some disorder.

All this might happen.

From this hypothesis to the desire of realising it, from this clear view, of things in minds inimical to popular fanaticism, to the wish to lay snares for the multitude or for the child, there would be but one step for vulgar natures who agitated themselves beneath the official world. But M. Jacomet was a functionary, and the morality of the police is sheltered from such suspicions. It is only evil-thinking minds that can believe in the existence of provocative agents.

XIII.

The following morning, the crowd assembled in front of the Grotto before sun-rise. Bernadette came there with that calm simplicity which neither the threatening hostility of some, nor the enthusiastic veneration of others had altered. The sadness and the anguishes of the previous day had left some traces on her countenance. She was afraid still that the Apparition would no longer reappear, and whatever was her hope, she did not dare to give it up.

She humbly went on her knees, placing one of

her hands on a blessed taper which she had brought or which was given to her, and holding her rosary in the other.

The weather was calm, and the flame of the taper did not ascend to heaven more direct than the prayer of that soul towards the invisible regions whence the blessed Apparition was accustomed to descend. It was thus no doubt; for scarcely had the child prostrated herself than the unspeakable Beauty whose return she invoked so ardently manifested herself to her eyes and ravished her out of herself. The august Sovereign Lady of Paradise cast upon the child of this world a look full of inexpressible tenderness, appearing to love her still more since she had suffered. She, the greatest, the most sublime, the most powerful of created beings; she, whose glory, ruling all ages and filling eternity, makes all other glory to pale or rather to disappear; she, the Daughter, the Spouse, and the Mother of God, she seemed to render altogether intimate and familiar the bonds that united her to this little unknown and ignorant girl, to this humble guardian of sheep. She called her by her name, with that harmonious voice the profound charm of which ravishes the ears of angels.

"Bernadette," said the Divine Mother.

"Here I am," said the child.

"I have to tell you for yourself alone, and concerning yourself, a secret. Do you promise me never to repeat it to any body in the world?"

"I promise you not to do so," said Bernadette.

The dialogue continued, and entered into a profound mystery, which it is neither possible nor

8

permitted for us to penetrate. Whatever it may
have been, when this sort of intimacy was established, the Queen of the Eternal Kingdom beheld
this child, who the day before had suffered, and
who was still to suffer for the love of her, and it
pleased her to choose her as the ambassadress of
one of her desires among men.

"And now my child," said she to Bernadette,
"go, go and tell the priest that I will that they
should erect here a chapel in my honour." And
in pronouncing these words, her physiognomy,
her look and gesture, seemed to promise that She
would scatter there graces without number.

After these words she disappeared; and the
countenance of Bernadette returned to the shade,
like the evening returns to the earth when the
sun has by degrees sunk into the depths of the
horizon.

The multitude pressed around the child, a little
before transfigured by the ecstasy. All hearts were
moved. Questions were put on all sides. No
one asked her if the Vision had taken place; for
at the moment of the ecstasy all had understood,
all were conscious that the Apparition was there;
but they desired to know what had been said.
Every one endeavoured to approach the child, and
to hear it.

"What has She said to you?"—"What has
the Vision told you?" was a question that issued
from every mouth.

"She has told me two things: one for myself
alone, and the other for the priests; and I am
going immediately to them," replied Bernadette,

who had hastened to resume the road to Lourdes in order to fulfil her commission.

She was astonished, that day as previously, that everybody did not hear the dialogue, and did not see the "Lady." "The vision speaks loud enough for persons to hear," said she; "and I also, I raise my voice as I usually do." Now, during the ecstasy it was clearly remarked that the lips of the child were in motion, but that was all; no word could be distinguished. In this mystical state the senses are in some way spiritualized, and the realities which strike them are absolutely imperceptible by the gross organs of our fallen nature. Bernadette saw and heard, she herself spoke; and nevertheless no one around her perceived the sound of her voice, nor the body of the apparition. Was Bernadette mistaken? No; she alone was right. She alone, aided by the spiritual help of extatic grace, perceived momentarily what escaped the senses of all others; the same as an astronomer, aided by the material help of a telescope, contemplates for a moment in the heavens an enormous star which is at a great distance, and invisible to ordinary eyes. Out of the ecstasy she no longer sees anything; in the same way as, without his powerful optical instrument, which centuples the power of the eye, the astronomer is, for the discovery of the hidden star, as powerless as any body else.

XIV.

What had been, however, that strange and intimate communication, that private secret, of which
Bernadette spoke without being willing to tell its
nature? Between the Mother of the all-powerful
Creator of Heaven and earth, and the humble
daughter of the miller Soubirous; between that
radiant majesty, the highest that there is after
God, between that supreme Queen of the realms
of infinity, and the little shepherdess of the hills
of Bartrès, what secret could there be? Assuredly
we shall not attempt to conjecture, and we should
consider it a sacrilege to listen at the gates of
Heaven.

However, it is permissible for us to observe the
profound and delicate knowledge of the human
heart, and the maternal wisdom which doubtless
determined the august speaker with Bernadette to
cause some words entirely of a secret nature to
precede the public mission with which she invested
her. Favoured in the eyes of all with marvellous
Visions, intrusted towards the priests of God with
a message beyond this world, this infantine soul,
hitherto so peaceable and so solitary, found herself all at once transported into the midst of
innumerable crowds and infinite disquiets. She
was going to be a mark for the contradictions of
some, the threats of others, the railleries of
many, and what was still more dangerous for her,
to the enthusiastic veneration of a large number of
people. The days were approaching in which the
multitudes were to receive her with acclamations,

and would dispute together to get the rags of her
garments as holy relics; in which eminent and
illustrious personages would go down on their
knees before her and ask her benediction; in
which a magnificent temple would be raised, and
in which whole populations would be stirred up,
and incessant processions take place on the faith
of her word. And it is thus that this poor girl
among the people was on the point of encounter-
ing the most terrible trial that could assail her
humility, a trial in which she might lose for ever
her simplicity and openness of mind, all those
modest and tender virtues which had germinated
and flourished in the bosom of solitude. The
graces themselves which she received became for
her a formidable danger, a danger under which
more than once chosen souls honoured with the
favours of heaven had succumbed. St. Paul himself, after his visions, was tempted by pride, and
needed an angel of Satan to buffet his flesh to
prevent him from being puffed up in his heart.

The holy Virgin wished, however, to shield this
little girl whom she loved, without permitting the
evil one to approach this lily of purity and innocence, brought forth in the rays of her grace.
Now, what does the mother when a danger
threatens her child? She clasps her more and
more strongly to her bosom, and she says to it in
a *low voice*, in the mystery of a word gently whispered into her ear, "Fear nothing, I am at hand."
And if she is obliged to quit her a moment, and
to leave her alone, she adds, "I am not going far
off, I am at a few steps from you, and you have
only to hold out your hand to take hold of mine."

Thus did for Bernadette the Mother of us all.
At the moment at which the world and its different temptations, Satan and his subtle snares,
were going to strive to snatch her away from her,
she desired to have more intimate relations with
her. She clasped her in her arms, and pressed
her more closely to her heart. To tell—she, the
Queen of Heaven—a secret to a child of the earth;
it amounted to all this; it was the lifting up of
Bernadette to the tips of her lips, and speaking in
a low voice; it was the founding in this infantine
memory an inaccessible place of refuge, an abode
of peace and intimacy which none could come and
disturb.

A secret, confided and heard, created between
two souls the closest of bonds. To tell a secret,
is to give an assured pledge of affectionate confidence and fidelity; it is to establish a closed and
as it were a sacred place of meeting between two
hearts. When any one of importance, when any
one very high above us, has revealed their secret
to us, we can no longer have any doubt about him.
His friendship has, through this intimate confidence, taken up a kind of domicile in us, and he
becomes thereby a constant guest, I was going to
say with more exactness, an indweller of our soul.
To think of this secret is, in a certain manner,
mysteriously to clasp their hand, and to feel it
present to us.

A secret confided by the Holy Virgin to the
daughter of the miller became thus for this latter
the most secure of safeguards. It is not a point
of theology which teaches us this; it is a study
even of the human heart that makes it evident.

BOOK III.

I.

When Bernadette reached the town, the crowd of people had rushed on before to see what she was going to do.

The child went down the road which crosses Lourdes, and which forms its principal street; then, stopping in the lower part of the town, before the wall of the enclosure of a rustic garden, she opened a green lattice-worked gate, and went towards the house to which the garden belonged.

The crowd, through a feeling of respect and propriety, did not follow Bernadette, and stayed in the street.

Humble and simple, clad in her poor clothes, that were mended in many places, her head and shoulders covered with her little white capulet of coarse cloth, having, in a word, no exterior sign of a message from on high, save perhaps that royal mantle of poverty which Jesus Christ has worn, the messenger of the Divine Virgin who appeared at the grotto presented herself to the venerable man in whom was personified at that quarter of the earth, and for that child, the indefectible authority of the Catholic Church.

Although it was still an early hour, Monsieur

the Curè of Lourdes had already said the Divine
Office.

We do not know if at the moment at which, for
the first time, he was going to hear this poor
shepherdess, so little in the eyes of flesh and the
world, so great perhaps before heaven, his memory
brought to his mind the different words which he
had pronounced actually that day at the Introit
and Gradual of the Mass: " *In medio Ecclesiæ
aperuit os ejus.......Lingua ejus loquetur judi-
cum.   Lex Dei ejus in corde ejus.*—His lips have
spoken in the midst of the Church.......His tongue
hath uttered what is just......The law of God is
in his heart."*

Mons. l'Abbè Peyramale, though quite fully
penetrated, as a faithful and devout son of the
Church, with the possibility of apparitions, had
some difficulty in believing in this extraordinary
vision, which, according to the word of a child,
had manifested itself on the banks of the Gave,
in the grotto till lately unknown, of the Rocks of
Massabielle.   The sight of the ecstasy would have
doubtless convinced him ; but he had seen none
of these things except through the eyes of others,
and great doubts still remained in his mind as to
the reality of the apparitions, and next as to their
divine character.   The angel of darkness transforms himself sometimes into an angel of light,
and a certain degree of anxiety is legitimate in
such matters.   He judged it necessary, besides, to
test by himself the sincerity of the girl who saw

* 22nd February, Feast of St. Peter Damian—Introit and
Gradual at Mass.

the apparition. So he received Bernadette with a mistrust, harsh enough in expression, and proceeding even to a degree of severity.

Although he had held himself, as we have said, aloof from these events, and had not in his life spoken to Bernadette, so recent, besides, among his sheep, he knew her however by sight, several persons having pointed her out to him, one or two days before, when she was passing in the street.

"Is it not thou who art Bernadette, the daughter of Soubirous the miller?" said he to her, when, after having crossed the garden, she presented herself before him.

The eminent priest, whose portrait we have drawn, was as familiar with his parishioners as a father, and he had a custom of seeking and knowing the little children of his flock. Only on this particular day was the tone of the father severe.

"Yes, it is I, Monsieur le Cure," replied the humble messenger of the Blessed Virgin.

"Well, Bernadette, what do you want with me? What are you come here for?" replied he, not without roughness of manner, and at the same time casting a look on the child, the cold reserve and the severe inquiry of which were assumed in order to disconcert a soul that had little confidence in itself.

"Monsieur le Curé, I am come on the part of the 'Lady' who appeared to me at the grotto of Massabielle."......

"Ah, yes," said the priest, cutting her speech short, "thou pretendest to have visions, and thou runnest all over the country with your stories. What does all this mean? What has been hap-

pening for several days ? What are these extraordinary things which thou dost assert, and for
which there is no proof ?"

Bernadette was pained and surprised perhaps in
her innocence, at the severe attitude, and the
almost harsh tone which Monsieur le Curé Peyramale had adopted in receiving her, he who
habitually was so paternal and so kind to his
parishioners, and particularly with the humble
and little.

Bernadette, having her heart somewhat op-
pressed, but without any commotion, and in the
peaceable assurance of the truth, related simply
what the reader already knows.

The man of God knew how to be superior to
his personal prejudices. Accustomed for a long
time to read in the depths of hearts, he admired
within himself, whilst he spoke, the astonishingly
truthful character of this little peasant girl, relating in her own language events so marvellous.
Through those limpid eyes, beneath that candid
countenance, he perceived the profound innocence
of that privileged soul. It was impossible for his
noble and upright nature to hear such an expression of truth, and to behold those harmonious and
modest features, in which all was goodness, without feeling himself interiorly led to believe in the
word of the child who spoke.

The infidels themselves, we have above explained, no longer questioned the sincerity of the
girl who saw the vision. In her ecstasies, the truth
that came from above seemed to light her within
entirely, and to enter into her very soul. In her
descriptions the truth seemed to come forth from

her person, and to shed its rays, warming hearts, and dissipating as well the clouds as the confused objections of the mind. This extraordinary child had, in a word, around her forehead, as it were, an aureole of truth, visible to the eyes of pure souls and even to others, and her words had the gift of chasing away all doubts.

However inflexible and decided was the character of M. Peyramale, whatever may have been his firmness of mind and soul, however strong was his distrust, his heart was strangely affected by an emotion—in appearance inexplicable—at the words of that Bernadette of whom people were speaking so much, and whom he heard for the first time. This man, so resolute, found himself conquered by this all-powerful weakness. Yet, he had too much command over himself, too much prudence, to allow himself to give way to an impression which, after all, might have been able to mislead him. As a private individual, he would have said, perhaps, to the child, "I believe thee." But as the pastor of a large flock, appointed as the guardian of truth, he had determined not to yield except to palpable and visible proofs. No muscle of his face betrayed his inward agitation. He had strength to keep up towards the child his rough and severe physiognomy.

"And dost thou know the name of this lady?"

"No," replied Bernadette, "she has not told me who she was."

"Those who believe thee," replied the priest, "imagine that it is the holy Virgin Mary. But dost thou know well," added he, with a voice that was serious and vaguely threatening, "that if thou falsely pretendest to see her in this grotto, thou art taking the way never to see her in heaven ? Here thou sayest thou alone seest her ; above, if thou liest in this world, others shall see her, and thou shalt be, for thy deception, for ever far from her, for ever in hell."

"I do not know if she is the Holy Virgin, Monsieur le Curé," replied the child ; "but I see a vision as I see you, and she speaks to me as you speak to me. And I am come, on her behalf, to say to you that she wishes that there should be erected a chapel at the Rocks of Massabielle, where she appeared to me."

The Curé looked at this little child, intimating to him this formal request with such a complete assurance ; and in spite of his previous emotion, he could not, before the humble and infantine appearance of the ambassadress of heaven, help smiling at this strange message. The idea that this child was under an illusion succeeded in his mind to the emotion of his heart, and doubt resumed the upper hand.

He made Bernadette repeat over the very words which the Lady at the grotto had used.

"After having confided to me the secret which concerns me, and which I cannot reveal, she has added : 'And now, go and tell the priests that I wish that they should build a chapel to me here.' "

The priest kept silence for a moment. "After all," thought he, "it is possible." And this thought, that the Mother of God had sent to him, to him a poor unknown priest, a direct message, filled him with agitation and trouble. Then he cast his eyes on the child, and asked himself: "Where then is the guarantee for this little girl, and what is it that can prove to me that she is not the sport of some illusion?"

"If the 'Lady' of whom thou speakest to me is truly the Queen of Heaven," answered he, "I shall be happy, according to my ability, to contribute to cause a chapel to be erected there; but thy word is not a certainty. Nothing obliges me to believe thee. I do not know who this Lady is, and before I can occupy myself about what she asks, I want to know what right she has to it. Ask her, therefore, to give me some proof of her power."

The window was open, and the glance of the priest, directed over the garden, observed the checked vegetation, and the momentary drought, which the rigours of winter cause to plants.

"The apparition, thou informest me, has at its feet a wild rose tree, a sweet brier that comes out from the rocks. We are in the month of February. Tell her, on my part, that if she wishes a chapel, she must cause the rose tree to grow."

And he sent the child away.

There was no delay in people knowing, in all its details, the interview which had taken place between Bernadette and the priest, who was venerated by everybody, and who was, at that period, curé of the town of Lourdes.

"He has not given her a good reception," said the philosophers and learned folks with satisfaction; "he has too much sense to believe in the reveries of an hallucination; he has extricated himself from a difficult position with infinite dexterity. On one side, to give his assent to such follies was impossible for a man of his intelligence and bearing ; and, on the other, to oppose to the whole affair a pure and simple negation, would have been to have turned his back altogether on this fanatic multitude. Instead of stumbling on these twofold rocks, in place of letting himself be taken amid the horns of a dilemma, he gets quietly out of the difficulty, and without running counter to the popular belief, he very craftily demands a visible, palpable, and certain proof of the apparition, a miracle, in a word, that is to say, an impossibility. He condemns the lie or the illusion to refute themselves, and with the thorn of a wild rose tree he causes the balloon to burst. It is very cleverly planned."

Jacomet, M. Dutour, and their friends, were rejoiced at this calling to account of the invisible being of the Grotto. " The apparition is summoned to show its passport," was the word which they repeated as they smiled with official consequence.

" The sweet brier will grow," said the most firm among the believers, those who had felt the impression of the spectacle, Bernadette in an ecstasy.

A great number, though having a full faith in the apparition, dreaded a trial. The heart of man is thus constituted, and the centurion of the Gospel spoke as the greater part of us do, when he said, " *Credo Domine, adjuva incredulitatem meam*—I believe, O Lord, help my incredulity."

Both one and the other awaited with impatience the morning of the following day.

III.

Among those whom a lofty contempt for superstition had hitherto prevented taking any part, in order to examine matters, with the crowds of people, several resolved to go henceforth to the Grotto, in order to assist at the popular deception. One of these was M. Estrade, that receiver of indirect taxes, of whom we have already spoken, and who was present, with M. Jacomet, when he examined the little girl who saw the vision. He had been then, we may remember, forcibly struck by the singular tone of sincerity displayed by Bernadette, and not being able to doubt the good faith of the child, he had attributed her statements to the results of hallucination. Sometimes, however, this first impression wearing off, he inclined to the solution by Jacomet, who continued to see nothing in the affair but a very skilful comedy and a miracle of trickery. His philosophy, being firm otherwise in its principles, oscillated between these two explanations, the only ones possible according to him. His contempt for such mystical extravagances and impostures was such that he had made it till this moment, in spite of his secret curiosity, a point of honour not to go to the rocks of Massabielle. He decided, nevertheless, that very day to go there,—partly to be present at a whimsical spectacle,—partly to observe, a little also through complaisance and to accompany his sister, who was much affected at these reports, and some

ladies of the neighbourhood. He has related to
us his impressions, that are beyond suspicion.

"I went," he told us, "fully determined to
examine, and I fully admit, to amuse myself, and
to laugh, expecting a comedy or some grotesque
extravagance. An immense concourse of people
collected together by degrees around these wild
rocks. I admired the simplicity of so many
simpletons, and I laughed to myself at the credulity of the servant women, who were devoutly on
their knees before the rocks. We came very early
in the morning, and, thanks to my elbows, I succeeded without difficulty in getting into the first
place. At the customary hour, towards sunrise,
Bernadette arrived. I was near her. I remarked
in her infantine features that character of sweetness, innocence, and profound tranquillity which
had struck me several days before at the Commissary. She went down on her knees, naturally,
without ostentation or embarrassment, without
confusion, or being put out by the crowd which
surrounded her, absolutely as if she had been
alone in a church, or in a lonely wood, far from
the sight of men. She took out her rosary, and
began to pray. Soon her face appeared to receive
and reflect an unknown light; it became fixed, and
remained full of admiration, ravished, radiant with
happiness, at the opening of the rock. I directed
my eyes immediately there, and I saw there
nothing else, absolutely nothing, but the branches
of the sweet brier stripped of its leaves. And,
nevertheless, what shall I say to you? In presence of the transfiguration of the child, all my
ormer prejudices, all my philosophical objections,

all my preconceived denials, fell down all at once,
and gave way to an extraordinary feeling which
took possession of me in spite of myself. I had
the certainty, I had the irresistible intuition, that
a mysterious being was there. My eyes did not
see her; but my soul, and that of innumerable
spectators at that solemn hour, beheld it as well
as myself, with the intimate light of evidence.
Yes, I attest it, a divine being was there. Suddenly and completely transfigured, Bernadette was
no longer Bernadette. She was an angel of
heaven plunged into unspeakable raptures. She
had no longer the same countenance; but another
intelligence, another life, I was going to say
another soul, were painted on her. She no longer
resembled herself, she seemed to be another person. Her attitude, her slightest gestures, the
manner, for example, in which she made the sign
of the cross, had a nobility, a dignity, a greatness
more than human. She opened quite wide her
eyes, that were insatiable in beholding, that continued fixed and almost immoveable; she feared,
it seemed, to lower the pupil, and to lose a single
instant the ravishing sight of the marvel she contemplated. She smiled at this invisible being,
and all this gave a powerful idea of her ecstasy and
bliss. I was not less moved than other spectators. Like them, I held my breath, to try and
hear the discourse that was taking place between
the vision and the child. She listened with an
expression of the most profound awe, or, to speak
better, of most profound adoration, mingled with
a love beyond bounds and the sweetest of trans-
ports. Sometimes, however, a tincture of sadness

9

passed over her countenance, but its habitual
expression was that of exceeding joy. I observed
that for some moments she no longer took her
breath. During all this time she had her rosary
in her hand, sometimes motionless, (for sometimes she appeared to forget it, to be in the abyss
of the contemplation of the divine being,) sometimes sliding more or less regularly through her
fingers. Each of her movements was in perfect
accord with her physiognomy, which expressed by
turns admiration, prayer, and joy. She made at
intervals those signs of the cross that were so
pious, so noble, so marked by a power of which I
have just spoken. If in heaven signs of the
cross are made, they are assuredly like to those of
Bernadette in her ecstasy. This gesture of the
child, restricted as it altogether was, seemed in
some manner to embrace the infinite. At a particular moment Bernadette advanced, moving on
her knees, from the point where she prayed, that
is, from the banks of the Gave, to the bottom of
the Grotto. This was about fifteen feet. Whilst
she mounted this declivity, which was somewhat
abrupt, those who were along her route heard her
very distinctly pronouncing these words : ' Penance ! Penance ! Penance !' "

"A few moments afterwards she got up, and
resumed the road to the town in the midst of the
crowd. It was a poor girl in tatters, who seemed
to have only had a common part at so surprising
a spectacle."

During all this scene, however, the wild rose-
tree had never flowered. Its bare and unsightly
branches twined themselves motionless along the

rock, and it was in vain that the multitude awaited the balmy and charming miracle which the first pastor of the town had demanded.

A circumstance worthy of remark! The belief of the faithful was little staggered by it; and in spite of this apparent protestation of inanimate nature against this all-supernatural power, several men of importance, amongst others he whose description we have just related, felt themselves converted to the faith by the unheard of spectacle of the transfiguration of the girl who saw the vision.

IV.

"Well then, hast thou seen it again to-day, and what did she say to thee?" demanded the Curé of Lourdes, when Bernadette presented herself to him on her return from the Grotto.

"I have seen the vision," answered the child; "and I said to her: 'M. le Curé asks you to give some proofs, for example, to cause the rose-tree which is beneath your feet to flower, because my word does not suffice for the priests, and they are not willing to trust to me.' Then she smiled, but without speaking. Then she told me to pray for sinners, and commanded me to descend even to the bottom of the grotto. And she cried out three times the words: 'Penance! Penance! Penance!' which I repeated while I drew myself on my knees to the bottom of the Grotto. There she revealed to me again a second secret which is personal to myself. Then she disappeared."

"And what have you found at the bottom of the Grotto?"

"I looked after she had disappeared, (for while she was there I paid no attention except to her, and she absorbed me,) and I only saw the rock, and some blades of grass which shot up in the midst of the dust."

The Curé remained lost in thought.

"Let us wait," said he.

In the evening M. l'abbé Peyramale related this interview to the Vicars of Lourdes, and to several priests in the environs. They joked their dean on the ill-success of his demand.

"If it is the Holy Virgin, most dear master," said they to him, "that smile, on hearing your request, seems to us unpleasant for you; an irony coming from so high above appears calculated to cause uneasiness."

The Curé got out of this argument with his usual presence of mind.

"That smile is in my favour," replied he. "The Holy Virgin mocks at nobody. If I had spoken amiss she would not have smiled, she would have been moved to pity at my reasons. She has smiled. Then she has approved."

V.

There was certainly some truth in the clever reply of M. l'abbé Peyramale, but perhaps a little less than he thought. Assuredly, if at this moment, with his profound sagacity and his elevation of soul, he had maturely reflected on the words which the heavenly Apparition had pronounced, a short time after she smiled, he would have comprehended the sense of that smile, which the poor child, though favoured with such visions, was unable to interpret.

"To pray for sinners, to do penance, to climb on one's knees the steep and painful ascent which ran from the rapid and tumultuous waters of the torrent to the immoveable rock, on which was to be founded one of the sanctuaries of the Church;" such had been the orders of the Apparition at the end of the prayer of the child; such had been her answer to the request to cause the wild rose tree to flower; such had been, in her own mouth, the clearest commentary on her smile. Who does not see, when reflecting on it, the admirable sense of this symbolic answer?

"And what! Though I am the Mother of God the Saviour, the Mother of that Jesus who went doing good and consoling the afflicted, must I be thus solicited, as a proof of my power, the idle and frail marvel which in a few days the rays of my servant the sun will accomplish? When a multitude of sinners, indifferent or hostile to the law of God, covers the surface of the globe; when populations that are guilty or gone astray quench their thirst in the poisoned waters of this world, in those troubled torrents that flow into the abyss; when they have, before all, need to mount upon their knees the rude path which separates from the immutable life of the spirit the fleeting and agitated one of the flesh; when the salvation of so many unhappy ones, and the cure of so many sick, are the constant anxiety of my maternal

heart ; have I not better testimonies to give of
my power and goodness than to cause roses to
flower in winter ?　And is it for so vain and
frivolous an object that I appear to a young child
on the earth, and that I open before her my hand
full of graces ?"

Such was, it seems to us, as much as it is permitted for a miserable man to penetrate and interpret things so high, the profound meaning of that
smile, and of those orders by which the Mother
of the human race replied to the demand of the
Rector of Lourdes.

God does not deign, above all in evil and
necessitous times, to sport in a manner with His
omnipotence over frivolous prodigies which only
strike the eyes, over ephemeral signs which fade
away from morning till night, and which the first
blast of the wind carries away.　God intends to
do things that are useful and good, and His
miracles are always benefits.　When He wills to
establish something that is eternal, He sustains it
forthwith upon an eternal proof which ages cannot
break asunder.

What was, however, the meaning of the order
given to Bernadette to mount the soil of the
Grotto upon her knees until the moment at which
she was stopped by the steepness of the dried up
rock ?　Nobody knew it ; and before this dry
rock, no one imagined that since the synagogue
had destroyed itself by thinking to kill Jesus, the
wand of Moses had passed as an inheritance to the
Christian people.

M. le Curé of Lourdes, in spite of his great
intelligence, did not see all at once the things

which the future would render evident. The emphatic doubt which there was at the bottom of his mind as to the reality of the apparition, hindered him from meditating with attentive care upon the different circumstances of the scene at the Grotto and to direct that clear perception which he was accustomed to direct to the things of God.

Though they were somewhat disconcerted in presence of the conversions that were made on the day itself at the Rocks of Massabielle by the extraordinary lustre of the transfiguration of Bernadette, the free-thinkers of the locality triumphed in a singular manner at the check experienced by the believers, on the subject of the humble and gracious proof exacted by the Curé Peyramale. They praised this latter still more than the day previously, for having exacted a miracle.

"Jacomet," said they, "was very unskilful in wishing to kill the Apparition; the Curé, much more skilful, compels it to kill itself." Incapable of understanding the genuine simplicity of that impartial wisdom which, without doubt, required proofs before believing, but also before denying; they call that cunning which was prudence, and they beheld a snare in the ingenuous prayer of an upright soul in search of truth. It required but little, we can see, for these gentlemen on this occasion to offer the Pastor of Lourdes the honour, very great perhaps, but assuredly not unmerited, of reckoning him as one of themselves.

VI.

The honourable M. Jacomet appeared nevertheless not to have detected as he wished the villany
in the very act of crime, and destroyed, by his
sole efforts, this rising superstition. He racked his
brains to guess the meaning of the enigma, for he
began to see clearly, by the demand even of the
Curé of Lourdes, that the clergy did not reckon
for nothing in the affair. He had then before his
mind only this little girl and her parents to deal
with. He doubted not, some way or other, to get
to the bottom of it.

When, by chance, Bernadette went out into the
street, the crowd pressed around her; they
stopped her at every step; each one wanted to
hear from her mouth the details of the Apparition.
Many, in the number of whom was M. Dufo the
advocate, one of the most eminent men in that
country, made her come to them and questioned
her. They offered no resistance to the secret
power which the Truth put into her words.

Many persons went during the day to call upon
the Soubirous, to hear the statements of Bernadette. She listened with all candour and complaisance to these endless enquiries; it was noticed
that to give testimony to what she had seen and
heard became henceforth for her her particular
function and duty.

In a corner of the chamber into which they
penetrated, a little chapel, adorned with flowers,
medals, and pious prints, and surmounted by a
statue of the Blessed Virgin, presented an appear-

ance of luxury and attested the piety of the family. All the rest of the chamber offered the spectacle of the most mournful nakedness. A truckle bedstead, some shabby chairs, a ricketty table, formed all the furniture of the lodging where people came to be informed of the splendid secrets of heaven. The greater part of the visitors were struck and moved by the sight of the extreme indigence everywhere visible, and did not resist the soft temptation of leaving some remembrance, some alms for these poor people. But the child and her parents always refused, and in such a manner that no one could insist on pressing them.

Among those visitors, several were strangers to the town. One of these came one evening, when the come and go of the day was a little calm, and when there was no longer but a neighbour or a relative seated at the fire. He carefully interrogated Bernadette, not wishing her to omit any detail, and appearing to take an extraordinary interest in the narrative of the child. His enthusiasm and his faith betrayed themselves at every moment by exclamations full of tenderness. He congratulated Bernadette on having received such a great favour from heaven, then he was moved with pity at the misery of which he saw the marks around him.

"I am rich," said he, "permit me to assist you."

And his hand deposited upon the table a purse which was half open, and which could be seen to be filled with gold.

The blush of indignation mounted into Bernadette's countenance.

"I wish for nothing, sir," said she, quickly.
"Take it back."

And she thrust back towards the unknown the
purse that was deposited on the table.

"It is not for you, my child, it is for your
parents who are in want, and whom you cannot
hinder me from succouring."

"Neither Bernadette, nor ourselves wish for
anything," said the father and mother.

"You are poor," continued the stranger, for a
moment; "I have disturbed you; I am interested
in you. Is it through pride that you refuse?"

"No, sir, but we wish to receive nothing, absolutely nothing. Take away your gold."

The unknown took back his purse and went
out, not being able to dissemble a physiognomy
that was very much disappointed.

Whence did this man come, and who was he?
Was he a compassionate benefactor, or was he a
skilful tempter? We are ignorant. The police
was so well trained at Lourdes, that Jacomet,
more fortunate than ourselves, knew perhaps this
secret, and knew better than any one else, the
meaning of the enigma.

Then, if by one of those hazards, as sometimes
are to be met with in police affairs, the very crafty
Commissary of police should learn the same evening the details of this scene between Bernadette
and this mysterious stranger, it would have to be
said that snares and temptations were as useless
against this extraordinary child as captious words
and violent threats. The knot of this situation

became more and more inextricable for that personage, so profoundly skilful notwithstanding, and so expert in things purely human. If the impossibility of causing the smallest contradiction to be made in the statement of Bernadette had surprised him, her absolute disinterestedness, her firmness in rejecting a purse of gold could not but plunge him into a perfect stupor.

Such conduct would be fully explained to police wisdom, if the demand of a visible proof of a miracle of the impossible flourishing of a wild rose-tree, made by the Curé, had not shown with the clearest evidence that the clergy were not concealed behind the girl who saw the vision. But Bernadette and her parents, *reduced to themselves*, poor, in want, needing bread, and deriving no profit from the popular enthusiasm and credulity, was an event altogether inconceivable.

Had the little girl invented her imposture to acquire for herself an empty fame? But, besides, such ambitious acts appeared scarcely probable with a rustic guardian of sheep, how was it possible to explain the indestructible unity of her statement, how explain that her disinterestedness should extend itself to her family, all so poor, and consequently so tempted without doubt to speculate upon the faith of the multitudes?

M. Jacomet was not a man to be staggered through some insoluble objections, and awaited with confidence the course of events, not doubting in any degree but that they had a triumph in reserve for him, and so much the more glorious, as it was beset, at first, with difficulties and obstacles.

VII.

The night had terminated the agitations of so many and such opposite minds, some believing in the reality of the Apparition, others remaining in doubt, a certain number absolutely denying it. The aurora had just risen, and the universal Church, over the whole surface of the globe, gently sounded in the depth of her churches, in the silence of lonely presbyteries, in the peopled shade of the cloisters, under the vaults of Abbeys and Convents, those words of the psalmist in the office of matins : " *Tu es Deus qui facis mirabilia. Notam fecisti in populis virtutem tuam....* Viderunt te aquæ Deus, viderunt te aquæ *et timuerunt, et turbatæ sunt abyssi.* Thou art the God that doest wonders. Thou hast made Thy power known among the nations.......The waters saw Thee, O God, the waters saw Thee, and they were afraid, and the depths were troubled."[*]

Bernadette, having arrived at the Rocks of Massabielle, went down on her knees.

An immense multitude had gone before her to the Grotto, and were pressing around her. Although there were a good number of sceptics, some who refused to believe, and others from simple curiosity, a religious silence all at once was manifested as soon as they perceived the child. A shiver, a strange commotion had passed over that crowd. All, by an unanimous instinct, infidels as well as believers, uncovered themselves

[*] Psalm, lxxvi. 15, 16, 17.

before her. Many went on their knees at the
same time as the miller's daughter.

At this moment the divine Apparition manifested
itself to Bernadette, who was suddenly ravished in
a marvellous manner. As on all occasions, the
luminous Virgin stood in the oval excavation of
the rock, and her feet trod upon a wild rose-
tree.

Bernadette contemplated her with a feeling of
inexpressible love, a sweet and profound feeling,
which inundated her soul with delights, without
troubling her mind in any way, and without
making her forget that she was still upon the
earth.

The Mother of God loved this innocent child.
She wished, through an intimacy more and more
close, to press her still more to her breast; she
wished to fortify still more the bond which united
her to the humble shepherdess, in order that this
latter might be sensible, in the midst of the agitations of this world, so to speak, that the Queen of
Heaven held her invisibly by the hand.

"My child," said she, "I wish to confide to
you, even for yourself alone, and concerning
you alone, a last secret; that, as well as the two
others, you will not reveal to any one in the
world."

We have explained above the profound reasons
which formed, through this intimate confidence,
the future safeguard of Bernadette, amid the moral
dangers to which the extraordinary favours of
which she had been the object, would infallibly
expose her. By this triple secret, the Holy
Virgin invested her messenger, as it were, with a

triple armour against the dangers and temptations of life.

Bernadette, in the joy of her heart, listened to, however, the ineffable music of that voice so sweet, so maternal, and so tender, which charmed, 1800 years ago, the ears of the Infant God.

"And now," replied the Holy Virgin, after some silence, "go, drink and wash yourself in the fountain, and eat the grass which comes forth by its side."

Bernadette, at this word "Fountain," looked about her. No spring existed or ever had existed at that spot. The child, without losing sight of the Holy Virgin, turned quite naturally towards the Gave, the tumultuous waters of which were rushing along at some paces distant, across the pebble stones and the broken rocks.

A word and a gesture from the Apparition stopped her in her walk.

"Do not go there," said the Holy Virgin; "I did not say go and drink out of the Gave; go to the Fountain, it is here."

And stretching out her hand, that delicate and powerful hand to which nature is submissive, she pointed with her finger to the child, to the right bank of the Gave, that same dried up corner, towards which, the morning of the day before, she had already mounted on her knees.

Though she saw nothing at the spot indicated that seemed to have reference to the words of the Divine Being, Bernadette obeyed the order of the heavenly Vision. The vault of the Grotto gradually became lower on that side, and the little girl climbed up upon her knees the space she had to get over.

When she had arrived at the place designated, she did not perceive before her any appearance of a fountain. Quite close up to the rock here and there were growing some tufts of short grass, of the saxifragous family, called *Dorine*.

Whether it was at a fresh sign from the Apparition, or whether it was through an interior movement in her soul, Bernadette, with that simple faith which so much pleases the heart of God, stooped, and scraping the soil with her little hands, began to scoop out the earth.

The innumerable spectators at this scene, neither hearing nor seeing the Apparition, did not know what to think of this singular work of the child. Already several began to laugh and to think there was some derangement in the brain of the poor shepherdess. How little is required to shake our faith !

All at once the bottom of this little cavity which was scooped out by the child became moist. Coming from unknown depths, across the marble rocks and thickness of the earth, a mysterious water began to gush forth drop by drop into the hands of Bernadette and to fill the hollow, to the size of a glass, which she had finished forming.

This new water, being mixed with the earth that was broken by the hands of Bernadette, at first did not make anything but mud. Bernadette, three times, endeavoured to lift to her lips this muddy liquid ; but three times, her disgust was so strong that she rejected it without having the strength to swallow it. However, she wished,

above all, to obey the radiant Apparition, who
presided over this strange scene; at the fourth
time, after a supreme effort, she overcame her
repugnance. She drank, she washed herself, she
eat a piece of a rural plant which grew at the foot
of the rock.

At this moment the water from the spring overflowed the banks of the little reservoir hollowed
out by the child, and began to flow in a little
stream, smaller perhaps than a straw, towards the
crowd who were pressing before the Grotto.

This stream was so very small, that for a long
time, that is, till the end of the day, the dried up
earth drank it up as it went along, and its progressive course was not traced save by the moisture
exhibited on the soil, and which lengthening by
degrees, advanced with extreme slowness towards
the Gave.

When Bernadette had accomplished, as we have
just related, all the orders which she had received,
the Holy Virgin cast upon her a satisfied look,
and an instant after, she disappeared from her
eyes. The emotion of the multitude was great in
presence of this prodigy. When Bernadette had
come out of her ecstasy, people rushed to the
Grotto. Every one wanted to see with his own
eyes the hollow out of which the water had started
up under the hand of the child. Every one wanted
to dip his handkerchief in it and bring a drop of
it to his lips, so that this rising spring, the earthy
reservoir of which was enlarged by degrees, soon
took the form of a puddle of water or of a liquid
mass of diluted mud. The spring, nevertheless,
as the water was drawn out of it, became more

and more abundant. The orifice through which
it came from the abysses insensibly enlarged itself.

"It is from water which will have oozed by
chance from the rock during the rainy season,
and which by chance also, will have formed under
the soil a little mass which the child will have
discovered, always by chance, when scraping up the
ground," said the learned men of Lourdes.

And these philosophers contented themselves
with this explanation.

The following day, the spring, stirred from
mysterious depths by an unknown power, and
increasing to the eyesight, issued from the soil by
a gushing more and more powerful. It flowed
already to the thickness of a finger. But the interior toil which it encountered through the earth
to trace for itself its first passage, rendered it still
muddy. It was only at the end of several days that,
after having augmented in some sort every hour,
it ceased to swell, and became absolutely limpid. It then flowed out of the earth by a very
considerable fall, which had almost the thickness
of the arm of a child. Let us not however antici-
pate events, but let us continue to follow them
day by day as we have hitherto done.

Let us resume them where we have just left
them, that is to say, on the Thursday morning,
the 25th February, at seven o'clock.

VIII.

Precisely at this very hour, at the moment at
which the spring, as a first divine testimony,
gushed up gently but irresistibly under the hand
of her who saw the Vision, the philosophy of
Lourdes published upon the events of the Grotto
a new article in the Free-thinking Journal of
the locality.

The Lavedan, which we have already quoted,
came from the press and was distributed in the
town just at the moment at which the astonished
crowd was returning from the Massabielle Rocks.
Now in this article, no more than in the preceding
one, no more than in any of the descriptions
which were written at that period, there was no
question raised as to any spring existing in the
Grotto.   So that, incredulity paralysed beforehand the audacious assertion, on which, after a
certain time, the free-thinkers might be tempted
to throw themselves, by saying that the spring
always flowed there.   Providence willed that besides the public testimony there might be opposed
to them, their own articles, their own printed
publications, authentic, irrefutable dates.   If before the 25th February, before the scene which we
have just described, before the order and indication given by the Holy Virgin to Bernadette in
ecstasy, there had existed those beautiful gushing waters which exist to-day, how have your
journals, whose eyes are so open, whose details
are always so minute, not been able to perceive
this powerful spring, and never spoken about it ?

We defy the free-thinkers to produce a single document—we say only one—speaking of a spring or of water, before the period at which the Holy Virgin ordered it and at which nature obeyed.

IX.

The popular emotion had assumed considerable proportions. Bernadette was received with acclamations as she passed by, and the poor child returned home with all haste in order to escape these ovations. This humble soul, who had lived hitherto unknown, in silence and solitude, found herself all at once placed in broad daylight in the midst of a tumult and a crowd, upon the pedestal of renown. This glory, which so many others seek, was for her the cruelest of martyrdoms. Her slightest speeches were commented upon, discussed, admired, contemned, mocked at, abandoned, in a word to the varying opinions of those who disputed about them. And it was then that she tasted the innate joy of not having to say everything, and of finding, in the three secrets that the Holy Virgin had revealed to her, as it were, a reserved sanctuary in which she might, in all peace, withdraw her heart and refresh it, in the shadow of that mystery and in the charm of that intimacy with the Queen of Heaven. Days were at hand in which the trial of popularity was to become still greater.

As we have just related, the flowing of the spring had taken place towards sun-rise in presence of a numerous crowd. It was the 25th

February, a Thursday, the third of the month, a
great market day at Tarbes. The intelligence of
the marvellous event which happened in the morning at the rocks of Massabielle, was then carried
to the chief town by a multitude of eye-witnesses,
and spread the same evening through all the
neighbouring departments. The extraordinary
movement, which for eight days attracted to
Lourdes so many pilgrims and curious personages, assumed from this moment an unheard of
development.

A great number of visitors came to sleep at
Lourdes in order to be there the next day ; others
walked all night, and at the first rays of the day,
at the hour at which Bernadette was accustomed
to arrive, from five to six thousand persons throng-
ing on the banks of the Gave, on the little hills
and rocks encamped in front of the Grotto. The
spring, more copious than the day before, was
already considerable.

When the girl who beheld the Apparition,
humble, peaceable and simple in the midst of this
agitation, presented herself to pray, the populations exclaimed, "Behold the Saint ! Behold the
Saint." Many sought to touch her garments,
considering as sacred every object that belonged
to her who was so privileged by the Lord.

The mother of the humble and the lowly was
desirous however that this innocent heart should
not yield to the temptation of vain glory, and that
Bernadette might not become proud for an instant through the extraordinary favours of which
she was the object. It was just that the child in
the midst of these acclamations, should feel that

she was nothing, and that she should ascertain
once more her utter want of power to evoke by
herself the divine Vision. Vainly she prayed.
People did not see spread over her countenance
the superhuman splendour of an ecstasy, and
when she rose up, after her long prayer, she
replied with sorrow to the enquiries of those who
surrounded her, that the Vision from above had
not appeared.

X.

This absence of the Holy Virgin had doubtless
for its purpose to maintain Bernadette in a state
of humility, and in a consciousness of her own
nothingness; but it contained also, perhaps, for
Christian people, a high and mysterious lesson,
the import of which will not escape souls accustomed to contemplate and admire the secret harmonies of works which come specially from God.

If heaven was that very day closed to the sight
of Bernadette, if the celestial creature who appeared in visible flesh had seemed to have
vanished for a time, the proof of the reality and
power of this superhuman being, the fountain
which had sprung up the day before, and was
increasing more and more, was visible to all
beholders, and was running down the inclined
soil of the grotto before the eyes of astonished
multitudes.

The Holy Virgin withdrew to allow in some
way her work to speak. The Holy Virgin retired
also and was silent to allow the Church of that

country to speak, whose words at the Introit of
the Mass and at the responses for Matins might
serve as a commentary on that strange fountain
which had started up suddenly under the hand of
Bernadette in an ecstasy.

While in effect this was taking place at the
Grotto, before the miraculous source which had
issued on the right side of the barren rock, there
was being celebrated in the diocese of Tarbes, and
several other dioceses of France, the memory of
another source, the most illustrious and the most
life-giving of all those which for six thousand
years have watered the inheritance of the children
of Adam.   On this very day, 26th February,
1858, Friday of the first week of Lent, was the
Feast of the Holy Lance and Nails of our Saviour.
And the source of which we are speaking, and of
which the special offices of the diocese proclaim
the remembrance, was the great divine source
which the lance of the Roman centurion, piercing   .
the right side of Christ when dead, had caused to
gush forth a river of life to regenerate the earth,
and save the human race.   "*Vidi aquam egre-
dientem de templo,* a latere dextro ; *et omnes ad
quos pervenit aqua ista salvi facti sunt.*—I have
seen a water flowing from the temple, *on the right
side,* and all those to whom that water came have
been saved," exclaimed the prophet, contemplating in the course of ages the prodigies of the
divine mercy.   "*On this day,*" said the priests in
the office of Matins, "*there will be, for the house
of David and the inhabitants of Jerusalem, a*

fountain opened, as an ablution for the sinner, and all others who are defiled."[*]

By these truly astonishing coincidences, and which we earnestly beg the reader to verify for himself, in the passage which we have pointed out in the note, by such coincidences the Church of this country replied with a striking clearness to the numberless questions which were raised around the marvellous spring, issuing out at the side of the Grotto of Massabielle. The source, which had just appeared at the base of the Pyrenees, arose, by a mysterious infiltration, from that immense river of divine graces which, under the nails of the soldiers and the lance of the centurion, began to flow eighteen hundred years since at the summit of Mount Golgotha.

Such was the innate principle to which we must go back to find the hidden origin of the miraculous spring, and it was meet that the offices which were celebrated at their point of departure, should lead of themselves the mind towards these mystic heights. As to the practical results, as to the exterior effects which this Fountain of the Apparition was to produce, we should very naturally enquire for the interpretation and secret, no longer in the centre or at the point of departure, no longer in a restricted society, and in the exceptional Feast of a particular diocese, but specially in the universal offices which the Catholic, Apostolic, Roman Church celebrated everywhere at that hour, throughout the Christian

* Order of the Diocese of Tarbes, Office of Matins, response for the second lesson of II. nocturn.

world. Now this same day, 26th February, 1858,
Friday in the first week of Lent, the Gospel at
the Mass contained these words, which need no
reflection :—"Now there is at Jerusalem a pond
called Probatica, which in Hebrew is named
Bethsaida, having five porches. *In these lay a
great multitude of sick, of blind, of lame, of
withered, waiting for the moving of the water.*
And an Angel of the Lord went down at a certain
time into the pond ; and the water was moved.
And he that went down first into the pond, after
the motion of the water, WAS MADE WHOLE OF
WHATSOEVER INFIRMITY HE LAY UNDER."*

XI.

Although without doubt very few would see
such analogies, the idea that the water that
issued from the spring at the Grotto might cure
the sick had succeeded of itself in coming into
the mind of all. From the morning of this same
day, the report of several marvellous cures began
to spread itself on all sides. In the midst of the
contradictory versions that circulated, amid the
sincerity of some, of the voluntary or involuntary
exaggeration of others, of the hesitation and
trouble of mind of a great number, of the universal emotion, it was difficult at the first moment
to discern the true from the false amongst the
miraculous facts which were alleged on all sides,
but which were related in different ways, some-

* St. John v. 4-6.

times mutilating their names, sometimes con-
founding the persons, sometimes mixing up the
circumstances of several episodes different and
strange to one another.

Have you ever, while walking in the country,
roughly thrown a handful of corn upon an ant-hill?
The affrighted ants run up and down in extraordinary agitation; they go, they come, they
cross one another, they knock against one another,
they stop, they resume their march, they turn
back their steps, they go away all at once from
the point to which they seemed to run, they
collect a grain of corn, then they leave it there,
wandering about everywhere in a feverish state of
disorder, a prey to an inexpressible confusion.

Such were the multitudes of inhabitants and
strangers at Lourdes, in the stupor into which they
were cast by the supernatural marvels that came to
them from heaven. Such is always elsewhere the
natural world, when it is visited all at once by
some fact in the supernatural world.

By degrees, nevertheless, order became established on the ant-hill, which was troubled for a
moment.

There was in the town a poor workman known
by all, who lingered out for many long years a
most wretched existence. His name was Louis
Bourriette. Some twenty years ago a great misfortune had happened to him. As he was working in the environs of Lourdes in getting up
stone along with his brother Joseph, a quarry-
man like himself, a badly managed mine had
made an explosion by their side. Joseph had
fallen dead on the spot. Louis, he of whom

we are speaking, had his face lacerated by the
blasts of the rock, and his right eye half crushed.
It was the most difficult thing in the world to
save him.   The frightful sufferings which followed this accident had been such that a burning fever set in, and it was necessary, during
the first days, to keep him in bed by means
of force.   He recovered, however, by degrees,
thanks to intelligent and devoted care.   Still,
medicine had been powerless, in spite of the most
delicate operations, and the most skilful treatment, to cure his right eye, which had unfortunately inflicted injury on his inward constitution.   This man had resumed his employment as
a quarry labourer, but he could not do any other
than common work, his wounded eye not rendering
him any service, and no longer perceiving objects
except in a misty way.   When he wanted to do
any work that required some care, the poor
labourer was obliged to have recourse to some
other person.

   Time had not brought any amelioration ; quite
the contrary.   Bourriette's sight every year grew
worse.   This progressive weakening had become
latterly more sensible, and at the moment at
which we have arrived, the evil had made such progress that the right eye was almost entirely lost.
When he closed his left eye Bourriette could no
longer distinguish a man from a tree.   The tree
and the man were only for him a black confused
mass dissolving on a dark night.

   The greater part of the inhabitants of Lourdes
had employed Bourriette one time or other.   His
state excited compassion, and he was much re-

spected in the confraternity of the quarry-men
and stone cutters, who were very numerous in
that country.

This unfortunate man, hearing speak of the
spring that had miraculously gushed forth at the
Grotto, called his daughter.

"Go and get me some of that water," said he.
"The Holy Virgin, if it is she, has but the will
to cure me."

A half-hour after, the child brought a vessel
with a little of that water, still dirty and earthy,
as we have explained.

"Father," said the child, "it is only muddy
water."

"Never mind," said the father, who began to
pray.

He rubbed his bad eye with this water, which,
a few moments before, he thought was entirely
lost.

Almost immediately he uttered a great cry and
began to tremble, so great was his emotion. A
sudden miracle was accomplished before his eyes.
Already around him the air had again become
clear and full of light. Yet objects seemed to
him still surrounded with a slight halo that
hindered him from perceiving their details.

The mists existed still, but they were no longer
black as they had been for twenty years. The
sun penetrated them, and in place of dark night,
it was before the eye of the infirm man the transparent vapour of the morning.

Bourriette continued to pray and to wash his
right eye with that beneficial water. Daylight

increased by degrees upon his sight, and he could plainly distinguish objects.

Next day, or the day after, he meets, in the public square of Lourdes, Doctor Dozous, who had always rendered, him every attention, since the commencement of his malady. He runs up to him.

"I am cured !" said he to him.

"Impossible !" exclaimed the doctor. "You have an organic injury, which renders your complaint absolutely incurable. The treatment which I have made you follow has for its object to ease your pains, but cannot restore you your sight."

"It is not you that have cured me," replies the quarry labourer, with emotion ; "it is the Holy Virgin of the Grotto."

The man of human science shrugged his shoulders.

"That Bernadette had unaccountable ecstasies, that is certain, for I have verified it with indefatigable attention. But that the water sprung up at the Grotto, through I know not what unknown cause, should suddenly heal incurable maladies, that is not possible."

In saying this he drew a note book out of his pocket, and wrote some words with a pencil.

Then, with one hand he closes the left eye of Bourriette, that is to say, the healthy eye, by which the latter could see, and presents to the right eye, which he knew was entirely deprived of sight, the little phrase which he had just written.

"If you can read this, I will believe you," said the eminent doctor, with a triumphant look, which strongly smacked of his great science and profound medical experience.

Some people who were walking in the square had assembled around them.

"'Bourriette has an incurable amaurosis, and he will never be well.'"

A thunderbolt, falling at the feet of the learned physician, could not more have stupified him than the voice of Bourriette reading as he did, quietly and without any effort, the only line of fine writing which he had slightly traced with a pencil over a page of a note book.

Doctor Dozous was more than a man of science he was a man of conscience. He frankly admitted and proclaimed without hesitation, in this sudden cure of an incurable malady, the action of a superior power.

"I cannot deny it," said he; "it is a miracle. A true miracle does not displease, neither myself nor my brethren of the faculty. This overwhelms me; but we must wholly submit to the imperious voice of a fact so evident, and so much out of the reach of what human science can accomphish."

Doctor Vergez, of Tarbes, admitted professor of the faculty of Montpellier, physician at the waters of Baréges, being called upon to give an opinion upon this event, could not hinder himself from equally seeing in it, in a manner the most undeniable, a supernatural character.*

* The conclusions which were written down by these two eminent physicians, both still living. as well as Bourriette, were inserted by them in two detailed reports separate from one another, which were demanded later by the Episcopal

We have said, the state of Bourriette was notorious during twenty years, and this poor man was
known by everybody. The marvellous cure had
not, besides, caused to disappear either the deep
marks or the scars of his terrible complaint, so
that every one could verify the miracle which had
just taken place. The quarry workman, almost
out of himself with joy, related its details to whoever was willing to listen to him.

He was not the only one to proclaim aloud
the testimony of an unexpected happiness, and
the expression of gratitude. Facts of the same
nature had been accomplished in other houses of
the town. Several persons at Lourdes, Marie
Daube, Bernarde Saubie, Fabien Baron, had all
at once left their bed of suffering, on which divers
maladies reputed incurable had kept them for
several years, and they published openly their
cure through the water at the Grotto. The hand
of Jane Crassus, which had been paralysed for
ten years, had been made straight again, and had
recovered the fulness of life in the miraculous
water.[*]

A precision as to the facts succeeded now the
vague reports of the first moment amongst the
statements that were made. The enthusiasm of
the people was at its highest, an enthusiasm
which was affecting and edifying, which mani-

Commission that was appointed to examine the events at
Lourdes.

[*] The account of these different cures has been officially
tested in the medical reports addressed to the Episcopal Commission.

fested itself in the Church by fervent prayers, around the Grotto by canticles of thanksgiving, bursting forth on the joyful lips of pilgrims.

Towards the evening, a great number of workmen of the association of quarry labourers, of whom Bourriette was one, marched to the Rocks of Massabielle, and traced out on the steep little hill which was opposite the Grotto a pathway for the visitors. Before the gap whence the fountain, already very strong, had gushed forth, they placed a trench of wood, beneath which they hollowed out an oval reservoir, about a foot and a half in depth, having almost the shape and length of an infant's cradle.

The enthusiasm increased every moment. The multitudes passed to and fro on the road to the miraculous fountain. After sunset, when the first shades of night began to fall upon the earth, it was seen that the same thought had occurred to a crowd of pious believers, and the Grotto was illuminated all at once with a thousand lights. The poor, the rich, the children, the women and the men, had spontaneously brought tapers and candles. During all the night, the other side of the Gave might be seen to radiate a bright and soft light, which these thousands of little torches had, placed here and there without any visible order, and answering on the earth to the twinkling and lustre of the stars that spangled the firmament.

There was not found among these people any priests, or bishops, or persons of any note; and, nevertheless, without any one making them any sign, at the moment at which the illumination

brightened up the Grotto and the rocks, casting
its reflection all dazzling into the little reservoir
of the Fountain, every voice was raised at the
same time, and was blended together in one
unanimous chant.   The litanies of the Holy Virgin were made to resound, interrupting the silence
of the night in order to celebrate the Admirable
Mother, before that rustic throne on which her
wisdom had deigned to appear in order to fill with
joy all Christian hearts.   "*Mater admirabilis,
Sedes sapientiæ, Causa nostræ lætitiæ, ora pro
nobis.*"

It was the hour when the enemies of superstiti-
tion were usually enjoying themselves at the cafés
and the clubs.   On this night trouble seized this
Sanhedrim.

"There never was a spring in this place,"
cried one.

"It is a pool of water, formed I do not know
how, in consequence of some accidental infiltration, which was discovered by the merest chance
when Bernadette scraped the soil.   Nothing can
be more simple."

"Evidently," was the general reply.

"But," one of those present ventured to say,
"they pretend that the water continues to flow."

"It is no such thing," cried out several voices
together; "we went there yesterday.   It is a
great puddle of water; it is nothing but a pool.
The people, with their usual exaggeration, pretend
that the water runs.   It is not true.   We examined the whole affair yesterday, when it was first
mentioned, and it is nothing but a muddy pool."

These declarations sufficed to convince the

world of philosophers and savants. It was the official thesis, accepted, certain, incontestable.

There is nothing easier than this: to deny everything, to be perfectly incredulous, and to take care to make no examination into the case in question. And so, six weeks after the bursting out of the waters, that is to say, on the 10th of April, the journal *L'Era Imperial*, referring to the subject of the Grotto, and the question of building a church on the spot, wrote as follows: "It would have been better to choose some other reason for building a sacred edifice, than the declarations of a child who is subject to hallucinations, and some other spot than the *pool* where she washes herself."

And this was put forth at the very moment when, as every one could, see for himself, there ran from the Grotto a strong stream of water, upwards of *one hundred thousand litres a day*. And so they persisted in denying that there was any running water to be seen; and this version of a "*pool*" was audaciously published in the free-thinking independent journals.[*] And as to the alleged miraculous cures, these they denied entirely, as they did the existence of the fountain, with contemptuous shrugs and laughter.

"Bourriette is not cured," said one.

"He never had anything the matter with him," declared another.

---

[*] We have discovered, on the authority of M. Lasserre, that the volume of water issuing from the miraculous fountain yields eighty-five litres per minute, which would be 5,000 an hour, or 122,400 litres a day. A litre contains about two of our ordinary pints.

11

"He imagines he is cured," said a third.

"Imagination has sometimes a surprising effect on the nerves," replied a physiologist.

"There is no such person as Bourriette," stoutly declared a new comer.

"And how comes it," they added, "that serious and well educated men, such as M. Dufo, a lawyer in a high position; as also Doctor Dozous, M. Estrade, the Commandant of the Garrison, and the *Intendant Militaire*, M. de Laffitte, have had the inconceivable weakness to allow themselves to be deceived and led away by all that has been taking place?"

During this eventful day Bernadette had been sent for to the Chamber of the Tribunal, and there examined by the *Procureur Imperial*, the Vice-President, and the Judges. All these had been equally unable, as M. Jacomet the Commissary of Police had been, to induce her to vary or contradict her statements.

The Procureur Imperial, followed by the Vice-President, had already pronounced on the matter, and nothing could disturb the conclusion at which he had arrived. He deplored this sudden influx of fanaticism, and energetically declared that he would perform his duty. Strange to say, notwithstanding this unusual concourse of people, no disorder whatever took place, so that the laudable zeal of M. le Procureur Imperial was condemned to complete inaction, and he simply preserved an attitude of watchful attention. Amid such tumultuous feelings, it seemed as if an invisible hand protected these innumerable crowds, and prevented them from giving (even innocently)

a pretext for violent intrusion on the part of the
men of justice, or for the interference of the men
of the law.   Whether they wished it or not, these
men had for the time their hands tied, and were
not set free until the mysterious Apparition of the
Grotto had completed her work.   The invisible
ægis of the Blessed Virgin defended these first
witnesses from all dangers.   "*Nolite timere,
pusillus grex.*"

The enemies of superstition made the most
urgent applications to the Mayor of Lourdes, to
induce him to decide on prohibiting by a Decree
all access to the Rocks of Massabielle, which
formed part of land that belonged to the Commune.   Such a decree, thought they, would in-
evitably be violated by the popular feeling, and
give rise to numberless cases before the court;
there would be many acts of resistance, and many
arrests would be made; and the authority of the
law, having come into question, would easily pre-
vail, for it would have all the force of the state for
its support.   Monsieur Lacade, Mayor of Lourdes,
was a very upright and honourable man, enjoying
and meriting the respect of the public.   Everyone
in the town of Lourdes did justice to his eminent
and rare qualities, his enemies and his rivals, in
their strongest language, never reproached him
except with a certain amount of timidity in adopting, between extreme parties, a firm attitude, and
a little too much leaning towards his functions as
Mayor, which he otherwise fulfilled, by the admis-
sion of all, with an air of superiority.   He refused
to grant the decree asked of him.

"I do not know, in the midst of so much

clamour, where the truth lies," replied he, "and I cannot pronounce yes or no. I shall let things proceed, so long as there is no disorder. It is an affair of the Bishop to decide the religious question; it is for the Prefect to determine measures that belong to the Administration. For myself, I wish as much as I can, to keep out of this, and I will not act as Mayor, except by the express order of the Prefect."

Such was, if not the text, at least the sense of his answer to the applications with which he was beset by the philosophers of the country, as the Christian creed has been by the philosophers of every age. The pretended liberty of thinking rarely tolerates liberty of belief.

From the day that the Fountain first appeared, the Apparition had not reiterated her order to Bernadette to go to the priests to demand the building of a church.

The following day the Vision had not manifested itself, as already stated, so that from this moment Bernadette had not reappeared at the presbytery. The Clergy, notwithstanding the rising tide of popular faith, and in spite of increasing rumours of miracles from all sides, continued to remain aloof from all these manifestations of enthusiasm.

"Let us wait," said the parish priest of Lourdes. "Even in human affairs prudence is necessary, but it is sevenfold more necessary in matters which pertain to God."

Consequently, not a single ecclesiastic appeared among the incessant processions which were made to the Grotto.

The Clergy, then, were resolved to hold themselves aloof, and the municipal authority refused to act, so that the popular movement was left free, and increased like the rivers of that country when the snows melted, and the rains fell in abundance in the spring-tide. It rushed onwards with invincible force; it increased every day; it overflowed on every side, always rising and covering the fields with its innumerable floods.

The partizans of repression began to feel their impotence against a current so formidable, and to see clearly that all resistance was powerless as a barrier of sand or straw against this sudden and sweeping inundation. They felt that they must resign themselves to inaction, and permit the multitudes thus set in motion by the inspirations of God to pass freely on their way.

XII.

Notwithstanding the immense concourse of people, all continued to proceed with the greatest order at the Grotto. They drank of the Fountain, they chanted Canticles, they prayed.

Moreover, the soldiers of the garrison had asked permission of their commanding officers to go to the place. With the instinct of discipline, developed in them by their military education, they marshalled the crowd, keeping open a free passage, and preventing the masses from pressing too closely on the dangerous banks of the Gave. They employed themselves on this side and on

that, assuming a certain authority which no one
thought of resisting.

Thus several days were passed, during which
the Apparition appeared as usual, and nothing remarkable or new occurred, except that the Fountain continued to increase in volume, and the
miraculous cures multiplied more and more.

At this period the world of freethinkers was
stupified with astonishment. Facts became so
numerous, so well attested, and so patent, that
defections took place continually from the camp of
the incredulous. Still there always remained a
determined nucleus of strong minds, who only
became more obstinate, and refused to believe in
the truth of events which were so apparent to an
unprejudiced mind. This would seem to be impossible if the whole universe did not know that a
great part of the Jewish people resisted the
miracles of Jesus Christ and His Apostles, and
that it required four centuries of prodigies to open
the eyes of the pagan world to the truth of
Christianity.

BOOK IV.

I.

On the 2nd of March Bernadette appeared again before the Parish Priest of Lourdes, and spoke to him for the second time of the Apparition.

" Her wish," said she, " is that a chapel should be built, and that processions should be made to the Grotto."

Events had now made great progress. The Fountain had gushed forth; cures had been effected; miracles had been wrought in the name of God, to attest the veracity of Bernadette. The priest required no further proof, and he demanded none. His mind was made up. His faith was now too firm to be clouded again by doubt.

The invisible "Lady" of the Grotto had never told her name; but the man of God had already recognised her by her maternal benefits, and had perhaps already added to his prayers, " Our Lady of Lourdes, pray for us."

At the same time, in spite of the interior enthusiasm which filled his heart at the spectacle of all these wonders, he had with rare prudence refrained from giving premature expression to the profound sentiments of love and gratitude that filled his mind at the thought that the Queen of Heaven had deigned to descend amongst his humble flock ; and this prudence had caused him to reiterate his directions to the clergy not to appear at the Grotto.

"I believe you," said he, to Bernadette, when she again presented herself before him. "But what you ask of me in the name of the Apparition, I am not able to perform. That rests with the bishop, and I have already informed him of what has occurred. I shall now go to his lordship and tell him what you have said of this new demand. It belongs to him alone to act."

II.

Monseigneur Bertrand Sèvère Laurence, Bishop of Tarbes, was a native of the Diocese, and therefore belonged to it by the double ties of nature and dignity. He had been born and educated there, and there also he grew up to man's estate. His high merit caused him to be rapidly appointed to various and important ecclesiastical dignities— he was successively Superior of the Little Seminary of Saint-Pé which he had founded, Superior of the Great Seminary, and Vicar General.

Nearly all the priests of the Diocese had been amongst the number of his scholars. He had been their preceptor before he became their bishop, he had directed them for nearly forty years.

The profound harmony, the great union of heart and soul, which reigned, through the force of circumstances, between the ancient Superior of the Seminaries and the Clergy whom he had formed himself for the sacerdotal life, was one of the causes of his promotion to the episcopate. When twelve years previously, the See of Tarbes became vacant by the demise of Monseigneur Double, the name of M. L'Abbé Laurence was in the mouth and hearts of all. The whole Diocese was filled with the same desire and hope, and a petition was signed, praying for the nomination of M. Laurence to the See of Tarbes. The bishop, as had frequently happened in the Primitive Church was thus chosen, and placed by universal suffrage in that high position for which he was so eminently qualified. From this statement it is evident that Monseigneur Laurence and his clergy formed but one great Christian family.

All the warmth of his nature concentrated itself in his excellent and paternal heart which beat so tenderly for all his children. But by a not irreconcilable contrast, his cool clear intellect submitted all things to the decision of unimpassioned reason. The bent of mind of the prelate, though open on all sides, possessed a tendency of a decidedly practical character. No one was more inaccessible to the illusions of the imagination, or less liable to be drawn away by hasty enthusiasm. He distrusted ardent and highly excitable natures. Passionate arguments had no effect upon his mind. If his heart was guided by feeling, reason alone was the law of his understanding.

The bishop, before acting, weighed with extreme care not only the circumstances of the case, but also the consequences which might ensue. Hence he occasionally evinced a certain degree of tardiness in pronouncing upon affairs of great importance which did not arise in any degree from in-

decision of character, but from that matured wisdom which deliberates slowly, informs itself fully,
and decides finally.   Knowing, moreover, that
truth is eternal, and one day or other will infallibly be made manifest, Monseigneur Laurence
exercised the rare virtue of patience, and knew
how to wait.

Monseigneur Laurence being gifted with a rare
sagacity of observation, was well acquainted with
human nature, and possessed to a high degree the
difficult art of managing and governing the human
mind.   He knew that the personal enemies of a
bishop soon became the enemies also of the whole
episcopate, and even in many cases of religion
itself, and unless under particular circumstances,
he was most careful to avoid anything that might
afford a pretext for a collision, a disagreement or
unpleasantness of any kind.   His prudence was
extreme.   Having through the extent of his
Diocese to direct the Bark of Peter, he was full of
a sense of his responsibility.   Attentive to the
state of the Sea and every breath of the wind, he
often looked down to the bottom of the water and
was careful to avoid its rocks.

Remarkable as an administrator, a man of order
and discipline, he reunited in his person the simplicity of an apostle to the prudence of a diploma-
tist, and from the reign of Louis Philippe up to
the period of the second empire, he was always
held in the very highest repute by successive
governments.   When Monseigneur Laurence made
a request, the authorities knew that it was likely
to be just and necessary, and they never refused
his applications.

Thus it happened that for a long time, the spiritual and temporal authorities lived in the most perfect unanimity in this Pyrenean Diocese, until the miraculous occurrences which form the subject of this history, happened at Lourdes.

III.

M. L'Abbé Peyramale laid before the bishop the surprising facts which had taken place at the Grotto of Massabielle and in the town of Lourdes during the last three weeks. He related the ecstasies and the visions of Bernadette, the words used by the Apparition, the gushing forth of the fountain, the sudden cures, the universal emotion.

His recital was without doubt lively and picturesque in the extreme, and it must have made an impression on the mind of the bishop, but could not produce immediate conviction.

Monseigneur Laurence was accustomed to receive the truths of religion through the medium of the Pope and the bishops, and he was by no means disposed to receive, without mature consideration, a message from heaven, which was presented to him all at once out of the ordinary rule, by an illiterate little peasant girl.

He was, however, too well versed in everything relative to the history of the Church to oppose an absolute negation to a matter that had, after all, its analogy in the secular annals of Catholicism, but he was at the same time too practical to be convinced without great difficulty. The bishops are the successors of the apostles. Monseigneur

Laurence was a holy apostle. He was a Saint Thomas. He desired to see before he believed, and that was fortunate, for when the bishop believed, all the world knew that they might believe in all security with him, and that proof had been obtained to the utmost clearness.

The parish priest of Lourdes had not himself been an eye-witness of most of the facts which he related, and as he had also forbidden his clergy to attend the meetings at the Grotto, he could only bring forward the testimony of laics, of whom many were sceptical and indifferent to religion, and did not observe even the laws of the Church.

On the whole, the proofs laid before the bishop were not such as to induce him to act upon them. In the midst of so many statements that had been made to him, the multiplicity and confusion of so many incidents, the inevitable gaps in his informations, and reports without number, it was impossible for him to take proper note of them for himself, and to trace the logical and providential course of events, with that method which it is so easy to do now. It happens in facts of the moral as with objects of the physical order; we must get to a distance to have a proper view of them. Abbé Peyramale might well analyse some facts that took place under his own eyes; but at this period neither the bishop nor himself could see their full extent, nor estimate their admirable synthesis; they were too near the events.

Monseigneur did not pronounce any opinion. Wiser in that respect than was St. Thomas, he did not positively deny the existence of the miracle, for he knew that such cases, although very rare, were not impossible. As a bishop, he required documents and attestations of an unexceptionable authenticity, and the second-hand proofs he had received from the parish priest of Lourdes did not seem to him to be sufficient. Might there not have been some illusion in the mind of the girl? Or some exaggeration in the recitals of the people? Have not souls been sometimes deceived by false miracles, whether arising from imposture, from hallucination, or from the artifices of the evil one?

All these questions he carefully considered, and made it a duty to proceed with extreme caution.

It is true that the thought of an official inquiry presented itself quite naturally to his mind, and public opinion, desirous of a solution, pressed for Episcopal authority to take this affair in hand and to pronounce its judgment. But with a discernment that was marvellous, the bishop felt that the very agitation of the people would be injurious to the deliberation and security proper for the inquiry. He had the wisdom, difficult to exercise, which enabled him to resist the popular pressure. He resolved to let things take their course, to allow new events to arise, and striking evidence to manifest itself in the cause of truth, whatever it might be.

" The hour is not come for episcopal authority to take cognizance of this affair. To sit in judgment, as is expected from us, we must proceed with a wise slowness, we must distrust the urging on of the first days, we must give time for reflec-

tion, and ask for lights for an attentive and enlightened observation."[*]

He repeated his orders to the clergy not to show
themselves at the Grotto.   But at the same time,
he took measures, in concert with the Curé of
Lourdes, to have himself well informed day by day
by incontestable witnesses, of all that passed at the
Rock of Massabielle, and of all the cures true or
false that might still happen there.

Such was the attitude full of reserve, assumed
by the Bishop, whilst the Civil Authority was at
the same time in the greatest perplexity.   Monsieur Massy was Prefect of Tarbes, and Monsieur
Rouland Minister of Public Worship.

M. le Baron Massy, Prefect of the Upper
Pyrenees, though a sincere independent Catholic,
was a declared enemy to superstition.   He professed to believe, as a good Christian should do,
all the miracles recorded in the Gospels, and in
the Acts of the Apostles, but beyond these marvels, of which the belief is obligatory, he did not
admit the possibility of any supernatural occurrences.   Miracles, he supposed, were indispensable
in the earlier ages of the Church, they were necessary and useful to strengthen her authority and to
increase her influence over the minds of men.
But when the Church was established on a firm
basis, she no longer required, he argued, these
supernatural aids, and God had then ceased to
work miracles on her behalf.   His faith in the

* Words from the Ordonnance published later by Monseigneur the Bishop of Tarbes.

supernatural ended, in fact, with the earliest ages of Christianity.

Up to this period, the Prefect and the Bishop had lived in perfect unanimity and friendship. M. Massy was a Christian, not only in belief, but in practice. He was universally esteemed for the purity of his life, and for his domestic virtues, which the bishop highly appreciated, nor could the Prefect fail to love and admire the many eminent qualities possessed by Mgr. Laurence, whose consummate prudence and perfect knowledge of mankind, led him to shun every occasion of conflict between the spiritual and temporal authorities, so that not peace alone, but also the most perfect harmony reigned between the chief of the Diocese, and the head of the Department.

V.

M. Massy was well informed of what was going on at Lourdes, by the reports of M. Jacomet, in whom he reposed the most implicit confidence, and instead of imitating the wise reserve of his bishop, he suffered himself to be influenced by his original prejudices, and not having the slightest belief in the possibility of such apparitions and miracles, but supposing that he was able to stem unaided the tremendous overflow of popular feeling, he took up a most decided position, and plainly declared his intention to put a summary end to this new superstition, which though now in its infancy, seemed likely to attain such gigantic proportions.

"If I had been Prefect of the Isère, at the time of the pretended Apparitions of La Salette," he used often to say, "I should very soon have brought the parties to reason, and that pretended Apparition would have ended, as this of Lourdes is about to do. All this Phantasmagoria is coming to nothing."

Instead of waiting for the religious authority, which was alone competent to deal with it, to decide upon the most fitting moment for taking in hand the examination of this extraordinary affair, Monsieur, the Prefect, at once decided in the sense of his anti-supernatural prejudices. The Bishop, patient as ever, took time to untie the gordian knot. M. Massy, in his impetuosity, preferred to cut it at once. The sword of Alexander might possibly have succeeded in such a trial of strength as this, but the little dress sword of a Prefect was likely to fail in the attempt. For a similar task, that of M. Massy, soon became rusty, and finally gave way and broke in his hand.

Although he had quite made up his own mind upon the subject, he must have known well that the question was one to be decided by the Episcopal Authority and not by the Civil Power, nor did he desire to offend the Venerated Prelate who conducted with consummate wisdom the affairs of the Diocese.

He commenced by setting a secret watch, we know not with what hope, over the Grotto night and day, as if any human power could possibly have been concerned in effecting this marvellous gushing forth of the miraculous Fountain, and of its rapid and progressive increase.[*]

On the third of March, in obedience to the orders which he had received from the Prefecture, the Mayor of Lourdes, Monsieur Lacadè, wrote to the Commandant of the Fort, desiring him to place at his disposal, the troops of the garrison, and hold them in readiness for the following day.[†] The soldiers under arms were to be drawn up in military array in the road, and at the approaches to the Grotto. The local Gendarmes and all the Officers of the Police had received similar instructions.

VI.

Notwithstanding the menacing attitude which had been assumed by the officials, the fame of these marvellous occurrences had spread into all the neighbouring provinces with the rapidity of lightning. Bigorre and Bearn had already been made acquainted with the earlier circumstances of the Apparition, and the subsequent news of the sudden appearance of the miraculous Fountain, and the marvellous cures which ensued, had stirred the population to its very depths. The whole department was aroused, and the roads were crowded with travellers, making all speed to witness these marvels for themselves. From all

[*] *Archives of the Mairie of Lourdes.* Letters of the Mayor to the Prefect, No. 61.

[†] Ibid. Letter of the Mayor to the Commandant of the Fort, No. 60.

12

sides, and by every road and little footpath which
led to Lourdes, vehicles of all kinds poured in;
the stream of travellers was increasing, and even
the darkness of night put no stop to this extraordinary movement, for the mountaineers made
their way down by the light of the stars, and the
earliest dawn of day found them at the Grotto.

The earliest travellers had most usually remained at Lourdes for some time, being unwilling
to tear themselves away from the scene of such
extraordinary events, so that the hotels, inns, and
even the private houses, were overflowing with
visitors, and it became almost impossible to find
room for them all.

Many passed the night in prayer before the
illuminated Grotto, that in the morning they
might be able to obtain the best places, in the
immediate neighbourhood of the girl who saw the
Apparition.

Thursday, the fourth of March, was the last day
of the fortnight.

When the first rays of dawn arose to brighten
the horizon, a crowd still more prodigious than
on the preceding days invaded the approach to the
Grotto.

A painter such as Raphael, or Michael Angelo,
might have drawn from this living spectacle the
subject for an admirable picture. Here, all
bent with age, was a venerable patriarch, an old
mountaineer, leaning with trembling hands on
his staff. Around him pressed his whole family,
from the grandmother, an ancient matron, with
her wrinkled face muffled in her black mantle
lined with red, down to the youngest grandson

raising himself on tiptoe in order to see the better.
With their hands fervently joined together, beautiful, peaceful, and grave, as the splendid virgins of
the Roman Campagna, were seen the young girls
of the mountains, praying singly, or in groups.
Many were busy with the rustic beads of their
Rosaries. Some were silently reading their books
of devotion. Others held in their hands, or upon
their heads, an earthen pitcher, to be filled with
the miraculous water, recalling to mind the Bibli-
cal figures of Rebecca or Rachel.

There was the peasant of the Gers, with his
enormous head, his bull neck, his face plethoric
like that of a Vitellius.

At his side was the fine head and profile of the
Bearnais peasant, which the innumerable portraits
of Henry IV. have rendered so popular and well
known.

Of middle height, but appearing tall from their
marvellous uprightness, the Basque peasants stood
around, in attitudes so absolutely motionless, as
to seem planted on the ground like statues; their
large foreheads, their small and prominent chins,
their whole features, in fact, bearing a distinctive
type, betokening the absolute purity of their race,
the most ancient, perhaps, of the whole country of
the Gauls.

Presenting forms less rude, but at the same
time less picturesque, were collected men of a
higher grade, of all professions, magistrates, mer-
chants, notaries, lawyers, and physicians, mixed
in great numbers among the crowd. Ladies in
hats and veils, with their hands buried in their
muffs, pacing to and fro, to warm themselves.

Calm and dignified, covered from head to foot
by their cloaks of ample fold, stood some Span-
iards, absorbed in prayer.

In several places the pilgrims, fatigued by travel,
or watching during the night, were seated on the
ground. There were some who, in their fore-
thought had brought with them their *havre-sacs*,
filled with provisions. Others carried by a strap
around them a gourd filled with wine. Many
children lay asleep on the ground, mothers deprived themselves of their *capulets* to cover them
up warmly, and protect them from the chill morning air.

Cavalry officers from Tarbes, or from the depot
at Lourdes, had arrived on horseback, and took up
their position in the running waters of the Gave,
to avoid the general press and confusion.

Many pilgrims and spectators had climbed up the
trees, to overlook the rest. The meadows, the
fields, the hills, every rising ground, and all the
rocks from whence a view could be obtained, were
literally covered with an innumerable multitude.
The soldiers and policemen paraded in the neighbourhood of this vast crowd, as well as in the
adjoining roads, they ran hither and thither, and
called to this person and that, in a state of
thorough anxiety and confusion. The vice-mayor,
in his scarf of office, stood quietly contemplating
the scene, while M. Jacomet and the Procureur
Imperial, were equally attentive to all that was
going on, and in readiness to repress the least appearance of disorder.

Upwards of twenty thousand persons were spread
along the banks of the Gave, and this multitude

increased incessantly by the arrivals of fresh pilgrims who came in on every side. Faith, prayer, curiosity, scepticism, were depicted on their varied countenances. All classes, all ideas, all sentiments, were represented in this immense multitude.

The simple Christian of the early ages was there, who knew that nothing was impossible with God. The Christian tormented by doubts, and coming to these savage rocks to seek arguments for his tottering faith. The believing woman asking of the Holy Mother the cure of some dear sick one, or the conversion of some beloved soul—the sceptic having eyes that see not, and ears that hear not—and the frivolous person, forgetful of his soul, and only in quest of some amusement, form a strange and unwonted spectacle. All these were to be found amongst that vast assemblage.

Around this crowd, with anxiety depicted on their countenances, paraded the *Sergents de Ville*, and the Gendarmes. The Deputy-Mayor, clothed in his scarf of office, was immoveable at his post. Attentive to all that was passing around them, and ready to repress the slightest disorder, were seen on a little wall Jacomet and the Procureur Imperial.

A loud, vague, confused sound came from the multitude, resembling the ceaseless tumult of the waves of the sea.

Suddenly the cry arose, " Here comes the saint! here comes the saint !"

Instinctively all heads were uncovered. Bernadette, accompanied by her mother, was seen on the path which the Confraternity of Stone-Cutters had traced out on the preceding days, quietly descending towards this ocean of human beings. Although she had the vast assemblage before her eyes, and was doubtless glad to see such devoted homage paid to the marvellous Lady, her whole thoughts were concentrated on the happiness that awaited her in seeing this incomparable beauty once more. When heaven is about to open, who is there that would look upon earth! She was so absorbed in the joyous expectation that filled her heart, that the cries, "Here comes the saint," did not seem to reach her ears. She was so full of the image of the vision, so perfectly humble, that she had not even vanity enough to be confused, and blush.

The gendarmes, however, ran towards the child, forming an escort for her, and clearing a passage to the Grotto. These brave fellows, as well as the soldiers, were believers, and their sympathetic attitude and religious demeanour, had prevented the crowd from being irritated at the display of armed force, and thus deceived the calculations of the crafty. A deep silence reigned. There is not a moment during the holy Sacrifice of the Mass, where greater recollection could have been observed. Even those who did not believe, were filled with respect. Every one held his breath. Had a blind person been there, he would have been unconscious of the presence of the vast assemblage; and, in the midst of the universal silence, nothing would have struck his ears save the gushing waters of the Gave. Those who were near the Grotto, heard the murmur of the miracu-

lous fountain as it ran peacefully into the little
reservoir, by the conduit of wood lately placed to
receive it.

When Bernadette knelt before the Grotto, all the
people, by one unanimous movement, fell upon
their knees. Almost instantly afterwards the superhuman rays of ecstasy illumined the transfigured features of the child. We need not again
describe this marvellous spectacle of which we have
so frequently attempted to give the reader an idea.
It was ever the same, yet always changing, like
the splendours of the rising sun. The powers of
a poor writer are limited, and his ideas weak and
unequal to treat of such high marvels. Though
Jacob in his sleep wrestled with the angel, the
artist in his infirmity, cannot wrestle with God.
And there is a time when he will find himself unable to describe the work of God. This is what
we now feel, and it must be left to those who read
this work, to picture to themselves the successive
joys, emotions, and blissful feelings of wonder and
delight which the beatific vision of the Virgin
Immaculate, of that admirable beauty which
charmed God Himself, impressed upon the heart,
and also upon the innocent countenance of the
enraptured Bernadette.

The apparition, as upon the preceding days,
had commanded the girl to go and drink, and
wash herself at the fountain, and to eat of the
herb already mentioned. She then again commanded her to go to the priests, and repeat her
wish that a church should be raised on that spot,
and that processions should be made to it.

The girl had entreated the Apparition to tell

her name; but the radiant "Lady" had not replied to this question. The moment had not yet arrived. The Queen of Heaven wished to be known by her benefits. She heard the grateful cries issue from every mouth, calling upon her and glorifying her before she answers, and says, "Your hearts have not deceived you. It is I myself."

VII.

Bernadette retook the road to Lourdes. In the immense crowd which we have described and which separated slowly, the question was asked with a thousand commentaries, what could be the meaning of the strange and mysterious order given by the Apparition to the child a week previously, an order many times repeated, and particularly that very day? All its details were examined, and every circumstance was weighed.

The Blessed Virgin addressing herself to a child among men, and speaking perhaps through her to us all, had ordered Bernadette to remove from the Gave, to mount the rock as far as the most remote corner of the Grotto, to drink, to eat the grass, and to wash herself in the Fountain, then invisible to the eye. The child, obedient to the heavenly voice, had performed these things. She had scooped up the earth. And the water had sprung forth, at first weak and muddy, then more abundant and less disturbed; and in proportion as it was emptied, it became in a few days a powerful and beautiful spring of water, clear as crystal, a river of life to the sick and infirm.

It was not necessary to be very skilful in the Science of Symbolism to understand the profound sense, the admirably actual sense of that order, in which philosophical imbecility could perceive nothing but folly and extravagance.

What is the evil of modern societies? In the order of ideas, is it not pride? We live at a time when man is making himself God. In the order of morals, is it not the most unbridled sensuality, the love of all that is passing around? What is the cause of that prodigious activity, of that astonishing industry which is upsetting the world? Man loves enjoyment. In the midst of so many fatigues, he seeks for physical well-being, he seeks for pleasures, he seeks for the satisfaction of his most material and egotistical instincts. He places his end here below, as if it was to be eternal. And therefore it is that he thinks not of going to the Church, never suspecting that she alone possesses the secret of true life and happiness without end.

O senseless mortals, says the mother of the human race, go not and quench your thirst in that Gave which passes; in those ephemeral passions which deceive when they say "always," in that apparent life of the senses which is only a death; in those material joys that kill the soul; in those waters which excite the thirst instead of appeasing it, in these powerless waters which hardly afford the illusion of a moment, and which leave you all your pains, griefs and miseries! Quit those tumultuous and agitated waves, turn your back on that flood which is flowing along, in that torrent which is precipitating itself into the

abyss. Come to the Source which quenches and
calms, which cures and restores to life again.
Come and drink at the Fountain of true joy and
true life, at that Fountain of the immutable Rock
on which the Church has laid her eternal foundations. Come drink and wash yourself at the
gushing Fountain....

"Drink at the Fountain! But where then is
it? Where then is found in the Rock of the
Church that Source of unheard of graces? Alas!
the time no longer exists in which the Church
makes the paralytic walk and the blind to see.
Vainly do our eyes look for the immoveable rock;
our eyes see it not, that Fountain of miracles at
which the sick and diseased are healed. Either it
never existed, or it is dried up these 1800 years."
So the world expresses itself.

"Ask and you shall receive," says the Word of
God. "If the prodigies do not arise in the midst
of you as in the days of the apostles, it is that,
turned towards the life of the senses, it is that,
not being willing to admit anything but what you
perceive with the eyes of the body, you seek not
the miraculous Fountain in the secrets of the
Divine Bounty. You do not see, you say, the
water gushing forth in the mysterious corner of
the Sanctuary. O Bernadette, O Humanity,
believe notwithstanding! Come and draw with
that entire faith which finds its nourishment while
it applies its lips to the maternal breast. Providence is a mother. And behold, how the Fountain issues forth, and behold how it augments in
proportion as men draw from it, absolutely as
happens with the milk for the lips of the child."

"Drink? But that water which gushes forth from the rock, passes over impure elements! The clergy have a thousand defects. They have ideas too of a particular kind which do not come from heaven. They have mixed the earth with the Divine Fountain. Wash myself? But I am more instructed, but I am less defiled, but I am more generous than this priest!"

Proud man, art thou not thyself formed of the slime of the earth? *Remember that thou art dust*...eat the grass, humble thyself, and be mindful of thy origin. Does not all that nourishes thee pass through the earth, and does not daily life itself come through that clay of which thou art formed?

Is the Fountain dried up? Humble faith will make it gush forth again. Is it muddy? Is it impure? Drink, drink, long and deep draughts, and it will become clear, transparent and luminous; and it will heal the sick and the infirm. The manifest instruction which is given to all the faithful. Would you ameliorate the condition of the clergy? Would you bring them to the practice of the apostolic virtues? Would you sanctify the human element of the Church? Participate in the sacraments which the priesthood administers. Be sheep, you will have pastors. Wash yourself in the soul of that priest, he will become purified in purifying you. You have allowed the Source of miracles to become lost, by not making use of it. It is by an inverse proceeding, it is by making use of it, that you must find it again. *Quærite et invenietis—Seek and you shall find.*

In order that it may be opened to you, you must knock. In order to receive, you must ask.

VIII.

Although the crowd, as we have said, was unusually great the morning of the arrival of Bernadette, we must not think that during the day there was a solitude at the Rocks of Massabielle. Persons were perpetually coming and going on the road leading to this Grotto, henceforth to be so celebrated. They examined it in every direction, some prayed before it, and some broke off fragments from the rocks as *Souvenirs*. On the evening of this day, there were not less than five or six hundred persons stationed on the banks of the Gave, where the Apparition appeared.

Whilst these events were taking place, a heart-rending scene was enacted around a cradle in a house at Lourdes, where dwelt a family of poor labourers. Jean Bouhoharts, and Croisine Ducouts, his wife.

In that cradle lay a child of about two years of age, so weak in constitution that it had never been able to walk, constantly sick, and exhausted by a low fever, a fever of consumption from its birth, that nothing could subdue. Notwithstanding the care of a clever physician of the country, M. Peyrus, the last hours of the child were apparently fast approaching. Death had spread his livid tint over it, and long suffering had reduced it to a frightful state of emaciation.

The father calm in his sorrow, the mother in

her despair, both watched over their dying child.
A neighbour, Françonnette Gozos, was then engaged in preparing the winding-sheet. At the
same time endeavouring to console the mother, so
overwhelmed with grief, they awaited with anxiety
the progress of the last agony. The eyes of the
child had become glassy, the body motionless, and
respiration had ceased to be observable.

"He is dead!" cried the father. "If he is not
dead," said the woman, their neighbour, "he is
on the point of death." And she endeavoured to
persuade the mother, who was weeping bitterly,
to go and sit at the fireside, whilst she made the
necessary arrangements for its interment. But
the mother seemed not to hear what was said to
her. A sudden idea rushed to her mind, and her
tears ceased to flow. "He is not dead!" she
cried suddenly, "and the Holy Virgin of the
Grotto will cure him for me."

"Grief has deprived her of reason," remarked
the husband, sadly.

The mother went to the cradle, and drew from
it the already motionless body of the infant,
which she folded in her apron. "I will run to
the Virgin," cried she, going towards the door.
The husband and their friend endeavoured to
turn the mother from her purpose. "My good
Croisine," said the former, "if our Justin is not
quite dead, you will kill him outright." But she,
as if beside herself, would not listen to them, and
went out, saying, "Whether he dies here or at
the Grotto it matters not. Let me go and implore the compassion of the Mother of God." So
saying, she took the road to the Grotto. Hur-

riedly passing on, and loudly invoking Mary, she
seemed to passers by to be insane.

It was five in the afternoon. Some hundreds
of persons were still at the Rocks of Massabielle.
Laden with her precious burden, the poor mother
forced her way through the crowd. At the entrance of the Grotto she prostrated herself in
prayer. Then proceeding on her knees towards
the miraculous fountain, her face glowing, her
eyes animated, and filled with tears, and her
whole person in a state of disorder, occasioned by
extreme grief, she reached the basin or reservoir made by the stone-cutters. The water was
icy cold.

"What is she about to do?" said they.

Croisine drew from her apron the naked body of
her child, who seemed to be in his last agony.
She made upon herself and upon him the sign of
the cross, and then without hesitation plunged
the whole body save the head into the icy water of
the Fountain.

A cry of horror burst from the indignant multitude.

"This woman is mad," they cried from all
sides, as they pressed around her, to prevent her
from repeating the action.

"Would you kill the child?" said some.

She seemed as one deaf, and remained like a
statue, a statue of grief, prayer, and faith.

Some one touched her on the shoulder. She
turned, still holding the child in the reservoir.
"Let me alone," she said, in a voice at once
energetic and suppliant; "I wish to do what I

can, the good God and the Holy Virgin will do the rest."

Many had remarked the complete immobility of the child, and its cadaverous appearance. "The child is already dead," said they. "Let her alone, it is a mother distracted with grief."

No, grief had not turned her brain; on the contrary, it had conducted her on the road to faith. Faith of the highest order, absolute, un-hesitating, and trustful, which God has solemnly promised never to disregard. This poor earthly mother knew in her inmost soul that she was addressing the heart of our mother in heaven. Hence her unlimited confidence overcame the terri-ble reality, as she held the dying infant in her arms. Doubtless, she as well as those who surrounded her, knew that a water so icy cold as that into which she had plunged her child was calculated beyond all doubt according to the laws of nature, to ex-tinguish completely the life of that beloved one. But no matter! her arm remained firm, and her faith failed not. During a full quarter of an hour, before the astonished eyes of the crowd, she held the child in that mysterious water. Oh! most sublime spectacle of Catholic Faith! This woman exposed her child to the most imminent danger to seek in the name of the Blessed Virgin Mary a cure from heaven. She placed him naturally on the road to death, in order to lead him super-naturally to life. Jesus praises the faith of the centurion. Truly the faith of this mother appears to us still more admirable.

Before an act of faith, so simple and so great, the heart of God could not but be moved. Our

Father, that Father so invisible but yet so manifest, bent down doubtless at the same time as the
Blessed Virgin over this touching and religious
scene, and He blessed this Christian believer of
the Primitive ages.

The infant, during this long immersion, had
remained immoveable as a dead body. The
mother wrapped him up again in her apron, and
came back with him in all haste.

The body was frozen.

"You see, surely, that he is dead," said the
father.

"No," said Croisine, "he is not dead! The
Blessed Virgin will cure him."

And the poor woman put him to bed in his
cradle.

Scarcely a few minutes had elapsed while the
attentive ear of the mother was stretched over
him.

"He breathes!" exclaimed she.

Bouhohorts cast himself down and listened in
his turn. The little Justin was actually breathing. His eyes were closed, and he was engaged
in a profound and peaceable slumber.

The mother, she sleeps not. All the evening
and night, she came every moment to hear that
breathing becoming gradually stronger and more
regular, and awaited with anxiety the moment of
his awaking.

It took place at the dawn of day. The emaciated state of the child had not disappeared, but
his complexion was coloured, and his features
calm. In his smiling eyes, turned towards his
mother, shone the two rays of life.

During this sleep, profound as that God had
sent to Adam, the mysterious and all-powerful
hand, that rules all matter, had reanimated and
repaired, we will not venture to say resuscitated,
this body so lately icy cold and motionless.

The child asked for his mother's breast, and
took long draughts with eagerness. And now
this child, who up to the present moment had
never walked, wished to rise, and go about the
room. But the mother, so courageous the evening before, and so *full of* faith, dared not believe
in the completeness of the cure, and trembled at
the thought of the banished danger. She resisted
the repeated solicitations of the infant, and refused
to take it from its couch. Night came, and was
peaceful as the last.

The father and mother left the house to go to
their work. Their Justin slept quietly in his
cradle.

When the mother returned home, an astonishing spectacle was presented to her. The cradle
was empty. Justin had arisen by himself, and
was going about the room, moving the chairs here
and there. The child so lately paralyzed could
now walk. The cry of joy that came from Croisine, the heart of a mother alone can divine.
She endeavoured to run to him, but could not,
so greatly was she overcome. Her limbs trembled. Joy had unnerved her, and she supported
herself against the door. A vague terror seized
her in spite of herself, and she cried out with
anxiety, "Take care, you will fall." He did not
fall, his step was firm and steady, and he ran to
his mother's arms, who embraced him weeping.

13

"You see now that he was not dead, and that the Holy Virgin has saved him," said she to her husband, on his return home.

Françonnette Gozos, who assisted the evening before, in preparing the winding-sheet for the little child, happened to drop in at this moment, and could scarce believe her eyes. She could not refrain from examining the child, so as to be assured of its identity. "It is indeed he!" cried the woman, "it is poor little Justin!"

They fell upon their knees. The mother joined .the hands of her infant together, and raised them towards heaven, and all gave thanks to the Mother of Mercy.

The malady has not returned. The child grew, and had no relapse. Ten years have passed. The writer of this account, M. Lasserre, went lately to see him. He found him strong, and in good health.

M. Peyrus, the physician who had attended the child, declared with the most entire good faith that it was beyond the power of medicine to account for the extraordinary cure that had been effected. Two doctors, Messrs. Vergez, and Dozous, examined this fact separately, and they, as well as M. Peyrus, could see no other cause for it than that of the operation of Almighty God.

They all attested three remarkable circumstances, which manifestly gave to this cure a supernatural character. The duration of the immersion; its immediate effect; and the power of walking manifested by the child immediately after leaving the cradle.

The conclusions in the report of M. Vergez

were formal in this respect. A bath of cold water
in the month of February, lasting a quarter of an
hour, given to a child in a state of exhaustion, and
agonizing, must, according to his opinion, and in
conformity with every data whether theoretical or
experimental in science, lead to an immediate
death. "For," added the skilful practitioner,
"if the ablutions of cold water above all when
repeated, can render great services in serious
adynamic affections, this method is subject to
rules the transgression of which does not occur
without real danger to life. As a general thesis,
the duration of the application of cold water should
not continue beyond a few minutes, because the
depression occasioned by the cold would destroy all
power of reaction in the functions of the organs.
Now the woman Ducouts, having plunged her
child into the water of the Fountain, kept it there
longer than a quarter of an hour. She has then
sought the cure of her son by a process absolutely
condemned by experience and medical reasoning,
and she has nevertheless obtained it immediately ;
for a few moments later, he fell into a calm and
profound sleep which did not cease till after about
twelve hours. And in order the most striking
light should be displayed over this fact, in order
that no uncertainty should remain over its reality
and the instantaneousness of its accomplishment,
the child, *who had never walked,* escapes from his
cradle and begins to walk with an assurance which
habit alone could give, showing thus, that his
cure had taken place without any convalescence,
and *in a way entirely supernatural.*"*

* Report of M. Doctor Verges, associated Professor of the

IX.

Other cures continued taking place on every
side. It would be impossible to report them in
detail, as well on account of their number as because the author of this book has imposed on
himself a law to relate nothing of this order of
facts, of which he has not himself ascertained its
certainty, not only by the deposition of direct witnesses of the event, but also by that of the parties
who were favoured by such marvellous graces.
We have been obliged, not without regret, to omit
in our narrative many of those admirable prodigies
which were fully proved, even by ourselves, and
limit ourselves to present a circumstantial history
of the most striking miracles. We notice, however, as we proceed, in the documentary evidence
of the Commission named later to examine these
events, some of the cures that occurred at that
period, that were authentically verified, and the
fame of which had spread from their origin over all
the country. The inn-keeper, Blaze Maumus,
by plunging his hand into the Fountain, had seen
disappear and become quite healed an enormous
wen at the joint of the wrist.

The widow Crozat, who had been deaf for
twenty years and unable to hear the offices of the
Church, suddenly recovered her hearing by using
this water. By a similar prodigy, Augustus
Bordes, who had been lame for a long time

Faculty of Montpellier, to the Commission of Enquiry appointed
by Monseigneur the Bishop of Tarbes.

through an accident, saw his leg grow straight
again, resuming its natural strength and shape.
All whom we have named were from Lourdes, and
each could render an account of these extraordinary
facts.

X.

In the supposition that it was in the cause of
truth that its party had taken up the side of negation, the Lawyers, whose anti-superstitious dispositions we have described, had, in these miracles
which we publicly attested and announced, an excellent opportunity for making a strict investigation, and of prosecuting, if there was room for it,
the authors or propagators of such news, which
was evidently of a nature to fill the public conscience with error and cause disturbance in minds.
Nothing even was more easy than to detect imposture in these matters in the very act of the crime.
These cures, in fact, were not hidden from each
one's observation, as the Apparitions which Bernadette perceived. They were open, patent, palpable—nothing could be easier than to take hold
of the imposture, if imposture there had been.
The cases were numerous, numbering already
twenty-five or thirty. They were within the
reach of anyone who wished to examine them.
All the world could verify them, study them,
analyse them, ascertain their truth or prove they
were falsehoods.

The supernatural quitted the invisible; it became material and palpable. In the person of the
sick restored to health, of the paralytics who

walked and were in motion, it said to all, as Jesus
Christ did to the Apostle Thomas : " See my feet,
see my hands.   Behold these eyes that were dead,
that have recovered sight.   Behold these dead
restored to life, these deaf who hear, these lame
who run with the activity of health and strength."
The supernatural was, so to speak, incarnate in
all these incurables who were suddenly healed,
and attesting itself publicly, it challenged enquiries, examinations, investigations.   It became
possible, may we use the expression, to seize it
body to body and lay hold of it by the collar.

It was there, everyone understood, that the very
heart of the question was to be found.   A reason was
to be discovered for the inconceivable events which
had just been thrown across preconceived ideas.
Thus there was no one who did not seek to conjecture the skilful and energetic means which
might be employed by that fraction of the official
world which hitherto had exhibited such a determined resolution unremittingly to prosecute and
crush fanaticism.

But what questions were put by the Police ?
What judicial instructions were issued by the
legal authorities ?   To what severe measures had
the administration recourse?   The administration,
the Lawyers, the Police did nothing at all.   They
turned another way, and considered it incon-
venient to hazard a public examination into facts
so notorious, the report of which had spread so
much about the country.

Why then did the free-thinking party abstain
from taking action in this matter ?   Why did they
so carefully refrain from investigating the extraor-

dinary facts which could not possibly have escaped
their notice? It was simply because they listened
to the dictates of prudence, and to that instinct of
self-preservation which sometimes preserves political parties from utter destruction by giving them
timely warning that their case is hopeless, and
that their only safety lies in immediate retreat.
The unbelievers ought to have been converted by
these miracles, but they remained unbelievers still,
they were only disconcerted and overcome by the
strength of the evidence alleged against them, by
the strong and sudden invasion made by these
supernatural events into the camp of the unbelievers. But we should possess very little knowledge of the human heart if we could suppose
for an instant, that determined partisans can be
brought humbly to acknowledge their error, by
means of the most certain and conclusive proofs
in the world. The freedom of the human will has
the terrible faculty of being able to resist everything, even God Himself. Brightly may the sun
shine in the heavens, illuminating the world with
its life-giving rays; but, if we choose obstinately to
deprive ourselves of its guiding light, if we are
determined to walk in darkness, what can be
easier than to close our own eyes? And just in the
same way may the soul render herself absolutely
inaccessible to the bright splendour of truth; but
in these cases, her darkness is not caused by her
own want of understanding or intelligence, it is
simply the result of her own free will, and spontaneous determination to shut her eyes to the
truth.

Thus, in the case of these miraculous cures, did

the free-thinking party act; they turned a deaf ear
to the facts which they could not deny; they
refused to debate the subject, and thereby pronounced their own defeat and condemnation.

XI.

However, the unbelieving philosophy of men
being irritated by the very circumstances which
they pretended to despise, and which they dared not
submit to the test of a public inquiry; they endeavoured to throw discredit upon them by other
means. They had recourse to a most profound
and subtle manœuvre; instead of examining the
true miracles, they invented false ones, which they
proposed hereafter to unmask, and proclaim as
open impostures; their papers made no mention
of Louis Bourriette, Blaise Maumus, Croisine
Ducouts, nor the widow Crozat, nor Marie Daube,
nor Bernard Soubie, nor Fabian Baron, nor the
others. But they perfidiously fabricated an imaginary legend, which they intended to circulate
widely by means of the press, and then to refute
it at their ease.

"You are not to be astonished," said the
journal of the Prefecture l'Ere Imperiale, "if
there are still to be found persons who persist in
maintaining that the young girl is predestinated,
and that she is endued with supernatural power.
For these persons aver—1st. That a dove hovered
over the head of the child during the time that
the ecstasy lasted. 2ndly. That Bernadette
breathed on the eyes of a little blind girl and

restored her to sight. 3rdly. That she cured another infant whose arm was paralyzed. And 4thly. That a peasant of the valley of Campan, having declared that he was not to be duped by these scenes of hallucination, the little girl had obtained that same evening, that the sins of the peasant should be changed into serpents—which serpents had devoured ·him ; and not a .trace of the limbs of the irreverent man was to be found." In regard to the real cures, in regard to the miracles that had undoubtedly happened, as to the springing forth of the fountain, the clever editor took good care not to speak. With not less craft, he gave no name, to avoid being contradicted. "Behold, to what we are come, and to which we should not have come, if the parents of the girl had followed the advice of the physician who asked them to send her to the hospital." It is observable that no physician had yet so advised. It was a trial balloon thrown out by a government journal. This appeared in the Ere Imperiale, dated March 6. After having invented these fables, the writer takes alarm in the name of reason and of faith, and goes on to say, "This is the opinion of all *reasoning* persons, who entertain sentiments of *true piety, who respect and sincerely love religion,* who regard the mania of superstitions as very dangerous, and *whose principle it is that they should not admit to the rank of miracles, any facts, except such as are pronounced to be true by the Church.*"

As to this reflection, we may say, in passing, the decision of the Church does not create the miracle, she pronounces on it. And on the authority of her examination, and her dictum, the faithful believe. But no law, neither in the order of faith, nor in the order of reason, prevents Christians, witnesses of supernatural manifestations, from recognizing their miraculous character. The Church has never exacted from believers this abdication of their reason and of their common sense. She reserves the right of judging, as a last resource, that is all.

The journal in question winds up the article thus :

"It does not appear, up to this moment, that the ecclesiastical authorities have judged what has passed to be worthy of any serious attention." The editor of the administrative journal, by this last remark, has, unintentionally, shown the truth of all that has been said, as regards the clergy, namely, that they were absolute strangers to the occurrences, and that they had been, and were continuing to be, accomplished without their having anything to do with the matter. As to the other poor journal, the "Lavedan," the journal of Lourdes, it was so crushed by the facts, that it was altogether silent. This silence continued during several weeks. It said not a word about these unheard of matters, and this concourse of people. One might have thought that this paper was printed at the other end of the world, if its columns had not been filled with articles, borrowed here and there, from public papers, directed against superstition in general.

XII.

During the period of the Apparitions, the most magnificent weather had favoured the popular movement. There had been an uninterrupted series of fine days such as they had not seen for many years. At the end of the 5th of March, the weather changed, and a thick fall of snow ensued. The rigour of the season naturally diminished the concourse of the people to the Grotto.

Miraculous cures continued, however, to happen.

Madame Benoite Cazeaux, of Lourdes, who had been kept to her bed for three years through a slow fever of a complicated character, accompanied with pains in the side, had vainly recourse to medical science. All had proved ineffectual. The waters of Gazost, where she had been to take the baths, had been also unsuccessful.

These repeated failures, these continual misfortunes had disconcerted the physicians, who, considering her as incurable, had ceased to come and see her. In this desperate condition, the poor woman had recourse to our Lady of Lourdes, and, behold her incurable malady disappeared after one or two glasses, and lotions, of the water of the Grotto.*

Another woman, Blaisette Soupenne, of Lourdes, about fifty years of age, was attacked for several years, by a chronic disorder in the eyes, and her

* Proceedings of the commission of inquiry appointed by the Bishop of Tarbes, 22nd proces-verbal.

state was very serious. It was, in technical language, a blepharite, complicated with atrophy. A
constant weeping of the eyes, smarting pains,
sometimes simultaneous, sometimes by turns;
eyelids exposed, completely turned inside out, and
stripped of their eyelashes, the two lower eyelids
being covered with a multitude of fleshy excrescences; such was the sad condition of that unhappy woman. Vainly had she applied several times
a day lotions of cold water upon her eyes; vainly
had she had recourse to all the medicaments prescribed by science, vainly had she sought some
relief from the waters at Barèges, Cauterets, and
Gazost, nothing seemed to succeed. Abandoned
by men, she turned at length towards the Divine
Bounty that had manifested itself at the Grotto.
Declared incurable by science, she had addressed
herself to faith, and she had asked of the miraculous Lady to remove from her, her cruel malady,
against which the skill of men and the agents of
nature had been powerless. From the first lotion
she had experienced relief. At the second, which
had occurred the following day, the cure had been
completed. The eyes had ceased to be full of
tears, the pupils were restored to their places, the
fleshy excrescences had disappeared. Ever since
that day the eyelashes had returned. According
to the physicians, summoned to examine this
case, the supernatural effect was so much the more
manifest in this wonderful cure, "that the material
injury," said they, "was more striking, because
to the rapid restoration of the fibres to their organic
conditions and vital state, had become added the
straitening of the eyelids. The bearing of this

fact is so much the more considerable, as the malady in question is one of the most obstinate, and, at the point to which it had reached with the woman, Soupenne, she absolutely required the intervention of surgical action, the cutting of the mucus membrane, or, at least, the energetic cauterisation of the swellings and fleshy pimples of that membrane.[*]

The marvellous became multiplied. God performed His own work. The Blessed Virgin exhibited her great power.

XIII.

Subsequently to the fifteenth day, Bernadette had returned several times to the Grotto, but, somewhat like the rest of the world, that is to say, without hearing in herself the internal voice that irresistibly called her.

This voice she heard again on the morning of the 25th of March, and she immediately took the road that led to the rocks of Massabielle. Her face was radiant with hope; she felt in herself that she was about to see again the Apparition, and that before her charmed eyes, Paradise was about to open for an instant its eternal doors.

Bernadette, as we may well suppose, had become in the town of Lourdes, the object of universal attention, and she could not move without being the centre of observation.

---

[*] Extract from the report of Dr. Vergez, professor of the faculty of Montpelier, to the episcopal commission.

"Bernadette is going to the Grotto," said they, on all sides, upon seeing her pass, and in an instant the people ran from their houses, and along the paths, pressing forward in the direction of the Grotto, arriving at the same time with the child.

In the valley, the snow had melted for two or three days, but it still crowned the crest of the surrounding heights; the weather was bright and fair. Not a spot in the peaceful blue of the firmament. The kingly sun seemed at this moment to arise in the bosom of those white mountains, and cast a splendour over their cradle of snow.

It was the anniversary of the day on which the Angel Gabriel descended to the most pure Virgin of Nazareth, and saluted her in the name of the Lord. The Church was celebrating the Feast of the Annunciation, while the multitude ran to the Grotto, among whom were the healed Bourriette, Crozat, Soupenne, Cazeaux, Bordes and twenty others. The Catholic Church at the end of the morning office, chanted these astonishing words:

"At this moment the eyes of the blind shall be opened, the ears of the deaf shall recover their hearing, the lame shall leap as the hart, *because the waters have risen in the desert*, and torrents in the solitude."

The joyous presentiments ·that Bernadette felt, had not deceived her. The voice that called her, was the voice of the Blessed Virgin. The moment the child fell on her knees, the Apparition manifested itself. As on all former occasions, an ineffable aureole shone around her, whose splendours were without limit, and whose sweetness is infinite as usual. Covered with a veil, her robe, in chaste folds, whiter than dazzling snow, fell around her. Two roses, full blown, were over her feet, their colour of that yellow tint such as is seen at the base of the horizon, at the first light of the virginal dawn. Her girdle was blue as the firmament.

Bernadette in ecstasy had forgotten the earth, in looking on the Beauty without stain. "O my Lady," said she, "will you have the goodness to tell me who you are, and what is your name?" The royal Apparition smiled, but replied not. But at this very moment the Universal Church, continuing the solemn prayers of her Office, cried, "Holy and immaculate Virgin, what praises can I give you? In truth, I know not, for thou hast carried, enclosed in thy womb, Him whom the heavens cannot contain." Again, Bernadette asked of the silent Vision, "O my Lady, will you have the goodness to tell me who you are, and what is your name?" The Apparition appeared still more radiant, as if her joy had increased, and yet replied not to the child's request. And the Church throughout all Christendom continued its prayers and chants, pronouncing these words: "Rejoice with me, all ye who love the Lord, because, being yet a child, the Most High loved me, and in my womb was conceived the God-Man. Generations will proclaim me ever blessed, because God has deigned to cast His regards upon His humble handmaiden, and out of my womb I brought the Man-God Incarnate."

Bernadette, with increasing fervour, renewed her prayers, and repeated these words a third

time. "O my Lady, will you have the goodness
to tell me who you are, and what is your name?"

The Apparition seemed to become increasingly
absorbed in her most blessed glory, and concentrated in her happiness, she continued silent.
But by a wonderful coincidence the choirs of the
Universal Church, at this hour chanted forth a
song of joy, pronouncing the name of the marvellous Apparition. "Hail Mary, full of grace,
the Lord is with thee, blessed art thou amongst
women."

Bernadette once more gave vent to these suppliant words: "O my Lady, I pray you, will you
have the goodness to tell me who you are, and
what is your name?"

The Apparition had her hands joined with fervour, and her face shone with the splendour of
infinite beatitude. It was Humility in its Glory.
At the same moment that Bernadette contemplated the Vision, the Vision doubtless contemplated in the bosom of the Divine Trinity, God
the Father, of whom she is the Daughter; God
the Son, of whom she is the Mother; and God
the Holy Ghost, of whom she is the Spouse.

At the child's last question, she opened her
hands, wherein was glittering a Rosary of golden
wire with beads of alabaster. She then unfolded
her arms, as if to show the earth her virginal
hands full of benedictions. Then, raising them
towards the eternal regions, from whence descended on the same day, the divine Messenger of
the Annunciation, rejoined them with fervour, and
looking up to heaven with an expression of unspeakable gratitude, pronounced these words:

"Je suis l' Immaculée Conception."—"I am the Immaculate Conception."

Having said these words, she disappeared, and the child found herself, like the multitude, in the midst of a rocky desert. At her side, the miraculous Fountain fell into its rustic basin through a wooden trough, and the peaceful murmur of its waters was heard.

It was the day and the hour, when the Church entoned in its Office the magnificent hymn,

| "O Gloriosa Virginum, | "O glorious of Virgins, |
| Sublimis inter sidera." | Sublime amid the stars." |

XIV.

The Mother of our Lord Jesus Christ had not said, "I am Mary Immaculate." She had said, "I am the Immaculate Conception," as if to mark the absolute character, the substantial character in some sort, of the divine privilege which she alone had had since Adam and Eve were created by God. It is as if she had said, not that "I am pure," but, "I am purity itself;" not that, "I am a Virgin," but, "I am virginity living and incarnate;" not that, "I am spotless," but, "spotlessness itself."

A thing that is white may cease to be so; but whiteness is always white. It is its essence, and not its quality.

Mary is more than conceived without sin, she is the Immaculate Conception itself, that is to say, the essential and superior type, the archetype of humanity itself without defilement, of humanity

14

which has come from the hands of God without
having been defiled by any original stain, by any
impure element which the fault of our first parents
introduced into the very source of that immense
river of generations which is flowing for upwards
of six thousand years, and of which each of us is
a fugitive wave. When you desire from a polluted
source to draw pure water, what do you do? You
take a filter, and by means of it the water becomes
disengaged from its grosser elements. You pass
it through a second, and then through a third,
and so on. Thus a moment comes when you
have a vessel of water perfectly pure and clear, a
liquid diamond. Thus did God when the original
source was troubled. He chose a family and
directed it in this world, from age to age, from
Seth to Noah, from Sem to David, from David to
Joachim and Ann, the parents of the Blessed Virgin. And when this human blood was thus, so
to speak, filtered, notwithstanding the accidents of
some intermediary offenders, down through fifty
generations of patriarchs and just, there came
into the world a creature absolutely pure, a creature without spot, a daughter of Adam entirely
Immaculate. Her name was Mary, and her fruit-
ful virginity brought forth, Jesus Christ.

The little shepherdess, to whom the Blessed
Virgin had deigned to appear, heard for the first
time these words, "Immaculate Conception," and
not comprehending them, made, in returning to
Lourdes, every effort in her power to retain them
in her mind.

"I repeated to myself the words Immaculate
Conception all the way, lest I should forget them,"

said she, one day, to the writer, "and until I arrived at the priest's house, where I was going, I said Immaculate Conception, Immaculate Conception, because I wished to convey to the Parish Priest the words of the Vision, in order that a chapel might be built."

FIFTH BOOK.

I.

The Apparition of Lourdes was investigated in the first instance by M. Jacomet, and afterwards by the Prefect, until at length it reached the Minister of State. From the twelfth to the twenty-sixth of March, the Préfet had made his reports to his excellency.

The Ministry of Public Worship was then united, not as at present to the department of Justice, but to that of Public Instruction. M. Rouland was the Minister.

Formerly Procureur Général, and now Minister of Public Instruction, M. Rouland, had at the same time, as regards religious matters, the traditional and shadowy formalism of old ideas and principles which were then current in the University. Dogmatic, and convinced of his own importance, his philosophy being of a sectarian character, as to his own wisdom, fanatical and opposed to all who did not run in the same groove of systematic ideas with himself; Mons. Rouland could not admit for a single instant, the realities of the visions and miracles of Lourdes. Living two hundred and fifty leagues from the spot, without other documents than two pre-

fectorial letters, he cut short the question in a
decided tone, and without even deigning to discuss
the matter. In spite of the prudent counsels he
had given to the Prefect, he allowed it to be seen
that his part was taken not to tolerate the Apparitions and miracles. As is always the case, in
similar circumstances, the minister made a show
as if he was however defending religion. On the
twelfth of April, he addressed to M. Massy, the
Préfet, the following letter :

"Monsieur le Préfet:—I have examined the two
letters you were so good as to send me, dated the
twelfth and twenty-sixth of March, respectively, on
the subject of a pretended Apparition of the Virgin alleged to have taken place at a Grotto in the
neighbourhood of the town of Lourdes.

"It is of importance, in my opinion, to put an
end to a matter which would finish by compromising the true interests of Catholicism, and weakening the religious feelings of the people. *The law
permits no one to erect an oratory for worship in
any place open to the public, without the joint
assent of the civil and ecclesiastical authorities.*
In accordance with this principle it is your business to have the Grotto closed immediately, inasmuch as it has been transformed into a sort of
chapel. But it might probably be open to grave
objections, were you *suddenly* to exercise this
right. It will be well then to confine yourself to
preventing the young visionary from returning to
the Grotto, and to take measures gradually to
wean the popular mind from the attractions of the

spot, and thus the visits will gradually become
less frequent.

"I am not able, M. le Préfet, to give you at
this moment more precise instructions. It is,
after all, a question of tact, firmness, and prudence; and in this respect any recommendations
on my part would be unnecessary.

"It will, however, be indispensable that you
should act in concert with the clergy; but at the
same time I cannot too strongly impress upon
you the importance of treating directly, in this
delicate matter, with the Bishop of Tarbes. I
therefore authorize you to say to the prelate, *in
my name, that I am of opinion that a free course
of action should no longer be permitted with
respect to a state of things that cannot fail to serve
as a pretext for fresh attacks against the clergy
and religion.*"

II.

On receipt of this letter M. Massy addressed
himself to the bishop, praying him to issue a
formal prohibition, to prevent Bernadette from
again visiting the Grotto. He reminded the
Bishop that the interests of religion would be
compromised by these hallucinations or these
frauds, if allowed to continue, and the deplorable
effect which similar things produced on serious
minds, who sought in good faith to reconcile
Catholicism with sound philosophy and modern
ideas, and took care, at the same time, to show his
lordship that neither he nor the minister be-

lieved in the reality of these apparitions. (Moreover the Prefet hinted that, if resisted, he would probably have recourse to violence.) Now Mgr. Laurence was too prudent not to make every effort in his power to avoid a collision. It was necessary, then, on the one hand, to resist the pressure of the temporal power, and on the other, not to irritate it, in order that harmony might be maintained. In the face of these difficulties Mgr. Laurence held a middle course.

As he resisted the popular enthusiasm, pressing him to declare for the miracle, so now he felt himself bound to oppose the minister and the prefect in their demands to condemn it without examination. He determined, therefore, not to give judgment until he had a full knowledge of the case.

III.

Mgr. Laurence, as already stated, hesitated as to what judgment he should give on the occurrences at Lourdes. Never having been himself on the spot, and knowing these things only from the clergy, who were not themselves eye-witnesses, his conviction was not satisfied. He waited under these circumstances; absolutely to forbid Bernadette to go to the Grotto, when she felt called by a voice from on high, would have been to attack the most sacred liberty of the soul, a liberty which Churchmen know how to respect even in a child. But he thought he might use the voice of counsel, and caution Bernadette not to go to the Rocks of Massabielle, unless called

by this irresistible agency; and therefore the
bishop deemed it prudent to direct the parish
priest of Lourdes to check her as much as possible, so that the civil power might have no
grounds for enforcing the violent measures
towards which it was manifestly tending.

The Prefect, on his part, was deterred by the
following consideration. With a prelate so universally venerated as Mgr. Laurence, and having
lived up to that moment with his lordship in the
most perfect harmony, he considered it advisable
to pause before a religious *coup d'etat*, which
would assuredly be occasioned by this invasion of
the bishop's prerogative. Baron Massy was too
politic in matters relating to administration not to
hesitate in breaking through that "*entente cor-
diale*," which had existed up to that time between
the first authority in the diocese, and the first
authority in the department.

IV.

Easter Day arrived, and in spite of the pious
apprehensions of the Minister of Worship, the
wonders accomplished at Lourdes had not " weakened the religious feelings of the populations."
Numberless conversations had taken place; the
confessionals were besieged; the faithful pressed
around the holy table; usurers and robbers had
made restitution; and certain scandals had ceased.

Easter Monday, the 5th April, the same day on
which the Prefect visited the Bishop, the Mother
of God had renewed her interior call in the heart

of the miller's daughter. The girl, quickly followed by a vast number of persons, arrived at the
Grotto, where, as on preceding occasions, the
heavens were unclosed to her enraptured gaze, and
she was permitted to see the Virgin Mary in her
glory.

On this day, before the wondering eyes of the
multitude, an astonishing spectacle presented itself. The candle that Bernadette carried was of
a very large size. She had placed the end of it
on the ground, while her hands, half closed, held it
close to the lighted extremity. When the Holy
Virgin appeared, by an instinctive movement of
homage, Bernadette fell into an ecstasy before the
Beauty Immaculate. In so doing, her hands
moved slightly upwards, and the flame played
through her fingers. Bernadette remained motionless, absorbed in heavenly contemplation, and did
not perceive the phenomenon that caused general
astonishment around her. Witnesses pressed one
on the other to observe more closely. Messrs.
Jean Louis Fourcade, Martinou, Estrade, Callet,
the ladies Tard'hivail, and a hundred other persons, were spectators of this extraordinary sight.
M. Dozous, the physician already mentioned,
declared that the flame continued to play through
her fingers for more than a quarter of an hour.
Suddenly a slight tremor was visible on the form
of Bernadette. Her features changed; the Vision
had ceased, and the girl returned to her natural
state. Her hand was taken hold of, and nothing
but what was usual was found upon it. The
flame had respected the flesh of the child, during
her ecstasy before Mary. The crowd, not without

reason, cried out, "A miracle!" One of the
spectators, however, wishing to make sure of the
matter, took the candle, which was still burning,
and applied it to the hand of Bernadette. Instantly she drew it away, crying out: "Ah, sir,
you burn me!"

The occurrences of Lourdes had caused such
a commotion throughout the country, that although they had no previous intimation, as
during the first fortnight, of the expected presence of the Vision, a crowd of nearly ten thousand persons was collected on this occasion round
Bernadette. In the archives of the Mayoralty of
Lourdes, the letter of the mayor to the Prefect,
written on this occasion, has been preserved.
The Mayor states that he placed his agents on all
the roads and approaches to the Grotto, to take
the numbers, which amounted to 9,060, of whom
4,822 were inhabitants of the town of Lourdes,
and 4,238 strangers.

V.

Some girls of great virtue, and amongst whom
we shall only mention one servant venerated
by all—Mary Courrège had, it seemed, at the
Grotto, on two or three occasions, and when
alone, the same vision as Bernadette. This was
vaguely rumoured, but had no influence on the
mass of the public. Little children had also their
visions, but entirely of a different class, of a
frightful nature. When the divine supernatural
appears, the diabolic supernatural tries to mix
itself with it. The history of the fathers of the

desert, and of the mystics, give at every page a proof of this truth. The abyss was troubled, and the evil angel had recourse to his delusions to cast disquiet and alarm into the souls of believers.

These different facts, that were not much noticed at the time, do not possess (now above all that certain details have been forgotten) an accuracy so trustworthy that we should be required to open up in their regard the gates of history. We simply mention them not entirely to neglect or overlook them. True visions alone have any individual importance; the rest fall to pieces of themselves.

VI.

A vast concourse of people continued to go to the Rock of Massabielle. There was no tumult among this crowd, and no undue agitation in this human current. Canticles and litanies were sung in honour of the Virgin. This is all that was heard, all that M. Jacomet and his police could take hold of. It was more than order, it was recollection.

The workpeople of Lourdes had enlarged the pathway, traced out some fifteen or twenty days previously by the quarry-men, on the brow of the Rocks of Massabielle. They had blasted the stone, and cut the rock in many places, and had formed on these abrupt slopes a road sufficiently large and passable. It was a work of considerable labour, time, and cost. These brave fellows worked at it after their hours of daily toil; their time for repose was occupied in making a road

which conducted to God. In toil there was repose. Towards nightfall, they were seen fastened
like ants on the side of a steep hill, digging up
the ground, wheeling their barrows, hollowing out
the rock, putting powder into it and blasting the
marble or the granite.

"And who will repay you for your toil?" they
were asked.

"The Holy Virgin," was the reply.

Before retiring from this labour, they all
descended together to the Grotto, and prayed.
In the midst of this superb of nature, under the
stars of heaven, these popular Christian scenes
possessed a simplicity and grandeur that were
perfectly primitive.

The Grotto by degrees changed its aspect. Up
to this time they had burned candles in token of
veneration and respect. They had placed there
vases of natural or artificial flowers, or statues of
the Blessed Virgin wrought by pious hands, "*ex
voto*" offerings, in sign of thanksgiving. The
workmen had made a little balustrade to protect these fragile objects from the involuntary
accidents that the press of the crowd might have
caused. Many persons, having received some
particular grace by the intervention of our Lady of
Lourdes, brought in homage to the place of the
Vision, their little crosses of gold with their
chains, and confided the keeping of their pious
offering to the honesty of the public faith. From
this moment the whole country cried out that
they should obey the Apparition, and construct a
chapel, and agreed to cast money into the Grotto.
Considerable sums, amounting to several thousand

francs, were in this way exposed, night and day, in the open air without protection. And such was the respect that this place inspired, (so lately unknown,) such was the moral effect produced on the people, that there was not to be found a single malefactor in the whole country who ventured to perpetrate the sacrilege of stealing the smallest article. And this is all the more wonderful, because, some months previously, many neighbouring churches had been robbed. The Holy Virgin desired that no criminal association should be mixed up with the origin of the pilgrimage she wished to establish.

VII.

A strange circumstance, which passed unperceived at this period, was subsequently brought to light, and struck many persons. One of the grandest privileges of a sovereign is the power of pardon; and when a king passes through his dominions he not unfrequently grants an amnesty to criminals. The Queen of Heaven could not do less. At the quarter sessions, which took place in the department immediately after the visit of the Apparition, not a single criminal was brought forward; there was neither a single crime. committed, nor a single criminal condemned, a case probably without a precedent in that locality. The session of assize in March had only to examine into one case, which was prior to the period of the Apparitions, and terminated in an acquittal. In the sessions following there were two cases to be adjudicated on, and both related to

occurrences *previous to the same period*. The
public journals of the 6th of March and the 8th
of June attest this extraordinary fact. The Queen
of Heaven had passed by, and left her blessing on
her way.

VIII.

Bernadette was constantly visited by numerous
strangers, whose piety or curiosity attracted them
to Lourdes. They were from all classes, and of
all professions. None found fault with her simple
and candid speech; none, after having seen and
heard the spectator of the Vision, dared to say
that she had uttered a falsehood. In the midst
of excited parties and numberless discussions, this
little child, by an inconceivable privilege, inspired all with respect, and was never an object of
calumny. The lustre of this innocence was such
that she was never accused or attacked, an invisible arm protected her. Of an intelligence
which was very ordinary in common matters, Bernadette was above herself on every occasion she
had to give testimony to the Vision. No objection put her out. When questioned on the subject she was always prepared with an answer. On
one occasion M. Le Rasséquier, Counsellor of the
Court of Pau, and formerly Deputy for the Basses
Pyrénées, went to see her, accompanied by several
ladies of his family. He made her describe the
circumstances, in very great detail, relating to the
Apparitions.

When Bernadette said that the Apparition expressed herself in *patois* Bearnais, he exclaimed,

"You do not tell me the truth, my child; the good God and the Holy Virgin neither speak nor understand your *patois;* they know nothing of that barbarous language."

"If they do not know it, sir," she replied, "how do we know it ourselves? And if they do not comprehend it, who has rendered us capable of understanding it ?"

She had also spiritual repartees. "How is it that the Holy Virgin could have ordered you to eat grass? Does she then take you for a beast?" said a sceptic one day to her.

Looking at her interrogator with a smile, she answered, "Do you think that you are one yourself when you eat salad ?"

She had her naïve replies also. This same M. De Rasséquier spoke to her of the beauty of the Apparition of the Grotto. "Was she as handsome as the ladies you see here ?" he asked.

Bernadette cast a glance around the charming circle of young ladies who had accompanied the visitor, then, with a disdainful glance, said : "Oh, she was very different from all them." "All them" were amongst the *elite* of Pau.

She disconcerted subtle persons, who sought to embarrass her. "If the parish priest were formally to forbid your going to the Grotto, what would you do ?" some one asked of her.

"I should obey him."

"But if you received at the same time from the Apparition an order to go, what would you do between these two conflicting orders ?"

The girl at once, and without the slightest

hesitation replied, "I should immediately go to the parish priest, and ask his permission."

Nothing, either at this period or later, caused her to lose this sweet and graceful simplicity. Never, unless interrogated, did she speak of the Apparition. She always considered herself the last and the lowest of the children in the sisters' school. They had the greatest trouble to teach her to read and write. The soul of this child was elsewhere, and if we could dare to penetrate into her interior nature, so exquisite, and visited by grace, we should perhaps venture to say that her soul, little curious doubtless in human affairs, was playing truant in the groves of paradise.

During the hours of recreation she mixed with her companions, and loved to play with them. Sometimes a visitor or stranger from a distance asked the sisters' permission to see this seer of the Vision, this privileged of the Lord, this well-beloved of the Holy Virgin, this Bernadette, whose name was even then so celebrated. "There she is," a sister would say, pointing her out amongst a group of children. The visitor would see a little, poor-looking, miserably clothed girl, playing at some of the various innocent games of childhood. But what she preferred to all, was to figure, either the thirtieth or the fortieth, in one of those immense rounds which children make, singing and holding each other by the hand.

When the Blessed Mother of God visited Bernadette, and chose her to bear testimony to divine and heavenly occurrences, when she made her the centre of interest to multitudes of people, who performed pilgrimages, one may almost say in

order to see and converse with her, she provided
for the preservation of her simplicity and candour
by a miracle greater than all the rest, and bestowed upon her a most astonishing gift, even the
privilege of continuing always a child, or the privilege of retaining her child-like heart and disposition to the end of her life.

IX.

It was not only at Lourdes that miraculous
cures occurred. Sick people who could not come
to the Grotto had procured the water, and had
seen their inveterate sufferings suddenly cease.
There was at Nay, in the Basses-Pyrénées, a boy
fifteen years of age, of the name of Henry Busquet, whose health was undermined. He had
had, in 1856, a violent and long attack of typhoid
fever, at the termination of which there was
formed, on the right side of his neck, an abscess,
that had extended by degrees to the upper part of
his chest, and the lower end of his cheek. This
abscess was as large as a fist. The physician, M.
le Doctor Subervielle, who had a great reputation
in that country, lanced that abscess about four
months after its formation, and there issued forth
from it an enormous quantity of sero-purulent
matter. But Henry was not cured. After several
powerless medical operations, the doctor thought
of the waters of Cauteret. In 1857, during the
month of October, at a period of the year at
which, the rich bathers being already gone, the
poorer people were going to these celebrated
15

baths, young Burquet bathed fifteen times in them. They had been more injurious than beneficial, and reopened his wounds. The malady became more and more aggravated, in spite of some momentary relief. The unfortunate child had, in the regions which we have just pointed out, an extensive ulcer, which was open, sending a considerable quantity of suppuration, covering the upper part of the chest, all one side of the neck, and threatening the face. Besides this, there were two new serious glandular obstructions which had declared themselves by the side of this frightful ulcer.

Such was the state of this poor child, when, hearing mention of the marvellous effects of the water of the Grotto, he thought of having recourse to it. He wished to travel, and make the pilgrimage thither on foot; but he was over-confident of his strength, and his parents refused to conduct him to it.

Henry, who was very pious, was strongly impressed with the idea that the Holy Virgin who had appeared to Bernadette would cure him. He asked one of his neighbours, who was going to Lourdes, to fill for him a little of the water from the Fountain. She brought him a bottle on the evening of Wednesday, the 28th of April, Feast of the Patronage of St. Joseph.

Towards eight o'clock at night, at the moment of retiring to sleep, the child went on his knees, and addressed his prayer to the Most Holy Virgin. His family prayed with him; his father, his mother, and several brothers and sisters. They were very exemplary, simple, believing people;

one of the daughters is at present with the sisters of St. Andrew.

Henry was in bed. Doctor Subervielle had often recommended him never to make use of cold water, under the penalty of a painful complication of his disease; but at this moment Henry thought of all else but the prescriptions of medicine. He takes away the bandages and lint which cover his ulcer and tumours, and by the help of a rag which he dips in the water of the Grotto, he bathes and washes his wounds with the miraculous water. Faith failed him not. "It is impossible," thought he, "but that the Holy Virgin should cure me." He fell asleep in this hope.

A profound slumber took possession of him.

On waking, his hope was a reality: all his pains had ceased; all his wounds were closed; the glands had disappeared; the ulcer was no longer anything but a solid scar, as solid as if the hand of time had slowly closed it. The eternal power that had interposed and cured him, had performed in a few moments the work of several months or several years. The cure had been complete, sudden, and without any convalescence.

The report of the physicians addressed to the commission, and from which we have drawn the technical terms of our narrative, is favourable to the manifest miracle that took place in favour of this child. "All the affections of this kind of nature," said one of them, "are slow in healing, because they reconnect themselves with scrofulous diathesis, and because they imply the necessity of profoundly modifying the organism. This sole consideration, placed by the side of the suddenness of the cure, suffices to prove that this fact exists out of the order of nature. We range it among the facts which possess fully and in an evident manner the character of the supernatural." See the report of Doctor Vergez, physician at the waters of Bareges, aggregate Professor of the Faculty at Montpellier.

The ordinary physician to the sick boy, Doctor Subervielle, declared this sudden cure to be marvellous and divine, as all the rest of the world; but the restless scepticism which there is often to be found at the bottom of the mind of the faculty, awaited the great proof of time. "Who knows," said M. Subervielle frequently, "if after eighteen years, this will not return? Till then I shall always be perplexed."

The eminent physician who spoke thus was not permitted to have the pleasure of seeing this cure confirmed by time. The country had the misfortune of losing him; he died some time after.

As to Henry Busquet, the author of this work, in compliance with his custom of verifying by himself, has sought to see and hear him.

Henry has told us his history himself, which we already knew by the official reports and several witnesses. He has related it to us as quite a simple matter, without astonishment or surprise. Through the strong good sense of this Christian people, the supernatural does not appear extraordinary, and still less contrary to reason. They find it conformable to true notions of common sense. If they are surprised sometimes that a physician restores them to health, they are never astonished that God, who has been all-powerful in

creating man, should be equally good in healing
him. They see with an upright glance that a
miracle, far from disturbing order, is, on the contrary, one of the laws of the eternal order. If
God, in His mercy, has given to certain waters
the virtue of removing such a malady, if He cures
indirectly those who make use of, according to
certain conditions, such material things, how
much, with still stronger reason, will He know
how directly to cure them who directly address
themselves to Him? Thus these poor people
reason.

We have desired to see with our eyes and to
touch with our hands the marks of this terrible
wound, so miraculously cured. A vast scar shows
the place at which it was ulcerated. A long time
has elapsed since the child has got over the crisis
of the eighteenth year, and nothing has reappeared of his cruel malady. No suffering, no
running, no tendency to glandular obstructions.
His health is perfect. Henry Busquet is at present a man of twenty-five years of age, full of life
and force. He follows, like his father, his trade
of a plasterer. On Sunday, in the band of the
Orpheon, he fills with ability his part of trom-
bone among the brass instruments. He has an
excellent voice. If ever you visit the town of Nay
you will be sure to hear him outside the windows
of some house, either building or repairing, for
on his scaffolding he has a habit of singing with
all his heart, from early morning till night. You
may listen to him without any fear that your ears
should be offended by some song of a gross description. His songs are usually lively and inno-

cent couplets, sometimes they are cantiques
which his charming voice modulates. He who is
singing has not forgotten that it is to the Blessed
Virgin that he owes his life.

X.

While all these miracles are being wrought on
every side, an incident occurred, in appearance
very foreign to the object of this history, but
which was to have, insignificant as it may appear,
the most decisive consequences on the progress
of the events we have been relating.

M. the Prefect of the Hautes-Pyrenees, discovered about this time that his saddle and carriage
horses were badly housed, and that it was convenient to have built spacious and elegant stables.
Now M. Massy determined, above all things, not
to disfigure, by his erections, his court or his
garden.

The official residence of the Prefect is in the
immediate vicinity of the cathedral. Between the
two edifices lies the old cemetery in which the
priests and canons belonging to this church were
formerly interred. Tradition reports that many
noble families of the country had their burial
vaults in that place, and that the ashes of illustrious personages reposed there. The Prefect
considered that this spot would perfectly suit the
purpose he had in view of erecting stables and
coach-houses. From the thought to the execution the distance was not great with Baron
Massey. Accordingly, he ordered the founda-

tions to be excavated among the tombs, and the ashes of the dead, and soon were seen in the cemetery the rising walls necessary for his official horses. The Prefect placed his buildings in front of one of the ancient doors of the cathedral, at three or four yards distance, so that the neighing from the stables could be strongly echoed even within the church. Such a forgetfulness of what was due to himself from one who professed respect for religion, could not fail to wound the bishop deeply.

Mgr. Laurence attempted in vain to make M. Massy comprehend that the ground was sacred, that it belonged to the Church, and that the tramp of horses should not be heard in that place, to disturb the repose of the dead, and the prayers of the living. M. the Prefect, as we have already said, knew not how to draw back. To dismiss the workmen, and to choose another site, would have been to acknowledge that he was in the wrong. And therefore, notwithstanding his strong desire to keep on good terms with the Bishop, he paid no heed to the remonstrances of the prelate. His pride would not succumb, and he continued his work in the ancient cemetery. This flagrant violation of the abode of the dead, induced Mgr. Laurence to abandon his reserve, and the bishop made an energetic protest. He addressed himself directly to the minister in Paris, requesting that his Excellency would give an order for the discontinuance of these scandalous erections.

The Prefect was wounded to the heart by the firm and dignified attitude of the bishop. Pur-

suing his accustomed habit, he persisted all the
more strenuously, and set off for Paris to endeavour to bring the minister round to his view of the
matter.   He tried to engage the Counseil Général
to favour him ; he consulted lawyers ; in short, he
determined on a desperate struggle.   This dispute lasted for several months, and was finally
decided in favour of the bishop.   The stables were
demolished ; grass now grows on the ground, and
a funereal tree marks the spot as one dedicated
to the dead.   But from the day on which the
bishop made his protest the harmony that had
hitherto existed between the head of the department and the head of the diocese was for ever
broken.   To this harmony succeeded, in the
heart of the Prefect, a violent feeling of irritation.
He was no longer disposed to conciliate.   The re-
straining power which had hitherto controlled
him was withdrawn.   Trivial causes sometimes
produce great effects.

XL

In the course of the months of March and
April, before and after the letter to the minister,
the Prefect endeavoured to discover the key to
these strange occurrences at Lourdes.   The interrogatories, renewed by the lawyers and M.
Jacomet, had been useless.   Neither the Commissary of Police nor M. Dutour were able to discover
any delinquency in the child.   This little girl, of
thirteen or fourteen years of age, ignorant, not
knowing how to read or write, or even to speak
French, disconcerted all the efforts of her most

clever and adroit interrogators, by her profound simplicity. A disciple of Mesmer and of Du Potet, coming from some unknown locality, had in vain attempted to put Bernadette into a magnetic sleep. His magnetic passes failed of their effect upon her calm phlegmatic temperament; they only resulted in giving the child a bad headache. She endured all these examinations and experiments in the most resigned manner. It was the Will of God that she should be exposed to every kind of trial, and come triumphant from them all.

We have heard that a very rich family were so charmed with the little Bernadette, that they offered to adopt her, offering a fortune of a hundred thousand francs to her parents, with the option of living close to their child. These disinterested and noble people were not even tempted by this; their desire was to remain poor.

It was now evident that all the deep-laid plans, enthusiastic attempts, and disputatious reasonings of the free-thinkers had completely failed. Notwithstanding his horror of fanaticism, the Procureur Imperial, M. Dutour, could not find, either in the code of criminal instruction, or in the Penal Code, any law enabling him to take severe measures against Bernadette, and to imprison her. To arrest her would have been illegal, and the chief magistrate who ordered it would have subjected himself to disagreeable consequences. In the eyes of the penal law Bernadette was innocent. M. the Prefect then thought of a mode to solve the difficulty.

XII.

The laws of France empower the Magistrate to seize, and put in confinement persons supposed to be insane—provided a certificate to this effect be obtained from two respectable physicians. The medical body, is in general, composed of honourable men, still this terrible power is liable to abuse. In learning that the Virgin had appeared anew to Bernadette, and that she had told the girl her name, the *Préfet* sent a commission to the house of the Soubirous, consisting of two physicians of the place, who were as much opposed to the Supernatural as the *Préfet* himself, one of them being, moreover, his particular friend. These gentlemen examined the girl, but could not discover in her any tendency to insanity. Her answers to the several questions put to her, were sensible, consistent, and devoid of peculiarity. And there was no undue excitement in her nervous system, but, on the contrary, an unusual calmness of temperament. Asthma frequently affected the girl's chest, but this infirmity had no connection whatever with derangement of the brain. These two physicians, in spite of their preconceived opinions, gave in their report to the effect, that the girl was in perfect health, save that she was subject to asthma. But, as upon the question of the Apparitions, she steadily persisted in the same unvarying recital, these gentlemen, who could not believe in the possibility of such visions, declared that she might probably be in a *state of hallucination.* Still they dared not state positively, notwithstanding their anti-supernatural ideas, that she was a case for confinement. However, the *Préfet* was determined to act upon this report, and make out a mere affirmative formula. Thus armed, and in virtue of the law of the 30th June, 1838, he resolved to have Bernadette arrested and conducted to Tarbes, at first to be placed in a hospital, and afterwards, no doubt, in a lunatic asylum.

The letter of the physicians, on this subject to the *Préfet*, is preserved in the Archives of the Mayoralty of Lourdes, dated the 26th April.

But it was not deemed sufficient to strike this blow at the child, it was necessary to oppose this extraordinary movement of the people. M. Rouland, the minister of public worship, had insinuated, in his letter to the *Préfet*, that it was possible to do this without overstepping the bounds of the law. For this purpose it was only necessary to consider the Grotto as having been turned into an Oratory, and thus a power was given to carry off the votive offerings of the faithful. If resistance were made by the believers, a squadron of cavalry would be held at a moment's notice, ready to be sent from Tarbes.

Matters were thus arranged against Bernadette, and against the people.

XIII.

The *Préfet*, M. Massy, had, at this juncture, occasion to go to Lourdes, where there was to be a general meeting of all the mayors of the canton. After having arranged the matters of business

relating to the conscription, M. Massy addressed
the meeting on the subject of the Apparitions.

The journal of the Prefecture, the *Ere Imperial*, on the following day, gave an account of
the proceedings, as also the speech of the *Préfet*
on the subject of the Apparitions. A part of
which was as follows:

"My sentiments," said this devout functionary,
"are above suspicion. Every one in the department knows my profound respect for religion. I
have given, I think, sufficient proofs of this to
prevent the possibility of my intentions being
misinterpreted.

"You will not then be surprised to learn, gentlemen, that I have given an order to the Commissary of Police, to carry off, and convey to the
Mayoralty, the articles at present placed in the
Grotto, where they will be left at the disposal of
the owners.

"I have also given orders, that those said to be
visionaries, shall be *arrested* and conducted to
Tarbes, *to be treated as insane persons*, at the
expense of the Department.

"I have further directed, that all those who
have contributed to circulate these absurd reports
now current throughout the country, shall be
prosecuted, under the act, forbidding the *propa-
gation of false intelligence*."

This occurred on the fourth of May, and it was
in this manner that this very religious Prefect
inaugurated his month of Mary.

These words were received with *unanimous
enthusiasm*, according to the Journal of the Prefecture. The truth is, that several highly dis-

approved the violent course which authority was
adopting, while others belonging to the sect of the
Free-thinkers, imagined that the hand of the Prefect would be enough to put a rough spoke in the
irresistible march of events.

Immediately after the delivery of this address
to the meeting, the *Préfet* of the Department
quitted the town, having taken measures to have
his orders put into execution.

The Mayor, and the Commissary of Police, were
ordered to carry out the designs of the *Préfet*.
The first had orders to arrest Bernadette, the
latter to go to the Rocks of Massabielle, and despoil the Grotto of all that the piety of the faithful had deposited in that place.

We shall follow both in their turn, commencing
with the Mayor.

XIV.

We have seen that, M. Lacadé, Mayor of
Lourdes, refrained from pronouncing on the extraordinary events passing in that place. He was,
in fact, strongly impressed by them, and it was
not without a certain amount of misgiving that he
saw the Administration enter upon these violent
courses. He was greatly perplexed. He knew
not what attitude the people would assume. It is
true that the *Préfet* had announced, that a squadron of cavalry should be kept in readiness, to
maintain the tranquillity of the town of Lourdes,
but even this did not allay his apprehensions. To
sustain his courage, he had recourse to the Procureur Imperial, M. Dutour, and both together

went to the house of the Parish Priest of Lourdes,
to communicate to him the order of arrest emanating from the Prefecture.   They explained to the
Abbé Peyramale how, according to the law of the
thirtieth of June, 1838, the *Préfet* acted in the
full plenitude of his legal powers.

The priest could not contain his indignation,
upon being told of this cruel and iniquitous measure.

"The child is innocent!" cried he, "and the
proof is Monsieur le Procureur Imperial, that as a
magistrate, you have not been able, in spite of all
sorts of questions, to find a pretext of any kind,
enabling you to act against her.   You know that
there is not a tribunal in France that would not
acknowledge her innocence, and that there is not
a Procureur General, who, under such circumstances, would not declare this proceeding to be
monstrous, and would positively refuse to arrest
her."

"It is not I who take action in this case,"
replied M. Dutour, "it is the *Préfet*, who upon
the report of the physicians, is about to shut up
the girl in consequence of the deranged state of
her mind; it is for her own good, in order that a
cure may be effected.   It is a simple administrative measure that does not in the least touch on
religion, since neither the Bishops nor the Clergy
have pronounced upon these facts passing around
them."

"Such a measure," replied the priest, becoming
more and more animated, "would be the most
odious of persecutions.   All the more odious, that
it assumes a hypocritical mask, that it affects a

wish to protect, and conceals under the cloak of
legality, the intention of striking a defenceless
being. If the Bishop and the Clergy, if I myself,
have awaited a clearer light to enable us to pronounce on the supernatural character of these
occurrences, we already know sufficient to judge
of the sincerity of Bernadette, and the soundness
of her intellectual faculties. And when they do
not affirm any cerebral injury, in what should
your two physicians be more competent to judge
of the state of folly or good sense than any one of
the thousand visitors who have questioned this
child, and all of whom have admired the full clearness and the upright character of her understanding? And your physicians themselves have not
dared to affirm her insanity, and conclude it only
from their own hypothesis. The *Préfet* cannot,
under any circumstances, arrest Bernadette."

"It is legal," said M. Dutour.

"It is illegal. As Pastor of Lourdes, I owe a
duty to all, and particularly to the feeble. If I
was to see an armed man attacking a child, I
should defend that child at the peril of my life,
for I know that the duty of protection is incum-
bent on the Good Shepherd of his flock. Know,
then, that I should act in the same manner were
this man even the Prefect himself. Go, then, and
tell him that his Gendarmes shall find me on the
threshold of the door, and they will have to pass
over my body, ere they touch a hair of the head of
this little girl."

"But nevertheless—"

"There is no nevertheless in the matter," interrupted the priest, "examine, make your inquiries,

you are free to do so. But if you intend to persecute, if you intend to strike the innocent, know
well, that before attempting anything against the
least, the very least among my flock, it is with me
that you must commence. You will have to commence with myself."

The priest had risen from his chair. His lofty
stature, his powerful features, lit up with the
plenitude of strength, his resolute gestures, his
face glowing with emotion, caused the Procureur
and the Mayor to listen in silence.

At length they spoke of the measures relative
to the Grotto.

" As for the Grotto," replied the priest, " if the
Préfet wishes, in the name of the law, and in
accordance with his private piety, to despoil it of
the objects which the innumerable visitors have
deposited there in honour of the Holy Virgin, let
him do it. The faithful will be saddened, and
even indignant. But he may set his mind at rest;
the inhabitants of this country know how to
respect authority, even when that authority is in
the wrong. I am told, that at Tarbes, a squadron
of cavalry is in the saddle, ready to rush to
Lourdes, upon a signal from the Préfet. Let the
squadron dismount. However ardent may be the
heads of the people, however wounded may be
their hearts, at the sound of my voice, I will
answer for it, that my people will be tranquil,
without the aid of armed force. In the presence
of an armed force I will not answer for their tranquillity."

XV.

The energetic attitude of the *Curé* of Lourdes, whom they knew to be incapable of yielding, in anything that he considered to be his duty, introduced into the question an unforeseen element, of which it was very easy to guess the result.

The Procureur Imperial, as soon as the matter took an administrative turn, had ceased to interfere, and it was only as a friend that he had accompanied M. Lacadé to the priest's house. All the weight, therefore, of decision, fell upon the latter.

M. Lacadé felt convinced that the *Curé* of Lourdes would undoubtedly keep his word. As to acting by surprise, and roughly arresting Bernadette unawares to the Pastor, that was a thing not to be thought of, now that the Abbé Peyramale was made aware of it, and would be on the watch. We have already said how strongly the mayor was impressed by the sudden appearance of supernatural events. The unimpassioned exterior of the magistrate, concealed an anxious and agitated mind.

The mayor informed the Prefect of the conversation which he and M. Dutour had had with the parish priest of Lourdes. The arrest of Bernadette, he added, might, moreover, in the present excited state of people's minds, raise the town, and provoke an unpleasant revolt against constituted authority. As for himself, in face of the determination so formally expressed by the Curé, and in presence of such extraordinary facts, he
16

felt himself, to his great regret, obliged to refuse
to act, were he, in so doing, to resign his office of
mayor. It was for the Prefect if he thought fit,
to give, with his own lips, the order to the Gendarmes for the arrest.

XVI.

Whilst the fate and liberty of Bernadette were
thus in jeopardy, M. Jacomet, in full uniform,
wearing his scarf of office, prepared to execute the
order of M. Massy, at the rocks of Massabielle.

The report that the Prefect had directed the
spoliation of the grotto, spread rapidly, and threw
the town into a state of confusion. The entire
population was astounded, as in presence of a
monstrous sacrilege, that the most Blessed Virgin
should have deigned to come amongst us, they
exclaimed, and to have wrought miracles, and then
to be received in this manner, it is enough to draw
down the vengeance of Heaven. The coldest
hearts were moved, and the excitement increased.

Previous to the occurrence we are now about to
describe, the Abbé Peyramale, and the priests of
the town had, one and all, endeavoured by words
of peace, to calm the irritation which prevailed.

"My friends," said the clergy, "do not compromise your cause by disorder; submit to the
law, though that law be unjust. If the Blessed
Virgin is in all this, she will know how to turn
these things to her glory. And your violence, if
you permit yourselves to be drawn into it, will be
regarded by her as a want of faith, injurious to

her power. Look at the martyrs, did they revolt against the emperors? Their triumph consisted in not combating."

The moral authority of the Curé was great, but the people possessed ardent minds, and indignant feelings. All seemed to be at the mercy of a chance.

The votive offerings deposited in the grotto, were of considerable bulk, and could not be transported by hand. M. Jacomet went to the hotel kept by M. Barioge, to hire a vehicle, in which to convey them away. "I shall not let my horses out to hire for any such purpose," answered the postmaster.

"But you cannot refuse your horses when you are paid for them," cried Jacomet.

"My horses are for the service of travellers, and not for such work as this. Serve me with a process if you please, I refuse my horses."

The commissary went elsewhere. In all the hotels, and at the houses of those who kept horses for hire, who were very numerous at Lourdes, on account of its vicinity to the baths; at the houses of private persons, wherever he went, he met with the same refusals. His situation was pitiable. The population, annoyed and disgusted, saw him thus going uselessly from house to house, followed by the sergents de Ville. The commissary heard the murmur, the laughter, and the jeers of the crowd. All eyes fell upon him, in the painful and useless search, which he made through all the streets of the town. He had in vain offered larger sums of money, increasing his offers as he went along. The poorest people had refused, although he offered thirty francs for a single horse and cart, and the distance was very short. The people, when they heard of this offer of thirty francs, compared it to the thirty pieces of silver. At length he found, at a blacksmith's, a woman, who for this sum, provided him with what he required. When he was seen leaving the house of this person with the cart, the multitude was all the more indignant, as no urgent necessity had induced the venal owners to comply. Those people were not poor.

Jacomet proceeded towards the Grotto, the Sergeuts de Ville conducting the cart. An immense crowd followed, silent and downcast. Arrived at the rocks of Massabielle, the cart could not be brought close to the spot, and was therefore halted at some distance.

Under the vault of the Grotto were the wax candles, fixed on chandeliers, and ornamented with moss ; whilst ribands, crosses, statues of the Virgin, religious pictures, rosaries, necklaces, and jewels lay on the ground, or, on the natural shelves of the rock. At certain places, under the pictures or images of the Blessed Mother of God, they had spread carpets. Thousands of bouquets had been brought thither in honour of Mary, by pious hands, and these first-fruits of the month of flowers, embalmed her sylvan sanctuary. In one or two osier baskets, and on the ground, shone pieces of money, in gold, silver, and copper, amounting to some thousands of francs, the first spontaneous gifts of the faithful for the erection in this place of a temple to the Virgin without stain. And, upon these pious offerings, whose sacred character had struck even the audacious malefactor with respect, notwithstanding the solitude of the place, no criminal had up to that moment dared to lay a sacrilegious hand.

M. Jacomet got over the balustrade formed by the workpeople, and entered the Grotto. He appeared confused. The Sergents de Ville were close to him; the crowd who had followed him kept their eyes on him, but were silent. The external tranquillity of the multitude was startling. The commissary commenced by first securing the money. He then extinguished the lights one by one, and picked up the chaplets, crosses, carpets, and the various objects that filled the grotto, and gave them to the Sergents de Ville to be carried to the cart. These poor officers looked dejected at their work, yet they evinced by their demeanour the utmost respect for the precious objects which they were employed to remove. In consequence of the distance that lay between the grotto and the cart, the work proceeded slowly. Jacomet said to a little boy, whom he found on the spot, "Here," said he, "take this picture to the cart." The child held out his hand to receive it, when another boy, at his side, called out to him,

"You wretch! what are you going to do? The good God will punish you."

The child was frightened, and drew back, and no fresh appeal from the commissary could induce him to come forward.

The movements of Jacomet were quite convulsive. When he picked up the first bouquet, considering it valueless, he was about to cast it into the Gave, but a vague murmur in the crowd arrested him. He appeared to understand that the measure of popular patience was at its height, and the slightest incident might cause it to overflow. The bouquets were then, together with everything else, transported to the cart. When the Grotto was cleared of everything, M. Jacomet proceeded to remove the balustrade. But being at a loss for an axe, he sent to some workmen at a saw-mill, close at hand, to lend him one, but they refused. A person, however, who was at work at a little distance, being afraid to refuse, allowed his to be taken.

M. Jacomet, with his own hands, cut away the balustrade, which, not being very solid, was easily demolished. At the sight of this man cutting away the wood with an axe, the effect on the multitude was such, that a menacing attitude, on the part of the people, was apparent. The river was at hand, and a few moments would have sufficed to precipitate the unfortunate commissary into the Gave.

Jacomet turned round, and his countenance was pale and disturbed. "That which I do," said he, with apparent distress, "is not of my own accord; it is with the greatest regret that I am forced to execute it; and I only act according to the orders of the Prefect. I must obey, whatever it may cost me, superior authority; I am not responsible, and the blame does not rest with me."

Some voices among the crowd called out, "Let us remain calm—no violence—leave all in the hands of God."

The advice and activity of the clergy had been effectual, there was no disorder.

The Commissary and the Sergents de Ville conducted the cart without further difficulty to the mayoralty, where they deposited the various articles collected at the Grotto, and the money was placed in the hands of the mayor.

That evening, as a protest against the measures of the Prefect, an innumerable crowd assembled at the Grotto, filling the place once more with lights and flowers. And, in order to prevent the police from seizing the candles, each person held his own, and in returning carried it home.

The following day, two remarkable coincidences happened, which made a lively impression upon the people. The woman who had let out her horse and cart on hire, fell from the top of a hayloft, and broke her ribs. The man who had lent his axe to the commissary, had both his legs broken by the fall of a beam, which he was about to place on his bench.

The free-thinkers saw in this an unfortunate and irritating coincidence, and the multitude considered this double occurrence as a punishment from heaven.

XVII.

The Prefect was but slightly affected by these
incidents. The bold and inflexible attitude of the
Abbé Peyramale occupied his mind far more than
these marks of celestial displeasure. God, in a
word, gave him less uneasiness than the Curé.
The refusal of the mayor, M. Lacadé, to proceed,
his proffered resignation, a circumstance very unusual on the part of a functionary, added to the
discontent manifested at the removal of the votive
offerings from the Grotto, the uncertainty in which
they were as to what was perhaps a passive obedience only in the Gendarmes, and the soldiery, who
participated fully in the popular enthusiasm and
veneration, all these things caused him to reflect,
and he felt that, under these circumstances, the
incarceration of the Visionary might produce the
most disastrous consequences. Not that he was
unprepared to brave an *emeute*, but a rising of the
population, accompanied by the resignation of the
mayor, a broil with one of the most respected
priests of the diocese, and followed probably
by a complaint to the Council of State, and by
an energetic protest of the Catholic or independent press, presented to his mind a character of
importance, which could not fail to have an effect
upon a man so intelligent, and so attached to his
functions, as the Baron Massy.

It would however have cost the haughty Prefect
very seriously to have to stop in the execution of
that radical measure which he had so publicly
announced the evening the counsel of revision was

held ; and certainly he would not have acted as
he did if the report of the physicians, instead of
being a simple and hesitating hypothesis, of itself
insecure, had attested the insanity of the Visionary.
But M. Massy, after all the examinations of Bernadette, understood that there could not be found
one serious physician but what acknowledged and
declared with all the world the perfect reason,
upright intelligence, and good faith of the child.

But should he, after all such evidence, resign
himself to this popular Superstition ? By no
means ; he would change his tactics ; he felt he
had gone too far to recede ; he had carried off
from the Rocks of Massabielle the votive offerings
of the people, and to revoke this measure was not
to be thought of for a moment.

He deemed it advisable, however, to allow the
Visionary to remain free—the idea of her arrest
was consequently abandoned.

Still he would eradicate this superstition, he
would defeat the Supernatural at once and for
ever, and M. Massy felt "certain" that his difficulties would soon end.   That he, a Prefect of the
Empire, he a Baron, the Baron Massy, should be
conquered by the silly stories of an infantine shepherdess, and be knocked down by a phantom,
would have been insupportable to his pride, and
appeared impossible to a man of his intellect and
intelligence.

Therefore, if he had given up, after his discourse of the fourth of May, the plan he had proposed of shutting up poor Bernadette as an insane
person, he was only the more violently disposed to
put a limit in one or another to the progress and

invasions of fanaticism.   The doctrines and explanations which for several days had become the
favourite topic of the free-thinkers of these southern
countries, suggested to his mind, already embarrassed, a new expedient, which seemed to him
completely decisive.   That we may understand
more fully how the Prefect came to change his
mode of attack, it would be well to cast a glance
on what was now passing in the camp of the Anti-
Christians.

SIXTH BOOK.

I.

The enemies of Superstition had lost considerable ground in their desperate struggle against the extraordinary events, which for the last three or four months, had scandalized their philosophy, and, in short, they were now standing at bay. In the same way as it had become impossible to deny the existence of the Fountain, whose limpid waters flowed before the eyes of the astonished multitude, so in the same way had it become impossible to deny any longer the cures that were being daily accomplished by the use of this mysterious water. At first they shrugged their shoulders at the account of the cures, and set themselves entirely and simply to deny their existence, refusing at the same time to make any examination into the matter. Then some of the clever ones of the party invented two or three false miracles, in order as they thought to achieve the more easy triumph. But incredulity had been very speedily outdone by the multiplicity of wonderful cures, of which we have not been able to relate but a small part. Facts had become imposing, startling, and so numerous, that it was necessary either to submit to the miraculous, or to find some

natural solution for these extraordinary phenomena.
The free-thinkers then felt, that, rather than deliver up their arms, or deny the plain evidence of
facts, it was urgent on them to have recourse to a
rapid evolution, and to discover new tactics. The
most intelligent amongst this little world felt,
that it was now very late in the day, and acknowledged the very grave fault they had at first committed, in prematurely, and without examination,
denying facts that had since become so obvious,
and so thoroughly substantiated. Such as the
gushing forth of the Fountain, and of the recovery of so many notable incurables, whom every
one could now see going about in perfect health,
in the streets of the town. And that which rendered the evil almost irreparable was, the unfortunate denial of evidence which had been authenticated, and officially announced, in all the journals
of the department.

II.

The greater part of the cures effected by the
water of Massabielle, had in them such a character of suddenness and rapidity as manifestly
pointed to the action of a supernatural power.
There were others, however, that presented in no
wise this very visibly supernatural character and
type, being effected by the use of lotions, or of
waters taken internally, with more or less fre-
quency, and following the ordinary course of natural remedies.

In a village near Lourdes, called Gez, a little

child, aged seven years, had been remarkable as the object of one of these cures of a mixed character, which according to the bias of mind, might be attributed to a special grace of God or the sole force of nature. This child, of the name of Lasbareilles, was born entirely deformed, with a double deviation of the bony frame on the back and chest; his legs, quite slender and almost dried up, were paralysed by their extreme weakness. This unhappy little thing was never able to walk. He was constantly on the sofa or sitting down. When he had to change his place, his mother carried him in her arms. Sometimes, however, the child, resting on the end of the table, or supported by the hand of his mother, succeeded in holding himself upright, and walking a few steps at the cost of violent efforts and great fatigue. The physician of the place had declared him absolutely incurable; through this essentially organic state of injury, they never had recourse to any remedy.

The parents of this unfortunate child, hearing the miracles of Lourdes spoken of, had obtained some of the water from the Grotto; and in the space of fifteen days, they had applied, at three different times, lotions to the body of the infant, without any result. Their faith was not, however, discouraged; if hope was banished from the world, it would be found again in the hearts of mothers. The fourth lotion took place on Maunday Thursday, that is the 11th April, 1858. On that day, the child walked by himself alone several paces. These lotions had become more and more efficacious, and the state of the child gradually improved. He then came after three or four weeks

to be able to walk almost like everyone else. We
say "almost like," for he preserved in his movements an awkwardness of manner that seemed to
be a remnant of his original infirmity. The slen-
derness of his legs had gradually disappeared at
the same time as the weakness, and his figure was
almost entirely straight. All the population of
the village of Gez, who knew the former condition
of this child, cried out, that it was a miracle.
Were they right or were they wrong? Whatever
may be our thoughts about this, it is certain there
is room for discussion on both sides. Another
child, Denys Bouchet, of the Burgh of Lamarque,
in the Canton of Ossun, was equally cured of a
general paralysis under conditions of a very similar
character. A youth, twenty-seven years of age,
named Jean Louis Amaré, an epileptic, beheld his
terrible malady completely subside, but subsiding
only by degrees, through the use of the water of
Massabielle.

III.

If we had not seen, since the Christian era,
marvellously varied forms of Supernatural cures,
we should perhaps be tempted to believe that
Providence thus disposed things at that moment
in order to lead human philosophy to be entrapped
in its own proper nets, and to destroy itself by its
own hands. But this very event was not, we
believe, a divine snare. God does not lay in
ambush for anyone. By itself, by its own normal
and regular developments, the logic of which is

unknown to human philosophy, Truth is an eternal snare for error.

When these cures were made known, the savants and physicians of the neighbourhood thought they had discovered an admirable opportunity for changing their tactics. This course was prudent, and had become necessary in consequence of the increasing amount of evidence. Abandoning their former mode of explanation in calling it "imagination," they now attributed the cures to the natural virtues of this singular water.

In giving this explanation, they showed at all events, that they recognized the truth and authenticity of the cures.

The reader will call to mind, how at the commencement of this history, the free-thinking journals, stated, that a little shepherdess, going to collect dry wood, had pretended that a luminous Apparition appeared suddenly before her. He will recollect the sneers of the wise heads of Lourdes, the shrugging of shoulders at the clubs, the transcendent disdain with which all strong minds received this silly child's play. Now, however, the miracle, if we dare so to express ourselves, had taken the initiative. The free-thinkers, lately so bold in their attack, were now obliged to defend themselves. The representatives of philosophy and science were not on that account less positive nor less disdainful towards popular superstition.

"Well, yes," they affected to say, in a tone of good humour; "well, yes, we acknowledge that the waters of the Grotto have cured certain maladies. What then? Where is the need of calling

out, 'A miracle,' and talking of supernatural graces,
and divine interventions? In order to explain
analogous action, if not identical, we have only to
turn to a thousand other springs of water, from
Vichy to Baden, down to Luchon, all acting with
efficacy on the human organization. The water
of Massabielle possesses purely and simply those
powerful mineral qualities which are generally to be
found in places higher up in the mountains, such
as the baths of Barèges, or Canterets. The
Grotto of Lourdes has nothing to do with religion,
but relates exclusively to the science of medicine."

The following letter will denote the attitude of
the savants of the country, in presence of the
miracles produced by the waters of Massabielle.
This letter was written by a physician of repute in
the neighbourhood, Dr. Lary, (who in no wise
believed in miraculous explanations,) and was
addressed to a member of the faculty.

"Ossun, 27 April, 1858.

"I am anxious, my dear colleague, to trans-
mit to you the details you have requested, relating
to the woman Galop, of our Commune. This
woman, in consequence of rheumatism in the left
hand, was unable to take hold of anything with it.
In attempting to lift a glass, she frequently let it
fall. She could not draw water from her well,
being unable to grasp the cord attached to the
pully. It was more than eight months since she
had been able to make her bed, or even to spin a
single skein of thread; now, since her first and
only visit to Lourdes, when she applied the water,
internally and externally, she can spin with ease,

she makes her own bed, draws water, washes plates and glasses, in a word, she can use that hand nearly as well as the other.

" The movements, however, of the left hand are not *altogether* so free as before the malady appeared itself; but compared with what they were before the use of the waters of the Grotto of Lourdes, *they are better by ninety to one hundred in difference.* This woman intends returning to the Grotto, and I shall ensure her attendance upon you, in order that you may see her, and then convince yourself of all that I now here tell you.

" You will find, when you examine the sick person in question, on her first finger, an ankylose swelling of the index. This is all that remains of her affection. If the reiterated use of the water of the Grotto causes this morbid state to disappear, *it will be another proof of the alkaline nature of the waters of the fountain.*

" I remain, praying you to believe me to be
" Your very devoted colleague,
" LARY, M. D."

This explanation once admitted, and taken for certain, *a priori,* showed that the physicians had less difficulty than the free-thinkers in believing in the cures produced by the waters of the Grotto. And from this moment they began to generalise their thesis, and apply it to every case.

The savants of the district extricated themselves from this awkward position by attributing qualities to the water of unexampled efficacy, a power hitherto unknown. Little cared they, if they
17

overturned all the laws of nature in their theories, provided it was not to the profit of heaven. And readily would they admit the *extra-natural*, in order to rid themselves of the *supernatural*.

Amongst those who believed, were some who occasioned great annoyance to the philosophers and savants.

"How has it happened," said they, "that this mineral fountain, so exceptionally powerful as to effect sudden cures, has been discovered by Bernadette when in ecstasy, in consequence of the celestial visions, and as a proof of the supernatural apparitions? How did it come to pass that this Fountain burst out at the very moment when Bernadette said she heard the divine voice telling her to go and drink, and wash herself at this fountain? How did it happen that this Fountain, springing out suddenly, in presence of the people, under circumstances so prodigious, and so astonishing, should pour out, not ordinary water, but water that, according to your own confession, has already cured so many grievous maladies in those who have resorted to it, not under medical direction, but in a simple spirit of faith?"

These objections repeated, under a thousand different forms, annoyed beyond measure the freethinkers, philosophers, and savants. Their replies were weak and miserable.

"What is there wonderful in all this!" they said, "a goat accidentally discovered the coffee plant; a herdsman, by chance, discovered the waters of the Luchon. Again, by chance, a peasant hoeing in a vineyard discovered the ruins of Pompeii. Why, therefore, should it be a matter of astonishment, that whilst this little girl was amusing herself in scraping a hole in the ground, during her hallucination, a spring should burst out, and its waters should happen to be mineral, and alkaline? and that at this precise moment she should have believed she saw the Holy Virgin, and heard a voice that told her of the fountain, is a simple coincidence, altogether fortuitous, which superstition would turn into a miracle. Now, as always, chance has done all, and has been the sole revealer of secrets."

But, believers were not to be shaken by such logic as this.

The other party now thought of the following expedient.

"If," said they, "the waters are miraculous, they belong to the state, or to the municipality, and no one can drink them without the advice of the faculty. And the building which is to be constructed in this place, should be an establishment for baths, and not a chapel."

This thought presented itself to the savants of Lourdes, at the period of the Prefect's unexpected proceedings with regard to the votive offerings in the Grotto, and the intended incarceration of Bernadette; an event which was, in the sequel, averted by the unexpected interference of the curé, M. Peyramale.

IV.

The explanations put forward by the medical and free-thinking sections, to be effective, required official support, and here M. Massy stepped in. Calling to his aid chemical seienee, he directed the mayor of Lourdes to address a well known chemist of the department, M. Latour de Trie.

Accordingly, M. Latour de Trie was directed to analyze this water. The chemist of the Prefecture set to work, and brought out an analysis entirely conformable to the medical explanation, the thesis of the philosophers, and the wishes of the Prefect. In his letter of the sixth of May to the mayor, the following analysis was transmitted by Monsieur Latour de Trie.

Chymical Examen,

" The water of the Grotto of Lourdes is very limpid, inodorous, and without any special savour. Its specific gravity is very near that of distilled water. Its temperature at the Fountain is of fifteen centigrades.

" It contains the following principles :

" 1. Chlorures of soda, of chalk and magnesia, which are abundant.

" 2. Carbonates of chalk and magnesia.

" 3. Silicates of chalk and alumen.

" 4. Oxide of iron.

" 5. Sulphate of soda and carbonate of soda.

" 6. Phosphate ; some traces.

" 7. Organic matter—ulmine.

"We attest that in the composition of this water there is a complete absence of chalk or selenite." .

"This particular fact, so remarkable, is entirely of advantage, and should make us consider it as very light, easy for digestion, and impressing on the animal economy a disposition favourable to the equilibrium of the vital action."

To this he added the following note:

"We do not think it will be going too far to say, when we consider the constitution and the quality of these substances, and their constituent parts, that medical science will not be slow, perhaps, to recognize the special remedial virtues of this water, and thus cause it to be classed with the waters that constitute the mineral riches of our department.

"LATOUR DE TRIE."

The civil order is less disciplined than the military order, and there happen in it, for want of a proper understanding, false manoeuvres. The Prefect, in the midst of his engagements, had neglected to give his orders to the editor's office of the official journal of the Prefect of the department, The *Era Impériale*, the result of which was, while the Chymist of the Prefecture said white, the Journalist of the Prefecture said black. While the first hailed in the Fountain of Lourdes, one of the future Therapeutic and mineral riches of the Pyrenees, the second qualified it as muddy water, and made a ridicule of the cures that were obtained.

"It is quite evident," writes he the very

day on which M. Latour de Trie sent his report,
that is to say, the sixth of May—"It is quite
evident that the famous Grotto pours out miracles
by torrents, and that our department is inundated. At the end of every turn, you will meet
people to relate to you a thousand cures obtained
by the use of muddy water. Soon the physicians
will have nothing to do, the rheumatic or con-
sumptive sick will have disappeared from the
department."

In spite of these disagreements, which he might
have avoided, it is just to acknowledge that M.
the Baron Massy was an active man. The fourth
of May, towards midday, he had made his address
to the mayor of the Canton of Lourdes, and given
his orders. On the fourth of May, in the evening,
the Grotto had been stripped of all votive offerings. The fifth of May, in the morning, he had
learnt the impossibility of arresting the Visionary,
and had renounced this measure. The sixth of
May, in the evening, he had in his hand the
Analysis of his chymist.

Furnished with this last and important document, he waited the course of events.

What was going to take place at Lourdes?
What would happen at the Grotto? What would
Bernadette do, whose smallest actions were watched
by the argus eyes of Jacomet and his agents?
With the heats which began to appear, would not
the water of the Grotto, as many said, be dried
up, which would cut short everything? What
attitude was the population going to assume?
Such were the reflections, the hopes and the disquiets of Baron Massy, Prefect of the Empire.

V.

At the Grotto, the miraculous Fountain still flowed, abundant and clear, with that character of perennial tranquillity which may be remarked in the beautiful streams which gush down the rocks.

The Supernatural Apparition ceased not to attest and prove itself by its benefits.

Sometimes rapid as the lightning which cleaves the clouds, sometimes slow as the light of the aurora which rises and becomes greater ray by ray, the grace of God continued visibly and invisibly to descend upon the multitude.

About three or four miles from Lourdes, at Loubajac, there lived a courageous woman, a peasant, formerly used to hard work, whom an accident had condemned for eighteen months to the most painful inaction. Her name was Catharine Latapie Chouat. In October, 1856, having got upon an oak tree to knock off some of the acorns, she had lost her balance, and received a violent fall which had caused a great disjointing of her right arm, and particularly her hand. The setting,—according to the report made and the proces-verbal which we have under our eyes,—the setting, which was immediately operated by a skilful physician, had only succeeded in restoring the arm to its normal state, without, however, having the effect of removing from it an extreme weakness. But the most intelligent and persevering efforts failed in consequence of the stiffness of the three most important fingers of the hand. The thumb, fore-finger and middle finger remained absolutely bent and paralysed, without its being possible, either to reset them, or cause them to perform a single motion. The unhappy peasant woman, yet young, for she was only thirty-eight years of age, could neither sew, nor spin, nor weave, nor attend to any of her house-keeping duties. After having for a long time in vain attended her, the doctor told her that she was incurable, and that she must be resigned no longer to have any use of her hand again. Such a decision, from one so competent, was to this unfortunate person an announcement of an irreparable calamity. The poor have no other resource but labour; for them a forced inaction is inevitable misery.

Catherine had become pregnant nine or ten months after her fall, and was drawing near her time at the moment when the divine events at the Grotto of Massabielle had suddenly occurred. One night, she was awakened all at once as if by a sudden idea.

"An interior spirit," said she to the author of this book, "an interior spirit said to me within myself, with an irresistible force, 'Go to the Grotto! Go to the Grotto, and thou shalt be cured!'" What was this mysterious being who thus spoke, and whom this ignorant peasant, ignorant, at least, as to all human knowledge, called "a spirit?" Her angel guardian knows without doubt this secret.

It was three o'clock in the morning. Catherine bids her two grown up children to accompany her.

"Remain for work," said she to her husband; "I am going to the Grotto."

"In this state of pregnancy, it is impossible," replies he. "To go and return from Lourdes is a journey of three good leagues."

"Everything is possible. I am going to be cured."

No objection could stop her. She started with her two children. The moon shone beautifully bright. The solemn silence of the night, disturbed every moment by unknown noises, the profound solitude of these countries, vaguely lighted up and peopled by indeterminate forms, alarmed the children. They trembled and stood still at every step, but Catherine encouraged them. She had no fear, and felt that she was walking towards the Life.

She reached Lourdes at break of day. She met Bernadette. Some one told her that she was the Visionary. Catherine made no reply, but advancing towards the child blest by the Lord and loved by Mary, she humbly touched her garment.

Then she continued her way towards the Rocks of Massabielle, where, notwithstanding the hour of the morning, a multitude of pilgrims were found already assembled and on their knees. Catherine and her children went on their knees also and prayed. And after having prayed, Catherine arose and went and quietly bathed her hand in the marvellous water. And immediately her fingers were straight again. They became supple, and were restored to their former living action. The Divine Virgin had just cured the incurable.

What does Catherine do? Catherine is not surprised; Catherine utters no cry, but she falls again on her knees, and returns thanks to Mary and to God. For the first time during eighteen months she prays with her hands joined, and crosses her fingers with those that had been healed.

She remained thus a long time, absorbed in an act of thanksgiving. Such moments are sweet ; the soul feels a joy in forgetting itself, and it seems to be in a paradise which it has found again.

Violent sufferings roughly reminded Catherine that she was still upon the earth, upon that earth of groans and tears, on which the malediction uttered originally against the guilty woman, the mother of the human race, had not ceased to weigh over her innumerable posterity. We have said that Catherine was at the last period of her pregnancy. As this poor woman was still on her knees, she felt herself seized all at once by the first and horrible pains of childbirth. She starts up ; she understands that she has no time to return to Lourdes, and that her delivery was on the point of taking place before the multitude around her. And she beheld for a moment that crowd with a terror full of anguish.

But this terror did not last.

Catherine turned herself towards the sovereign Virgin whom nature obeys.

"Good Mother," said she to her with simplicity, "you who have just obtained for me so great a grace, spare me the shame of being delivered before the world, and cause at least that I may be able to go home before bringing into the world the infant I bear."

And immediately all her pains ceased, and the spirit, that interior spirit of whom she spoke to us, and whom we believe was her Angel Guardian, said to her:

. " Be tranquil. Depart with confidence; you will get back without any accident."

"Let us get up now and go," said Catherine to her two children.

And behold her resuming, while holding them in her hand, the road to Loubajac, without allowing any one to suspect the imminent crisis in which she had been, and without manifesting any uneasiness, not only to the assistants, but even to the midwife of her village, who was accidentally there, and whom she perceived in the midst of the pilgrims. Happppy beyond what we can say, she passed over quietly and without any hurry the long journey and the bad roads which separated her from her house. The two children had no longer any fear as during the night; the sun had risen and their mother was cured.

When she had reached her home, Catherine wanted again to pray; but immediately her pains seized her again. A quarter of an hour after, her delivery was accomplished. A third son was born to her.

At the same period, a woman from Lamarque, Marianne Garrot, had seen disappear in less than ten days, by simple lotions of the water of the Grotto, a milky ring-worm, which covered the whole of her face, and which for two years had resisted every mode of treatment. Doctor Amadou de Pontacq, her physician, had attested the

fact, and was later an irrefutable witness before
the episcopal commission.*

* We give also, in a note, on this fact the conclusions of the
commission.

"A ring-worm affection may not in itself present any high
degree of gravity, nor inspire any fear of a serious danger of
some disastrous consequence. However, that with which the
woman Garrot has been attacked, would denote, by its duration,
by its resistance to prescriptions which have been ordered and
faithfully attended to; by its continual and progressive invasion,
a powerful extent of malignity, an inoculation, so to speak, of a
virus deeply rooted, which, to succumb, would have required a
long perseverance of care, a patient continuation of treatment
already adopted, or of a new mode more appropriate and efficacious.

"The disappearance, not instantaneous, but rapid, of the
milky ring-worm from the woman Garrot, is beyond therefore
the habitual mode of action of chymical preparations, since the
first lotion has produced *instantaneously* a sensible amendment,
or partial cure, which the second, administered four days after,
has developed, causing this improvement to progress, and
advanced this cure already began, and which, without the help
of any other remedy, these two lotions have brought, by a rapid
and gradual progress, in a few days to a complete cure.

"Now the liquid, the use of which has procured this prompt
result, is always the same water, without any special virtue,
without analogy or co-relation with the affection which was
conquered, which for the rest, if it had possessed any, would
have long since produced this effect by the daily use which the
sick person would have made of it for her own sustenance and
cleanliness every day.

"We cannot then attribute this cure to the special efficacious
character of the water of Massabielle, and everything concurs,
it seems here, tenacity, the invading activity of the ring-worm
affection, the promptitude of the cure, the inappropriate nature
of the element that produced it, in order to cause us to acknow-

At Bordères, near Nay, the widow Marie Lanou-Domengé, aged eighty years, was for three years attacked on her left side with an incomplete paralysis. She could not walk a step without the assistance of another, and she was, on account of her infirmity, quite incapable of work. Monsieur, the Doctor Poueymiroo, of Mirepoix, after having uselessly employed some remedies to restore life in the members thus suffering from atrophy, had discontinued to prescribe for her, and had altogether ceased coming to see her. Hope nevertheless departs with difficulty from the minds of the sick.

"When shall I be cured?" said the good woman to Monsieur Poueymiroo, every time she met him.

"You will be cured when the Good God shall will it," replied the doctor, invariably, who was far from doubting, when he spoke thus, that he was uttering a prophetic word.

"Why should I not believe that word, and why should I not address myself to the divine goodness?" said the old peasant woman to herself, when she heard speak of the Fountain of Massabielle.

She sent some one to Lourdes to get at the Fountain itself a little of that water which would effect her cure.

When they brought it to her it was received with great emotion.

"Let me get out of bed," said she, "and keep me standing upright."

ledge in it, a cause foreign and superior to natural active causes."
—*Extract from the fifteenth Procès-Verbal of the Commission.*

They lifted her up, they put her dress on in all haste, almost in a feverish manner. The spectators and actors in this scene were in a commotion.

Two persons raised her up, and kept her standing while supporting her under the shoulders.

A glass of water from the Grotto was presented to her.

Marie stretched out her trembling hand towards the liberating water, and plunged her fingers into it. Then she made upon herself a large sign of the cross, after which she brought the glass towards her lips and slowly drank its contents, absorbed without doubt in some fervent prayer which she made to herself. She was pale, so pale that it was believed for an instant she was going to faint. But, while an effort was made to prevent her from falling, she got well again, leaped up and looked round her. Then she uttered, as it were, a triumphal cry of joy. "Loosen me! Loosen me quickly. I am cured."

Those who supported her half withdrew their arms, and in a hesitating way. Marie darted away immediately, and began boldly to walk, as if she had never been unwell. Someone who retained, in spite of all, some fear, offered her a stick to help herself. Marie looked at the stick with a smile. Then she took it, and with a disdainful jerk, cast it to a distance, as if it had been an object heretofore of no use. From this day, she returned to the rough toils of the fields.

Some visitors, having come in order to verify the fact, asked her if she could walk in their presence.

"Walk, gentlemen!" exclaimed she, "why I can run!" And saying these words, she began to do so before them.

This happened in the month of May. In the month of July following, Mary was exhibited from one to another as a phenomenon, a vigorous octogenarian, who courageously was cutting down the corn, and was far from being the last in the fatiguing toils of the harvest.

Her physician, the respected Doctor Poueymiroo, praised God for this evident miracle, and later, signed, with the Commission of enquiry, the procès-verbal of the extraordinary facts which we have described, and through which he hesitated not to acknowledge "the direct and evident action of the divine power."

VI.

The press of Paris and of the Province began to notice the events at Lourdes ; and far beyond the Pyrennean districts, public attention was by degrees turned towards the Grotto of Massabielle.

The measures of the Prefect were loudly praised by the Free-thinking Journals, and not less severely criticized on the Catholic side. The latter was at the same time reserved on the subject of the reality of the Apparitions and miracles, and pretended that such a question should be judged by ecclesiastical authority and not prematurely decided by the arbitrary will of a Prefect.

The innumerable cures accomplished, whether at the Grotto or at a distance from Lourdes, attracted an immense number of sick persons and

pilgrims. The analysis of M. Latour de Trie,
and the pretended mineral properties of the new
fountain, as recognized by the official chymist,
enhanced still more the credit of the Grotto, and
tended to draw to it still greater crowds, who
counted, not on its miraculous agency, but on the
sole force of nature in effecting cures. All the
means taken by incredulity turned directly against
the end it had in view.

The number of visitors to the Grotto now increased. The frosts of winter had disappeared,
the month of May had returned, and with it genial
days. Spring-tide seemed to invite the pilgrims
to the Grotto. They arrived by all the flowery
roads and paths which traversed the woods, the
meadows and the vineyards in this abrupt mountainous country.

Disappointed and powerless, the Prefect saw
that this pacific and prodigious rising continued
to increase, bringing Christians ceaselessly to
kneel at the foot of a solitary rock, and to drink
the waters of its little bubbling Fountain. What
was he to do in the face of this multitude, not
only inoffensive and peaceful, but meditative, singing canticles, or praying in silence? Before he
could act or take any coercive measures, he must
at least be provided with a pretext. And this pretext was still wanting.

Contrary to the hopes of the Free-thinker, to
the fears of the believer, and to the expectations
of all, no disorder arose. An invisible hand
seemed to protect the innumerable crowds left
without chief or guide to direct them.

The magistracy, represented by M. Dutour, and

the police, in the person of M. Jacomet, looked on in amazement at this extraordinary spectacle. Baron Massy had indeed given orders, that all objects deposited in the Grotto should be removed, but there was no law interdicting the making of such offerings. And therefore, in spite of the orders for spoliation, by Monsieur the Prefect, the Grotto was often filled with lighted candles, flowers, votive offerings, and even money, which was given for the erection of the monument demanded by the Holy Virgin. The piety of the faithful, desired by this means to show their good will, their zeal and their love to the Queen of Heaven, useless though the manifestation might be.

"But what matter," said they, "if the money be carried off? The offering will have been made. The candles shall burn, though they may only give out a momentary light in honour of our mother; and flowers shall perfume for an instant the blessed rock where she placed her feet."

Such were the thoughts of these Christian souls.

Jacomet and his agents continued to carry off everything, and the Commissary had become more daring since the fourth of May, sometimes disdainfully casting the offerings into the Gave before the scandalized gaze of the believers. Sometimes also, in spite of himself, he was observed to be forced to retain for the holy places, their festival character. When the ingenious piety of the believers having stripped off the leaves of countless roses round the Grotto, it was impossible for him to collect the thousand scattered frag-

18

ments of the flowers of this bright and perfumed carpet. The crowd, however, continued to kneel and
pray without taking any notice of these provoking
proceedings, letting all pass with a patience that
God alone could have inspired.

One evening there was a report that the Emperor or the Minister had asked Bernadette's
prayers. M. Dutour utters a cry of triumph, and
prepares to save the state. Three poor women, who
had formed, it appeared, such a project, were
brought up before the Tribunal of Justice, and the
Procureur demanded that upon them the full rigor
of the French Law should be inflicted. In spite of
his fury and his eloquence, the Judges acquitted
two of them, and only fined the other five francs.
The Procureur exclaims against this weakness,
pursues his suit, and makes an exasperated or
desperate appeal to the Imperial Court at Pau,
which, smiling at his rage, not only confirms the
acquittal of the two women, but refuses to sustain
the very trifling condemnation pronounced on the
third, and dismisses her entirely from the charge.

This little fact, so discreditable in itself, only
appears in this history in order to show to what
extent the Bar of the Court was lying in wait,
how much it was looking about to find some
offence, some pretext to display its severity, since
it had recourse to such measures, and since it
could employ its time in getting up prosecutions
against poor and simple women, whose innocence,
the Imperial Court, a short time after, was obliged
solemnly to proclaim.

The people remained calm, and a pretext to act

with vigour, in the name of the law, did not present itself.

One night in the midst of thick darkness, some unknown hands removed the pipes from the miraculous Fountain, and caused the waters to lose themselves under large heaps of stones, earth and sand. Who had raised this dark monument against the divine work? What impious hands, and cowardly in their impiety, had committed, when concealing themselves from men, such a profanation? No one knows. But when the day dawned and the sacrilege was known, a smothered indignation, as might have been foreseen, ran through the numerous crowds that flocked to the place of the scandal, and there was seen to be moving on the roads and in the streets a people that was agitated, and like the agitated sea which is foaming, is full of froth, and roars under the blast of a hurricane. The Police, the Magistracy, the Sergents de Ville were on the watch, observing, looking about, listening, but they could not detect any violence nor seditious cries. The superior and divine influence that maintained these angry crowds in order, was evidently invincible.

Who then, once more, had committed this nocturnal act? The Law and the Police, notwithstanding their active and blustering inquiries, were never able to succeed in discovering him! and it happened that some unjust spirits had the boldness to suspect the Law authorities and the Police, evidently in the wrong, for having, by such an act, sought to provoke disorders in order to have a pretext for severe measures.

The municipal authority strongly denied all

connivance in this indignity. The same evening,
or the next day, the Mayor gave an order to
replace the pipes, and to free the soil of the
Grotto from all the heaps with which the new
Fountain had been obstructed. The policy of the
Mayor was to disengage himself *personally* from
all hostile attitude, and to keep things as they
were. He was ready to act, but only as a sub-
ordinate, upon the express command of the Prefect.

Sometimes, the populations fearing that they
might not always control their excited feelings,
took precautions against themselves. The association of stone-cutters, to the number of four or
five hundred, had resolved to make a peaceful
manifestation at the Grotto, and to go there pro-
cessionally singing canticles on the occasion of the
Feast of their Patron, which was celebrated on the
day of the Ascension, which fell that year on the
thirteenth of May. Nevertheless, feeling their
hearts becoming indignant, and their hands trembling with rage at the acts of authority, they distrusted themselves and gave up their project. They
limited themselves to suppressing on that day,
in honour of the Holy Virgin that appeared at
Lourdes, the ball which they gave every year at
the conclusion of their Feast.

"We do not wish," said they, "any disorder
even involuntary, or any rejoicing of which the
Church disapproves, to afflict the eyes of the Holy
Virgin who has visited us."

VII.

The Prefect felt more and more that all coercive measures had failed in consequence of the surprising tranquillity that prevailed amongst the multitudes. Not even an accident had happened. Nothing. He must retrace his steps over the track he had hitherto followed, and frankly leave the population free, or descend purely and simply to violence and persecution, and raise arbitrary barriers before these multitudes, by inventing some pretext. He must either advance or retire.

On the other hand, the variety and suddenness of the cures that had been worked, appeared to many honest minds to be ill explained by the therapeutic and mineral properties of the new Fountain. There were some who disputed the accuracy of the scientific decision given by Monsieur Latour de Trie. A chymist of the neighbourhood, M. Thomas Pujo, pretended that this water was only ordinary water, and that of itself it had no medicinal property.

Several very competent professors in that country confirmed these assertions. Science began to declare the analysis of Mons. de Trie to be entirely erroneous. These reports assumed such a form that the municipal Council of Lourdes was excited. The mayor could not, in presence of the unanimous feeling, refuse to cause a second attempt at analyzing the waters of the Fountain. Without consulting the Prefect, which seemed useless for him to do, (so much was he personally convinced of the accuracy of the examination of

M. Latour,) he caused the municipal Council to adopt a decision authorizing M. the Professor Filhol, one of the great chymists of the day, to make a new and definitive analysis! The Council voted at the same time the necessary funds to remunerate this learned Professor.

M. Filhol was a man of weight and authority in modern science, and his verdict was evidently to be without appeal.

What was his analysis going to be? M., the Prefect, was not chymist enough to know. But we believe, without great fear of deceiving ourselves, that he must have been uneasy. The verdict of the eminent Professor of Chymistry of the Faculty at Toulouse, might upset, in fact, the combinations and plans of M. Massy. It was urgent to make haste. There again, he must fall back or go forward.

In the midst of these different passions and multiplied calculations, the world did not fail to tempt Bernadette with new trials as useless as the foregoing.

She was preparing for her first communion, and she made it on the third of June, the feast of Corpus Christi. It was the very day on which the municipal Council of Lourdes gave Monsieur Filhol the commission to analyze the mysterious Fountain that had recently sprung up under the hand of the Visionary in ecstasy. God entering into the heart of a child and of a young girl, made also the analysis of a pure stream, and we may imagine that He must have admired and blest in that virginal soul, a source the most fresh, and a crystal the most pure.

In spite of the retreat in which she loved to be concealed and recollected, people continued to visit her. She was always the innocent and simple child of whom we have endeavoured to trace the portrait. By her candour, by her shining good faith, by her delicate perfume of peaceful holiness, she charmed everybody who came near her.

One day, a lady, after conversing with her, desired, in a moment of enthusiastic veneration, easily to be conceived by those who have known Bernadette, to exchange her rosary of precious stones for that of the child.

"Keep yours, madame," replied she, showing her modest instrument of prayer. "Here is mine; I do not wish to change it. It is poor like myself, and suits my indigence better."

An ecclesiastic tried to make her accept a piece of money. She refused—he insists. A new refusal so formal that any longer to insist seems useless. He, however, does not hold himself beaten. "Take," says he; "it will not be for you, it will be for the poor, and you will have the pleasure of bestowing an alms."

"Do it with your own hands for my intention, Monsieur L'Abbé, and it will be better than if I did it myself," replies the child.

Poor Bernadette understood that she was to serve God gratuitously, and to fill, without quitting her noble poverty, the mission which she had received on high. And nevertheless, she and her family sometimes wanted bread. At this very time, the salary of Monsieur the Prefect, Baron Massy, was raised to 25,000 francs. M. Jacomet received a bounty. The Minister of Worship, in

a letter which was communicated to several Functionaries, testified to the Prefect his high satisfaction, and praising him for all he had hitherto
done, pressed him to adopt energetic measures,
and added that he must finish at all costs with
the Grotto and miracles at Lourdes.

On this side as on all others, he must either
go back or go forward.   What was there however
to be done ?

VIII.

The plan of the Divine work unfolded itself by
degrees with its admirable and powerful logic.
But no one at this moment, and M. Massy less
than any one else, could perceive, how manifest
soever it was, the invisible hand of God which
directed all things.   It is not in the midst of the
fray that we can judge of a battle.   The unfortunate prefect being engaged on a false track, did not
see in all that was passing anything but an irritating series of unpleasant incidents and an unaccountable fatality.   Take God out of certain questions, and you meet with what cannot be explained.

The march of events, slow but irresistible, over-
threw successively all the theses of incredulity, and
forced such miserable human philosophy to beat a
retreat, and to abandon one by one all its entrenchments.

The Apparitions had taken place.   The Free-
thinkers had altogether absolutely denied them,
while they accused the Visionary of only being an
instrument, and of giving herself up to an in-

terested imposture. This suggestion could not
be sustained in face of the examination of the
child, whose veracity was self-evident.

Incredulity, dislodged from this first position,
had hit upon the ideas of hallucination and catalepsy: "She thinks she sees; she does not see.
It is nothing."

Providence in the meantime had collected
together from the four quarters of the horizon,
thousands and thousands of witnesses around the
child in ecstasy; and when the moment arrived
the truth of Bernadette's recital was proved by a
solemn attestation, by causing a miraculous fountain to gush forth before the astonished eyes of the
collected multitudes.

"There is no fountain," said the incredulous.
"It is only an exudation from the rock, a little
pool; anything you please except a fountain."

But, as soon as they denied publicly and
solemnly that there was a spring in the Grotto,
it increased in a manner like a living being, and
took such large proportions, that more than one
hundred thousand *litres* a day ran from the strange
rock. "But it was chance! a fortuitous circumstance!" stammered incredulity in dismay, and
losing ground hour by hour. And, behold how
events follow out their inevitable course; cures the
most astonishing at once attested the miraculous
character of the water, and gave a fresh and decisive proof of the divine reality of the all-powerful
Apparition by whose indication a living fountain
had issued forth under the hand of a simple mortal.

The first act of the philosophers had been to

deny the cures, in the same way as they had at
first denied the sincerity of Bernadette, and as
they also denied the reality of the Fountain.   And
forthwith the cures became so numerous, so notorious, that incredulity was forced to give way, and
to admit them.   " Well, be it so, there have been
cures, but these are mineral waters ; the Fountain
has therapeutic virtues."   Such was the cry of unbe-
lief, when holding in his hand the official chymical
analysis.   And upon this astounding cures multiplied, absolutely inexplicable by any such hypothesis.   At the same time from divers quarters
several conscientious and enlightened chymists
came forward, loudly declaring that the Fountain
of Massabielle had in itself no mineral virtue
whatever, that it was mere ordinary water, and that
the analysis of M. Latour de Trie, was without
any foundation in fact.

Driven in this way from all their entrenchments,
where they had encountered defeat after defeat,
pursued by the overwhelming evidence of facts,
and crushed by the weight of their own avowals,
openly published in their own journals, what had
the philosophers and free-thinkers to do ?   They
had only to surrender their arms to truth, and
believe.

The author of *Des Essais*, Montaigne's Essays,
says : " It happens with men, just as it occurs to
the ears of corn.   When they first shoot out, their
heads are erect and proud, as long as they remain
empty, but when they become heavy, from the
grain approaching maturity, they begin to bow
humbly down, and to bend their heads towards
the ground.   In like manner men, who have tried

everything, searched into every deep thing, are
found to have renounced their presumption, and
acknowledged their natural condition." Perhaps
the philosophers of Lourdes had not sufficient intelligence to receive, and hold fast, the good seed
of truth ; and it may be, that pride had rendered
them inflexible, and rebels to clear evidence, causing them to persist in maintaining an attitude
erect and proud, like the empty heads of corn. Not
only their attitude remained in this state, but impiety, shamefully driven from one subterfuge to
another, chased from sophism to sophism, from
falsehood to falsehood, forced even to the confines
of absurdity, at length threw off the mask and
appeared in her true colours. She passed from
the domain of discussion and reasoning, into that
of pure intolerance and acts of violence, which are
her own proper element.

Baron Massy perfectly aware of this state of
minds, felt that he would have considerable moral
support in adopting arbitrary measures, and in
giving a loose rein to persecution, in the exasperated state of the free-thinkers now vanquished
and humiliated. As for himself, he too had been
defeated in a struggle analogous to, if not identical
with, that which he had undertaken against the
supernatural power. All his attempts had fallen
to the ground. Issuing from the depths of a desert
rock, and announced by the voice of a child, the
supernatural had stepped forth, overturning in its
path all obstacles, drawing crowds together, and,
in its passage, conquering enthusiastic shouts,
prayers, cries of thanksgiving, and acclamations of
popular faith. And what once more remained for

him to do? It remained for him to harden himself against all evidence, and to offer violence to the tenderest feelings of the people.

IX.

In the midst of these succeeding portions of the drama, the questions of the stables of the prefecture had assumed a character more and more serious, so that the Prefect was driven to a state of exasperation. The month of June had arrived. The season of the baths had commenced, attracting the bathers and tourists of Europe to the Pyrenees, who would be witnesses of the scandal of the supernatural, so discreditable to the department under the administration of the Baron Massy.

The instructions of M. Rouland had become more pressing, urging on the Prefect to carry out rigorous measures. On the 6th of June, M. Fould, minister of finance, returning to his country seat, situated in that part of France, stopped at Tarbes, and had a long conference with M. Massy. The report was spread, that their conference related to the Grotto.

The mere fact of drinking at a Fountain, on a common belonging to the town, had in it nothing criminal in the eye of the Law. Therefore the genius of the adversaries of superstition was imperatively obliged in the first instance, to invent a pretext for interference. The laws of France do not sanction the arbitrary indictments of persons, as in Russia or Turkey, and so it was necessary to have some show of legality for proceeding further in this matter. A very ingenious and lucky idea now occurred to the clever Prefect in this matter. The lands in question belonged to the Commune of Lourdes, the mayor, as administrator, could forbid entrance upon them without assigning any motive, just as an owner of lands or houses could act with regard to his own private property. Once adopted, this astute measure would turn an act, perfectly innocent in itself, into an offence, punishable by law. Baron Massy's entire plan gravitated towards this idea, and once thought of, the Prefect decided on this despotic course of proceeding. The following day the Mayor of Lourdes was pressed to inhibit persons from entering these grounds. And an order to this effect was drawn up for his signature and approval.

" The Mayor of the town of Lourdes," &c., &c.

" Seeing that he has received instructions addressed to him by the Superior Authority," &c.

The remainder of the order was in substance as follows :—Considering that it is of importance "to the interests of religion," to avert the deplorable scenes now passing at the Grotto of Massabielle,—Considering also that it is " the duty of the mayor to watch over the public health of the locality,"—Considering the vast number of strangers that come to use the water of the aforesaid Fountain—and considering that there *are grave reasons for supposing that this water contains mineral qualities*—it is expedient before permitting its use, that there should be a scientific analysis made. *Mineral waters being under the previous control of the state,* therefore,—It is for-

bidden to use the water of the aforesaid fountain,
and all passage on the Commune to the rocks of
Massabielle, is forthwith interdicted, and a barrier shall be erected at the entrance to prevent
access to the place.   Boards shall be put up with
the words :   *It is forbidden to enter on this property.   All violation of this present decree shall be
prosecuted according to Law.*   The order was
dated on the eighth of June, 1858.   The Commissary of Police, the Gendarmerie, the Rural
Guards, and authorities of the Commune, are
charged with the execution of this decree.

The Mayor A. LACADE.

[Seen and approved]
The Prefect O. MASSY.

X.

It was not without hesitation, that M. Lacadé
consented to sign this order, and take upon himself the execution of such a measure.   Wavering
in character, and a friend to a middle course of
action, the mayor at the same time liked his
functions and as some maliciously said, was in
love with his official scarf. But now he must
either be made the instrument of Prefectorial
tyranny, or resign the honour of remaining Mayor
of Lourdes.   In this embarrassing position, M.
Lacadé tried to conciliate all parties, and with
this view demanded as a condition before signing
the order, that the words before mentioned, should
head the proclamation.   This being acceded to,

the mayor thought he was in a position to say, that he was relieved from all further responsibility with the public. "I do not," he said, "take the initiative, I remain neutral. I do not command, I obey. I do not give this order, I receive it; and it is my duty to execute it. The burthen rests with my immediate chief, the Prefect." On the part of a soldier of a regiment in the line, such reasoning would have been just. Thus armed, M. Lacadé issued the Prefectorial Mandate. At the same time, under the protection of armed force, and under the direction of M. Jacomet, notices were posted around the Rocks of Massabielle, to warn persons against approaching the Grotto and miraculous Fountain. Prohibitory placards were posted up wherever any entrance could be made into the communal land that surrounded the venerated rocks. The Sergents de Ville and guards watched day and night, being relieved every hour, and legal proceedings were taken against several persons who entered in order to kneel at the Grotto.

XI.

There was at Lourdes a Juge de Paix or Justice of the Peace. This man was named Duprat. He was as inveterate against superstition as the Jacomets, the Massys, the Dutours and the other constituted authorities. This judge not being able under such circumstances to condemn the delinquents but in the smallest penalty, planned a crooked method for rendering the fine enormous, and truly formidable for the poor people who came from all sides, to pray at the Grotto and ask the Holy Virgin—this one, the restoration of health that was lost ; this other, the cure of a child that was beloved ; a third, some spiritual favour, some consolation in a great grief.

M. Duprat, acting as a severe magistrate, condemned these malefactors to five francs penalty. But through a conception worthy of his genius, he included in one single judgment all together who had violated the Prefectoral prohibition, whether 'in forming a part of the same crowd, or whether, as it appears, in even going to the Grotto during the course of the same day. And he pronounced against them all a condemnation involving the whole of the expense of the fines. So that for the small act which one or two hundred persons might perform in going to the Massabielle Rocks, each of them would find himself exposed to pay not only for himself, but for the others, that is to say, that he would have to pay from 500 to 1000 francs, from £25 to £40, and nevertheless, as each individual condemnation was only five francs, or four shillings, the decision of this magistrate was without appeal before a higher tribunal, and there would be no means of causing it to be set right. The Judge Duprat was allpowerful, and it is thus that he used the plenitude of his power.

XII.

Such an arbitrary intervention of power in the grave question which had been set in motion for some months on the banks of the Gave, implied on the part of the government not only the denial of the supernatural event, but a denial even of its very possibility. Having admitted for a moment, the *possibility* of the Apparition, the measures which the Administration would have adopted would have been different. They would have had for their object an enquiry, while they only tended visibly to a stifling of the question.

There was a fact absolutely certain; the cures. Whether they were produced by the mineral and therapeutic nature of the waters, by the imagination of the sick persons, or rather in virtue of a miraculous action, these cures were more manifest and officially recognized by the incredulous themselves, who not being able to deny them, endeavoured only to explain them by natural means.

There were witnesses amounting to hundreds and thousands that were truthful and beyond all suspicion, who declared that cures had been worked by the use of the waters of the Grotto. Not a single person could be found to whom they had been fatal, or who had experienced any injury from them.

Why then these prohibitory measures, these raised barriers, this armed and threatening force, these persecutions? Why, then, since such measures were adopted, did they not carry out their logic to the end? Why not shut up every pil-

'19

grimage where a sick person had found his health
restored, every church where a man in prayer had
believed he had received a grace from God?

This was the language employed on all sides.

"If Bernadette," said some, "had, without saying anything of Visions or Apparitions, discovered
purely and simply a mineral fountain possessing
strong healing qualities, what barbarous authority
would have hindered the sick from going to drink
at them? Under the reign of Nero they would
not have dared to do so; under all governments
they would have voted a reward for such a child.
But here, the sick go on their knees beforehand to
pray, and subalterns with lace of wool, silver or
gold, who go down flat on their faces before their
masters, are not pleased when men prostrate before their God. Such is the cause. It is prayer
that they persecute."

"But superstition!" said the free-thinkers.

"Is not the Church there to watch over it and
defend the faithful against error? Let it act in
its own domain, and transform not into a Council
a meeting at the Prefecture, and into an Infallible Pope, a Prefect or a Minister. What disorder has it produced? None. What evil has
taken place to justify your measure and your prohibitions? None. The mysterious Fountain has
done nothing but good. Let the believing populations go and drink at it, if it so pleases them.
Leave them the liberty of believing, praying, and
of being healed; the liberty of turning themselves
to God, and of demanding from the powers on
high the alleviation of their sufferings. Free-
thinkers, tolerate the liberty of prayer.

But neither anti-christian philosophy, nor the pious Prefect of the Hautes-Pyrénées would consent to have any regard for this unanimous cry, and their career was marked by severity.

The intolerance with which the enemies of Christianity, so wrongfully reproach the Catholic Church, is their predominant passion. They are essentially tyrants and persecutors.

SEVENTH BOOK.

I.

The clergy continued not to go to the Grotto,
and to keep themselves entirely aloof from the
movement. The orders of Monseigneur Laurent
on this subject, were strictly observed throughout
the diocese.

The population, cruelly agitated by administrative persecution, turned themselves with anxiety
towards the ecclesiastical authorities which were
charged by God with the direction and defence of
the faithful, and they expected to see the bishop
protest energetically against the violence offered
to their religious liberty.

Vain expectation. Monseigneur observed an
absolute silence, and left the prefect to do as he
pleased. Still further, Baron Massy published in
his journals that he was acting in concert with the
ecclesiastical authority, and, to the general amazement, the bishop gave no contradiction to the
assertion. The spirit of the people was in great
trouble and agitation.

Already, at the commencement, the burning
faith of the multitude was at a loss to understand
the extreme prudence of the clergy at the point
to which the event had reached, after so many

proofs of the reality of the Apparitions of the
Holy Virgin, after the gushing forth of the Fountain, after so many cures and miracles, the excessive reserve of the Bishop in presence of a persecuting power appeared to them an unaccountable
defection. The respect which they had for his
character as for his person was not quite sufficient
to keep under restraint the expression of the popular dissatisfaction.

Why not pronounce upon the fact, when the
elements of certainty were overflowing on all sides?
Why not, at least, order an enquiry, a study of
the question, some examination or another to
guide the faith of all, and hinder it from being
misled? Events which sufficed to throw the
civil power into confusion, and to raise innumerable populations, were they not worthy of the attention of the Bishop? Did not the obstinate silence
of the Prelate authorize the Prefect to act as he
had done? If the Apparition was false, ought
not the Bishop to enlighten the faithful and check
the error at its outset? If it was true, ought he
not to oppose himself to the persecution against
the believers, and defend with courage the work of
God against the malice of men? A simple step
of the Bishop, an enquiry, would it not hinder the
Prefect from entering on the path of persecutions
on which he was engaged? Were the priests and
the Bishop then deaf to so many prayers and cries
of gratitude which were raised at the feet of that
ever-celebrated rock, where the mother of a cruci-
fied God had placed her virginal step? Had the
letter killed the spirit? Where they, as the
Pharisees of whom the Gospel speaks, blind to the

brilliant splendour of so many miracles? Were
they so busy with the affairs of the Church, and so
absorbed in their clerical functions, that the all-
powerful hand of God, appearing out of the
temple, should be for them an unperceived fact,
or an event without importance? Was it then
under such circumstances, when God intervened,
and when persecutors were rising up, that the
Bishop, as at processions, should walk the last?

This clamour arose from the midst of the crowds,
and went on increasing. The clergy was accused
of indifference or hostility, the Bishop of timidity
and weakness.

By the logic of events, and the natural bent of
the human heart, this vast movement of men and
ideas, so essentially religious in its principle,
threatened to become anti-ecclesiastical. The multitudes, full of faith towards the Blessed Virgin
and the Holy Trinity, but full of discontent, irritated at the prolonged abstention of the clergy,
tended by the same stroke to rush towards the
Church in which the Divine strength abides, and to
desert the sacristy, where, under the sacerdotal
costume, are to be found too often the defects of
man.

Monseigneur Laurence continued, nevertheless,
to persist in his immoveable reserve. What were
the prelate's reasons for resisting the voice of the
people, which is sometimes the voice of heaven?
Was this prudence divine, or was it human? Was
it wisdom? Was it weakness?

II.

To believe is not easy. In spite of so many striking proofs, Monseigneur Laurence still had doubts, and hesitated to act. His very enlightened faith did not proceed at so rapid a rate as the faith of the simple. God who, so to speak, shows Himself all at once to ingenuous and ignorant souls, whom human studies could not enlighten, is pleased sometimes to impose a longer or more patient enquiry on cultivated and instructed intellects, who are capable of arriving at truth by the path of toil, examination, and reflection. As the Apostle Thomas, refusing to believe on the testimonies of the other disciples and holy women, Monseigneur Laurence would have wished to see all things with his eyes and touch them with his hands. Of a precise mind, inclined rather towards what was practical than what was ideal, of a disposition naturally distrustful of popular exaggerations, the prelate was one of those who, by I know not what particular instinct, become cold before the passionate sentiment of others, and who willingly take it for granted that emotion leads astray and enthusiasm is deceiving. Although, at moments, he was forcibly struck by so many extraordinary events, he was so afraid too readily to affirm the supernatural, that he would perhaps have risked mistaking it or only confessing it too late, if the grace of God had not tempered in him and preserved within the limits of a just measure this natural disposition which we have pointed out.

Not only Monseigneur Laurence hesitated to give a decision, but he hesitated even to order an official enquiry. As a Catholic Bishop, powerfully impressed with a sense of the exterior dignity of the Catholic Church, he had a certain fear of compromising the gravity of that mother of the human race, in engaging her prematurely in a solemn investigation of those singular facts, of which he had not a sufficient personal knowledge, and which might, after all, have only as their basis the childish fancies of a little shepherdess and the vain illusions of poor fanatics.

Assuredly, the Bishop had never counselled the measures that had been taken by the civil authority, and he highly disapproved of them. But, since this evil had happened, was it not prudent to draw from it the accidental good which might result from it ? Was it not wise, if by chance there was any error in the popular belief and narratives, to abandon the pretended natural fact to itself, to struggle all alone against the hostile examination and persecution of M. Massy, the freethinkers and savants, leagued together to crush superstition ? Therefore he would wait, and not be in a hurry to engage perhaps in a useless conflict with the civil power. " I deplore, like you, the measures which they are taking," said the Bishop, in his private discourses, to those who pressed him to interfere. " But not being charged with the duties of the police, nor consulted, I can only allow the matter to go on. Each one answers for his own acts......I have nothing to do up to the present," added he, " with the acts of the civil authority, relative to the Grotto, and I congratulate

myself on keeping myself so. Later the ecclesiastical authority will see if there is anything to
do."*

In this spirit of prudence and expectation, the
Bishop ordered the clergy of the diocese, earnestly
to preach calm to the populations, and employ their
influence to cause them to submit to the decree of
the Prefect. To avoid all material disorder, not
to create any new embarrassment, even to favour,
out of respect for the principle of authority, the execution of measures adopted in the name of power,
and watch the coming of events, appeared to the
Bishop the wisest of courses.

Such were the thoughts of Monseigneur Laurence, as they manifest themselves in his correspondence at that period. Such were the considerations which determined his attitude and inspired
his conduct.

If Monseigneur Laurence, in his high prudence
as Bishop, placed himself at the point of view of a
possible error, God, in His infinite clear penetra-
tion, placed Himself at the point of view of the
immutable certainty of His acts, and the truth of
His own work. Now, if the man of the Church,
if the Bishop had believed from the beginning in
the reality of so many apparitions and miracles,
would he have been able to resist the generous
impulses of his zeal as an apostle, and hesitate a
single instant in interfering with energy against
the persecutors of the faithful, against the enemies of the divine work? If he had had the

* Letter of Monseigneur Laurence, to the Curé of Lourdes,
dated June 11.

faith that the Mother of God had truly appeared
in his diocese, demanding a temple for her glory,
and curing the sick, would he have been able to
balance a second between the will of that eternal
Queen of heaven and earth, and the miserable
opposition of a Massy, or Jacomet or a Rouland?
No—assuredly. With such a faith in his heart, the
Bishop, as formerly St. Ambrose at Milan—could
not but stand up with his crozier in his hand and
his mitre on his head, and confront the civil
power. Publicly, at the head of the believers,
without any fear of men, he would have gone to
drink at the divine Fountain, bend his knees
before the blessed rock which the Holy Virgin had
sanctified by touching it with her feet, and lay, in
those desert places, the first stone of a magnificent
temple in honour of Mary Immaculate.

But, in defending thus the work of God then at
that moment, the prelate would have infallibly
weakened it for the future. The support which he
would have lent to it at the origin, would have
compromised it later, and rendered it open to suspicion of emanating not from God, but from men.
The more the Bishop kept himself out of the
movement, the more rebellious, or, rather, hostile to the popular faith,—the more the supernatural work showed its force by triumphing without any exterior aid, by itself, by its own intrinsic
truth, by its own power, and in spite of animosity
or abstention on the part of all that bears in this
world the name of Power.

Providence had determined that it should be
thus, and that the grand fact of the Apparition of
the ever Blessed Virgin visiting us in the nine-

teenth century, should, like early Christianity, be
subject to trials and persecutions. It was the will
of Almighty God that faith should commence with
the humble and the weak, as in the kingdom of
heaven, the last should be first, and the first last.
It was necessary, then, that the Bishop, so far
from taking the initiative, should be almost the
last to yield to the irresistible evidence of facts.
And this is why God had, in His secret designs,
placed on the episcopal seat of Tarbes a man so
eminent, and withal so reserved, whose character
we have described. This is why it had pleased
Him not to give, in the first instance, to Mgr.
Laurence faith in the Apparition, and to keep him
in doubt, notwithstanding so many astounding
facts. The people had the virtue of faith, but
their impatient ardour would have sought to urge
the clergy to a premature interference. The
Bishop had the virtue of prudence, but his eyes
were not yet open to the truth of the supernatural
work which was happening before him, and which
every one saw. The complete wisdom and the
just measures of all things were as always in God
alone, who guided events, and whose all-powerful
hand made subservient to His ends, the fury of
the multitudes and the hesitation of the Prelate.

III.

The people, carried away by enthusiasm, were
less prudent than the Bishop, and they were also
unchecked by the arbitrary measures of the administration. The more ardent among them braved

the tribunals, and fines, and broke through the barriers, to kneel before the Grotto, giving their names to the guards who watched around the communal lands. Amongst the guards were many believers, who, on entering the venerated precincts, fell on their knees before taking up their position. Placed between the morsel of bread they gained by their petty offices as Sergents de Ville, or Cantonniers, on the one side, and the disagreeable duty they had to perform on the other, these poor men, in their prayer to the Mother of the weak and infirm, cast the responsibility of their disagreeable functions upon the authorities who compelled them to act. Notwithstanding, they strictly fulfilled their duty, and regularly proceeded against the delinquents.

Though in their impetuous zeal, many of the believers exposed themselves voluntarily to peril, in order to go publicly to invoke the Holy Virgin at the place of the Apparition, the jurisprudence of M. Duprat, whose fine, in appearance but five francs, might have been raised, as we have explained, to enormous sums, was put on to frighten the people. For a great number, for all those of the poorest class, such a condemnation would have been a complete ruin.

Thus, the greater part endeavoured to escape the rigorous vigilance of the persecuting power.

Sometimes the believers, respecting the barriers, where the guards at the frontier of the communal land were stationed, reached the Grotto by bye paths. Some one amongst them, left behind, was on the watch, and warned them, by a preconcerted signal, of the arrival of the police. The sick were thus painfully carried up to the Miraculous Fountain. The official authority, when informed of these infractions, doubled the posts, and intercepted all the paths. Some were then seen, in spite of the violence of the waters, swimming across the Gave, to come and pray before the Grotto, and drink the waters of the holy Fountain. The night favoured such infractions, which became more and more multiplied, in spite of the good will and activity of the agents.

The influence of the clergy was diminished, almost compromised, through the reasons which we have assigned. In spite of the efforts they made to comply with the orders of the Bishop, the priests were powerless in calming agitated minds, and in making them understand that even the arbitrary acts of power should be respected. "We ought only to respect what is respectable," was a revolutionary word which found its echo everywhere. The personal ascendency of the Curé of Lourdes, so beloved and venerated, began to receive a shock through the popular irritation.

Order was threatened through the same measures which had been taken under the pretext of maintaining it. The populations, wounded upon the most cherished points of their belief, oscillated between submission and violence. If on the one side petitions were signed to the Emperor, to demand, in the name of liberty of conscience, the withdrawal of the Decree of the Prefect, on the other, three or four times, the planks which shut up the Grotto, were broken and thrown into the Gave. Jacomet strove in vain to discover the believers, who showed such little respect for autho-

rity, who had committed this crime hitherto unknown in our code; prayer by night, with dam-
aging and breaking down of enclosures.

Often people went, to avoid this crime, to prostrate themselves by the fences at the exterior
boundary of the communal land.

It was a mute protestation against the measures
of the civil Authority, and as it were a mute appeal
to the Omnipotent God.

The day on which the court at Pau quashed the
condemnation pronounced by the tribunal at
Lourdes against one of the three women prosecuted for innocent purposes on the subject of the
Grotto, and confirmed the acquittal of the others,
the crowd was enormous at the entrance of the
fences. It cried out, "Victory!" It could not
contain itself, and broke down the barrier in com-
pact masses, without making any answer to the
demands and bewildered exclamations of the
agents. The police, who were disconcerted by the
check experienced at Pau, and in disorder before
these thousands of people, fell back and allowed
the torrent to pass. On the following day, the
orders and remonstrances of the Prefect arrived to
reassure the police, and to enjoin a more severe
vigilance. The force was augmented; the agents
received a hint that they would be superseded.
Rigour was then redoubled.

Sinister reports, absolutely false, but craftily
spread and readily accepted by the multitude,
spoke of a prison for the delinquents. The real
penalty not sufficing, an attempt was made to
raise in the minds of the believers a kind of terror
through imaginary threats.

By one means or other they succeeded in preventing for several days any open breaches of the decree.

Sometimes sufferers, who had come from afar, unfortunate persons who had been a prey to paralysis, to blindness, or some one of those sad infirmities which medicine abandons, and which God alone has the secret of healing, went to the Mayor, and supplicated him with their clasped hands to permit them to go and seek a last chance of cure at the miraculous Fountain. The Mayor, —obstinate with his Prefectorial countersign, and showing, in the execution of measures now taken, that energy in detail by which feeble characters deceive themselves—the Mayor refused, in the name of the superior authority, the permission demanded. Exhibiting cruelty without excuse, he made a legal process against sick people.

The greater part of the people then went on the right bank of the Gave, fronting the Grotto. There was there, on certain days, a countless multitude over whom there was no hold; for the land they trod upon belonged to private individuals, who thought they would draw on themselves the benediction of heaven by authorizing the pilgrims to come and kneel on their meadows, and to pray on them, with their eyes turned towards the place of the Apparitions and the Fountain of the miracles.

During this prodigious concourse, young Bernadette, exhausted by her asthma, fatigued without doubt also by so many visitors, who wanted to see and hear her, fell ill.

In his strong desire to calm the minds of

people, and to remove all cause of agitation, Monseigneur profited by this circumstance to advise
the parents to send Bernadette to the waters of
Cauterets, which are in the neighbourhood of
Lourdes. It was an expedient to withdraw the
Visionary from those dialogues, enquiries, and
narratives of the Apparition, of which all the
world was to hear an account, and which kept
up the popular emotion. The Soubirons, uneasy
at the state of Bernadette, and finding, on their
part, that these perpetual visits were. wearing her out, confided her to an aunt, who was
going herself to Cauterets, and who took on herself the cost of the little expenses of their journey,
which besides did not amount to very much at
this period of the year, at which the springs were
still almost deserted.

The privileged classes and the rich only came a
little later, and there were few at Cauterets during
the month of June, save some poor people from
the Montagne. Unwell, seeking for silence and
repose, striving to get out of the way as much as
possible from public curiosity, Bernadette took
the waters there for two or three weeks.

IV.

In proportion as June was drawing near to its
close, the great period for the waters of the Pyre-.
nees was commencing. Bernadette had returned
home to her parents at Lourdes. From all quarters of Europe there came to the mineral station,
bathers, tourists, curiosity seers, travellers, ex-

plorers, and savans. These severe mountains,
solitary and wild during all the rest of the year,
were by degrees peopled with a world, generally
belonging to the high society in the great cities.
At the close of July the Pyrenees are a faubourg
of Paris, London, Rome, and Berlin. French and
foreigners meet each other at the refreshment
rooms, elbow each other in the saloons, walk on
the promenades, ride up and down on all sides,
on the borders of the gushing Gave, on the abrupt
ridges, or on the flowery carpet of the shady
valleys. Ministers of State, fatigued by their
labours, deputies and senators worn out with
making or hearing speeches, bankers, diploma-
tists, commercial men, ecclesiastics, magistrates,
writers, and men of the world, came for the purpose of recruiting their health, not only from
these illustrious sources, but also, and above all
perhaps, from the fresh and pure atmosphere of
the mountains, which gives to the blood a more
powerful activity, and to the mind greater alert-
ness and elasticity.

This society, so varied, this cosmopolite world,
essentially undulatory and varying, represented all
the beliefs and unbeliefs, all the grave and frivolous philosophies, all opinions and systems. It
was a microcosm; it was an abridgment and
summary of Europe;—Europe, which, by the
natural consequence of things and at the hour
that was appointed, Providence placed in presence of supernatural events and miracles which
were accomplished at the gate of the Pyrenees.
God followed out His eternal designs. The same,
as heretofore at Bethlehem, He showed Himself to

20

the shepherds before He showed Himself to the
Magi Kings; the same at Lourdes, He had at
first called the humble and the little, the mountaineers and the poor, and it was only after these
that He convoked the rich and brilliant world, the
sovereigns of fortune, of intelligence and art, to
the spectacle of His works.

From Cauterets, from Barèges, from Luz, from
Saint-Sauveur, from the Eaux-Bonnes, from Bag-
nères-de-Bigorre, strangers were resorting to
Lourdes. The town was furrowed by dashing
equipages, drawn, as is the custom of these countries, by four strong horses, harnessed and set off
with showy colours and tinkling little bells.

The greater part of the pilgrims, or the travellers, took care to respect the order forbidding entrance on the sacred precincts. There were persons who braved all legal proceedings and went to
the Grotto—some through a feeling of religious
faith, others by a strong sense of curiosity. Bernadette had innumerable visits. People wished to see,
and they saw those who were cured. In all the
saloons of the mineral waters, the events which we
have described were the object of every conversation. By degrees public opinion became formed,
no longer the opinion of this corner of the earth,
of forty or sixty leagues which is stretched out at
the base of the Pyrenees, from Bayonne as far as
Toulouse, or to Foix, but the opinion of France
and Europe, represented at this moment in the
midst of the mountains by visitors of all classes,
of all ideas, and of all countries.

The violent measures of Baron Massy, as vexa-
tious for the curiosity of some as for the piety of

others, was highly blamed on all sides. Some parties declared them to be illegal, others found them to be inopportune ; all agreed in denouncing them as absolutely powerless to overcome the prodigious movement of which the Grotto and the miraculous Fountain were the centre. The discovery of this evident want of power rendered severe towards the Prefect even those who entertained the same horror for the supernatural, and who, at the commencement, would have willingly applauded his policy. Men in general, above all of the caste of freethinkers, judge acts of power much more by visible results than by philosophical principles. Success is the surest means of being approved. To fail is a double misfortune, for universal blame almost always comes to be added to the public humiliation of want of success. M. the Baron Massy was assailed by this double misfortune.

Illustrious personages passed the limits. On one occasion a stranger was suddenly accosted when about to cross the forbidden grounds and evidently bent upon going to the Rocks of Massabielle.

"No one is permitted to enter here," said the guard.

"You will soon see that," replied quickly the unknown, advancing with a determined air on the communal land, and directing his steps towards the place of the Apparitions.

"Your name, you shall be prosecuted."

"My name is Louis Veuillot," replied the stranger, the well-known editor of the *Univers* Journal in Paris.

The same day, a lady passed the limits, and was found kneeling at the barrier formed by planks that enclosed the Grotto. Through the openings of this palisade she could see the miraculous Fountain, and there she prayed. What did she ask of God? Did her soul turn to the present or the future? Did she pray for herself or for others who were dear to her, and whose destiny was confided to her? Did she implore the benedictions and protection of heaven for an individual or a family? It matters not. This woman had not escaped the vigilant eye of the Prefectorial agent. The Argus leaves M. Veuillot, and runs towards the person on her knees.

"Madame," said he, "no one is permitted to pray here. You are taken in the fact. You will have to answer before the *Juge-de-Paix*. I hereby serve you with a process. Give me your name."

"Willingly," replied the lady. "I am Madame Bruat, Governess to His Highness the Prince Imperial."

The terrible Jacomet entertained the most profound respect for the great, and made no official report on this lady.

Such scenes as these were of frequent occurrence; they alarmed the agents of the Prefect, and probably frightened the Prefect himself. Deplorable was it that the powerful were suffered to violate the order with impunity, whilst severity was exercised towards the weak. They had two, weights and two measures.

V.

The question raised by the supernatural facts, by the Apparitions, true or false, of the Holy Virgin, by the gushing forth of the Fountain, by the miraculous cures, real or disputed, could not nevertheless, in the opinion of all, always remain in suspense. It was necessary that everything should be submitted to a competent and strict examination. Strangers, who were only in these parts for a rapid season, who had not been present at the outset of these extraordinary events, and who could not have been able, like the people of the country, to form a reasoned conviction, were unanimous, in the midst of the various narratives and judgments they heard on all sides, in being astonished at the complete silence and apparent indifference of the ecclesiastical authority. As much as they blamed the intermeddling of the civil power, so much did they condemn the prolonged abstention of the religious power personified in the bishop.

The freethinkers, interpreting at their own will the long hesitation and attitude of the prelate, thought themselves sure of his verdict. The friends of M. Massy began to cry very loud that Monseigneur Laurence was in accord with the Prefect in his judgment of events. They cast upon the Bishop all the responsibility of the violent measures which had been taken. "The Bishop," said they, "might with a word stop the superstition. He had only for this purpose to

pass his high judgment upon it.   The civil authority was only forced to act through his default."

The believers, having before them the evidence
of the miraculous facts, considered themselves as
equally certain of a solemn judgment in favour of
their faith.

Others in great number among the strangers
had no conviction or settled mind, and demanded
to be freed from their uncertainty by a definitive
inquiry.   "Of what service is a religious authority," said they, "if it is not to judge in similar
disputes, and to fix a faith for those who, on
account of distance, or want of documents, or any
other cause, are unable to examine and decide for
themselves ?"

Incessant applications reached the Bishop's
residence, to this purport.   To the murmuring
of the multitudes was united the voices of classes
which are by custom called enlightened, although
often the little lights of the earth may cause them
to lose sight of the Great Luminary of the Heavens.   On all sides an enquiry was demanded.

The supernatural cures continued to be produced.   On a hundred sides were addressed to
the Bishop's Palace authentic testimonials of
these miraculous cures, signed by a great number
of witnesses.

On the sixteenth of July, the Feast of our Lady
of Mount Carmel, Bernadette heard the secret
voice that had been silent within her for some
months, and which called her, no longer to the
Massabielle Rocks, then shut up, but on the right
bank of the Gave, in those meadows where the
crowd was praying, that they might be sheltered

from the legal proceedings and vexations of the police.

It was eight o'clock in the evening. Scarcely had the girl placed herself on her knees, and commenced to recite the Rosary, than the ever-blessed Mother of Jesus Christ appeared to her. The Gave, which separated her from the Grotto, had disappeared to the eyes of the ecstatic. She did not see anything before her but the blessed rock, which seemed to be as equally near to her, as on former occasions. The Immaculate Virgin smiled sweetly upon her, as if to confirm all that had passed, and illuminate the future. No words issued from her heavenly lips. At a particular moment she bowed her head towards the child, as if to say a " very long farewell or a supreme adieu." Then she disappeared, and returned to the heavens. It was the eighteenth Apparition, and the last.

In a sense of an opposite character, strange facts occurred, which it is important to notice. On three or four occasions some children and women pretended to have visions like Bernadette. Were these visions true? Did diabolic mysticism endeavour to mix in the divine mysticism, to cause trouble? Was there simply at the bottom of these singular phenomena a derangement of the mind, or excitement to perverse trickery among some mischievous children? or must we seek for it in some party, hiding himself in a perfidious shade, or certain hostile hands who put forward these visionaries to throw discredit on the miraculous events of the Grotto? We know not.

The multitude, with its thousands of eyes fixed

on every detail, with its intuitions and desires for
a solution, was less reserved than we in its judgments.

The hypothesis that the self-styled visionaries
were set on by the dull manœuvres of the police,
assumed immediately, right or wrong, among the
public who had become very distrustful, a very
serious consistency. The two or three children
who pretended to have apparitions, mixed up with
their story, otherwise very incoherent, all sorts of
extravagance. They scaled one day the barrier of
planks which enclosed the Grotto, and, under the
pretext of offering their services to the pilgrims,
to draw water for them, or to cause their rosaries to
touch the blessed rock, they received and appro-
priated the offerings. A remarkable detail;—
Jacomet, who could have so easily arrested them,
did not disturb them. He affected, sometimes,
not to perceive these strange scenes, these
ecstasies, these infringements of the prohibition,
and sometimes to be out of the way when they
happened. From this surprising behaviour of
the very crafty and shrewd Commissary, each
one had surmised one of those dark villanies, of
which the world too often, perhaps, considers the
members of the police to be capable, as well as
those of the administration. "Monsieur the Baron
Massy," said they, " seeing public opinion going
away from him, and convinced by experience of
the impossibility of arresting events openly by
means of violence, attempts to dishonour them in
their principle by fomenting false visionaries, of
whom he will make a great noise and parade in

the journals and with the government. *He has done what is of advantage.*"

Whatever be the value of these suspicions, which were very probably unjust, such scenes were calculated to trouble the minds of men. M. the Curé of Lourdes, moved at such scandal, hastened to drive disgracefully away from the catechism the pretended visionary children, at the same time declaring, that if similar acts were repeated again, he would know how himself to make a severe enquiry, and discover the true originators of them.

The attitude and threat of the Curé produced a sudden and radical impression. The pretended visions entirely ceased, and there was no longer any question about them. They only lasted four or five days.

The Abbé Peramale informed the Bishop's court of this incident. As to M. Jacomet, he addressed, on his side, to the competent authorities, an hyperbolical and romantic report, of which we shall have occasion later to speak.

This audacious effort of the evil and hostile spirit, endeavouring to pervert and dishonour the movement, operated as an addition to all the peremptory reasons which urged the Bishop to act. Everything combined to show that the moment for interfering was come, and that the religious authority were in arrears for examining and deciding the case.

Men who were distinguished in the Christian world, such as Monseigneur de Salinis, Archbishop of Auch ; Monseigneur Thibaud, Bishop of Montpellier ; Monseigneur de Garsignies, Bishop of Soissons ; M. Louis Veuillot, chief editor of the

Univers; other personages less known, but o great respectability, Monsieur de·Ressegnier, formerly a deputy; M. Vène, Engineer in chief for the mines, Inspector-general of the mineral waters of the Pyrenees, and a great number of eminent Catholics, were at that time in that country. All had studied the extraordinary facts which form the subject of this history; all had seen and examined Bernadette; all had believed, or were disposed to do so. A Bishop is cited, one of the most venerated of men, who was unable to contain his emotion at the narrative so striking, so simple, and shining with truth, of the young girl who had beheld the vision. In contemplating this little child, on the forehead of whom the unspeakable Mother of God had fixed her looks, the prelate did not know how to resist the first emotion of his feelings which were so deeply affected. He, a prince of the Church, cast himself down before the majesty of that humble peasant.

"Pray for me, bless me, me and my flock," said he, with a voice that was smothered, tottering when he bent his knees.

"Rise up, Monseigneur! It is for you to bless this child," exclaimed the Curé of Lourdes, who was present at this scene, and took the Bishop quickly by the hand to help him to stand up again.

However rough and rapid may have been the act of the priest, Bernadette had already anticipated him; and, quite confused at his humility, she bent down her head under the hand of the prelate. The Bishop blessed her, not without shedding tears.

VI.

The total effect of these events, the testimony of so many persons of weight, the spectacle of their conviction after an examination, were calculated to produce a powerful impression on the clear and sagacious mind of the Bishop of Tarbes. Monseigneur Laurence judged that the hour was come to speak, and he gave over at length being silent. On the 28th of July, he published the following pastoral decree, which was immediately published throughout the diocese, and which caused an immense emotion ; for every one understood that the extraordinary state of things with which their minds had been for so long a time taken up, was now on the way at last to a solution.

" ORDINANCE OF MONSEIGNEUR THE BISHOP OF TARBES, CONSTITUTING A COMMISSION CHARGED WITH INVESTIGATING INTO THE AUTHENTICITY AND NATURE OF THE FACTS THAT HAVE OCCURRED DURING ABOUT SIX MONTHS, ON THE OCCASION OF AN APPARITION, TRUE OR PRETENDED, OF THE MOST HOLY VIRGIN IN THE GROTTO, SITUATED ON THE WEST OF THE TOWN OF LOURDES.

" Bertrand - Sévére - Laurence, by the Divine Mercy and the favour of the Holy Apostolic See, Bishop of Tarbes.

" To the Clergy and the Faithful of our Diocese, Health and Benediction in our Lord Jesus Christ.

" Facts of a serious gravity connected with

religion, which greatly move the diocese and are
heard from afar, have taken place at Lourdes since
the 11th of last February.

" It is said that Bernadette Soubirous, a young
girl of Lourdes, aged fourteen years, has had
visions in the Grotto of Massabielle, situated on
the West of that town; that the Immaculate Virgin
has appeared to her, and that a Fountain has risen
up there.   That the waters of this fountain, when
used for draught or for lotions, has worked a great
number of cures; that these cures are reputed to
be miraculous.   That crowds of people have come,
and are still coming, whether from our diocese, or
the neighbouring dioceses, to ask at that water the
cure of their different maladies, through the invo-
cation of the Immaculate Virgin.

" The civil authority is in motion at it.

" On all sides, and since the month of March
last, the Ecclesiastical Authority has been called
upon for an explanation of this unexpected pilgrimage.

" We at first considered that the hour was not
come to occupy ourselves to any useful purpose
with this affair; that, to sit on the judgment
which was looked for from us, it was necessary to
proceed with a wise deliberation and caution, to
distrust the impulse of its earliest stages, to allow
minds to calm, to give time for reflection, and
seek for lights from an attentive and enlightened
observation.

" Three classes of persons are appealing to our
decision, but with different views.   They are first
those, who, refusing all examen, see nothing in
the facts of the Grotto, and the cures attributed to

the water of the Fountain, but imposture, jugglery, and a means of making dupes. It is evident that we cannot be of their opinion, *a priori*, and without a serious examen ; their journals have exclaimed from the first, and very loudly, that it was superstition, imposture, bad faith ; they have affirmed that the facts of the Grotto have had their causes for existence in a sordid interest, culpable cupidity, and have thus wounded the moral sense of our Christian populations. That the party which denies everything, and accuses motives and intentions, is the easiest to adopt for cutting through difficulties, we admit ; but, besides its being dishonest, it is unreasonable, and more adapted to irritate than to convince them. To deny the possibility of supernatural facts, is to follow a superannuated school, it is to abjure the Christian religion, and to have oneself dragged along the track of the incredulous philosophy of the last century. We cannot, as Catholics, take counsel in such circumstances, among persons who deny to God the power of making exceptions to the general laws which He has established to govern the world, the work of His hands, nor enter into discussion with them in order to arrive at the knowledge if such or such a fact is supernatural, when it is understood, beforehand, that they proclaim the supernatural to be impossible. Is it that we repel, upon the facts of which there is question, a discussion which is frank, sincere, conscientious, and enlightened by science and its progress? No, certainly, we appeal to it, on the contrary, with all our hearts. We desire that these facts should be first of all submitted to the severe rules of

certainty,. which a sound philosophy admits ; that
next, in order to decide if these facts be supernatural and divine, there be summoned to the discussion of these grave and difficult questions,
special men who are versed in the sciences of
mystic theology, medicine, physics, chemistry,
geology, &c., &c.   In fine, that. science should
be heard, and that she should pronounce.   We
desire, above all things, that, to arrive at truth,
no means shall be omitted.

" There is another class of persons, who neither
approve nor blame the facts which are stated, but
who suspend their judgment ; before pronouncing,
they desire to know the decision of competent
Authority, and solicit it most earnestly.

" There is, in · fine, a third class which is the
most numerous, and which has already formed,
though premature, convictions, on the facts before
our attention. It awaits with a lively impatience for
the bishop of the diocese to pronounce in the first
resort on this grave affair.   Although it expects
on our part a decision favourable to its pious sentiments, we know enough of its submission to the
Church, to be assured that it will receive our judgment, whatever it may be, when it shall be
known.

" It is then to enlighten the religion and the
piety of so many thousands of the faithful, to
satisfy a public want, to fix uncertainties, and to
tranquillize minds, that we yield this day to the
applications that have been repeatedly made for
a long time on all sides ; we appeal for light ·
upon facts which interest in the highest degree a
faithful devotion to Mary, to religion itself.   We

have resolved for this end, to institute in the diocese a permanent commission to collect and ascertain the facts which have occurred, or which may still take place in the Grotto of Lourdes, or through occasion of it; to signalize them to us, to make us acquainted with their character, and to furnish us also with the elements indispensable for arriving at length at a solution.

"For these causes,

"The Holy Name of God being invoked,
"We have ordered and do order as follows :—
Art. I. A Commission is instituted in the Diocese of Tarbes, for the purpose of enquiring:

"1. If cures have been worked by the use of the water of the Grotto of Lourdes, whether by drinking or by lotions, and if these cures could be explained in a natural manner, or if they should be attributed to a Supernatural cause.

"2. If the visions which the girl Bernadette Soubirous pretends to have had in the Grotto are real, and in this case, if they can be explained in a natural manner, or if they reveal a supernatural and divine character.

"3. If the object that appeared has made any requests, manifested intentions to the child. If she has been charged to communicate them; if so, to whom? and what might be the requests or intentions manifested?

"4. If the Fountain which flows this day in the Grotto existed before the Vision which Bernadette Soubirous pretends to have had.

" Art. II. The Commission will only present to us facts established upon solid proofs ; it will present to us upon these facts circumstantial reports containing their opinion.

" Art. III. Messieurs the Deans of the Diocese will be the principal correspondents of the Commission.   They are requested to bring under its notice :

    " 1. The facts that shall be brought forward in their respective Deaneries ;

    " 2. The persons who might be able to give evidence of these facts ;

    " 3. The physicians who shall have had the care of the sick before their cure.

" Art. IV. After taking informations, the Commission will proceed to enquiries.   The evidence shall be received under the faith of an oath. When the inquiries shall be made in the localities two members at least of the Commission shall attend there.

" Art. V. We earnestly recommend to the Commission to summon frequently amongst them men versed in the sciences of medicine, physics, chymistry, geology, &c., in order to hear them discuss the difficulties that might arise before them on certain points of view, and to know their opinion. The Commission should neglect nothing to surround themselves with lights, and to arrive at the truth, whatever it may be.

 " Art. VI. The Commission is composed of nine members of our Cathedral Chapter, the Superiors of our Great and Little Seminaries, of the Superior of the missionaries of the Diocese, of the Curé of Lourdes, and the Professors of Dogmatic and Moral Theology, and of Physics, belonging to our Seminary. The Professor of Chymistry belonging to the Little Seminary shall be often consulted.

"Art. VII. M. Nogaro, Canon-Archpriest, is named President of the Commission. Messieurs the Canons Tabariès and Soulé are named Vice-Presidents. The Commission will name a Secretary and two Vice-Secretaries among themselves.

"Art. VIII. The Commission will commence its labours immediately, and will meet as often as it shall judge necessary.

"Given at Tarbes, in our Episcopal Palace, under our signature, our seal, and the counter-signature of our Secretary, the 28th July, 1858.

"✠ BERTRAND S.
"BISHOP OF TARBES.
"By order,
"FOURCADE, *Canon-Secretary.*"

Monseigneur had scarcely issued this ordinance when a letter from Monsieur Rouland, Minister of Worship, reached the Bishop's Palace. His Excellency conjured his Lordship to interpose and stop the movement.

VIII.

Whether the police or the Administration had fomented the false visionaries, or they were the innocent victims of universal suspicion, it is impossible to know in a manner beyond doubt; and it is a fact which it would be still more impossible

21

to establish by regular documents. In similar cases, when there are proofs, they are almost always destroyed by interested parties. There remains then, for the attainment of truth, nothing but the general physiognomy of the events, and the unanimous feeling of the contemporary public, a feeling sometimes assuredly very just, but often also impressed with passion, and often infected with error. In the presence of these incomplete elements, of this shadow mixed with light, and this light mixed with shadow, the historian has only to relate facts that are authentic and proved, and to express his doubts and scruples as to the rest, and leave the reader to cut the knot and settle the question in the most probable way.

Therefore, whatever was the cause or the unknown hand which urged two or three low street boys to play the visionaries, M. Jacomet, M. Massy, and their friends, were eager to exaggerate before everybody, and to parade in a blustering manner these boyish tricks. They endeavoured to draw off in this direction the attention of the multitudes, and to turn it aside from grave events, such as the divine ecstasies of Bernadette, the gushing forth of the Fountain, the cure of the sick, which had captivated the popular faith. When a battle is lost on one point, great strategists endeavour by some feigned demonstration to draw the enemy over ground full of snares and mined beforehand. This is what is called causing a diversion.

The hasty disappearance of the false visions and false visionaries before the watchful attention and the clear-sighted menaces of the Abbé Peyramale, baffled from the first the hopes conceived by the profound tactics of the free-thinkers.

The good sense of the public continued firm on the true platform of the question, and never allowed itself to be deceived. It was not so with the high judgment and reason of Monsieur the Minister Rouland. The following statement will show how it happened that this strong mind was led astray.

Attempting in opposition to the triumphant and irresistible force of things a desperate effort, employing the last resources of their genius to cause to issue at all cost and sacrifice out of these smallest incidents, a supreme chance of escaping a defeat, and resuming the offensive, Messieurs Jacomet and Massy had presented to the Minister of Worship the most hyperbolical and fantastic picture of these childish scenes.

By an illusion scarcely credible on the part of a Minister of State, M. Rouland suffered himself to be led away blindly, and at once, by these official reports. The Rouland philosophy had no faith in Notre-Dame de Lourdes, but he had faith in Jacomet and Massy. These two gentlemen induced him to believe that, under the Rocks of Massabielle, children had come to play at the office of priests, and persons of ill repute, crowned them with laurels or flowers, who represented the people and formed a congregation of mock worshippers, &c. They did not conceal from the minister their own impotence, notwithstanding the violent measures they had adopted—according to them the material force was vanquished and civil authority at its last gasp—and ex-

plained to him that the only mode of solving
the difficulty was through the intervention of the
Bishop. This was in entire accord with the
views of his Excellency; for to interfere in religious questions, and to allow himself the desire to
trace out a programme for the Bishop, was, in
point of fact, the well-known tendency of M. Rouland. The Minister, although he had formerly
been Procureur General, did not pause to enquire
how it came to pass that the Magistrates at
Lourdes had not taken measures to have the
actors in these profanations brought before their
tribunal. So strange a non-interference of the
magistrates in presence of such pretended disorders, did not awaken any distrust in his mind.
Accepting then with unministerial frankness the
romantic stories of the police and the Prefect,
imagining that he saw the matter clearly, and
believing himself to be a high theologian, rather
more so than an archbishop, because he was
Minister of Worship, M. Rouland, sitting in his
cabinet, took an off-hand view of the situation,
and wrote a letter to Mgr. Laurence, worthy of
being classed with that which he had originally
addressed to the Prefect, and which we have
already cited. It was even impregnated with
official piety. Reading this in the light of a true
history, one cannot forbear a smile, while observing
how Ministers of State are sometimes grossly
deceived, we might almost say impudently
mocked and laughed at, by the inferior agents of
their administration. It is with a melancholy yet
ironical spirit that one contemplates the following
letter, written by the very same Minister who

some time later signed the authoritative order to raise a noble church on the Rocks of Massabielle, to the eternal memory of the Blessed Virgin Mary.

"Monseigneur," writes M. Rouland, "The accounts I have recently received of the occurrences at Lourdes, appear to me to be of a nature highly calculated to afflict all persons imbued with the sentiments of religion. The mock blessings of rosaries by children, the conspicuous appearance of women of bad repute, the crowning of visionaries, and the grotesque ceremonies that parody religion, cannot fail to give a handle for attacks on the part of the Protestant press, and other publications, unless the central authority quickly endeavours to interfere. These scandalous scenes do not less throw discredit on religion in the eyes of the populations, and I believe it to be my duty, Monseigneur, to call your most serious attention again to these facts. Such deplorable manifestations appear to me sufficient to induce the clergy to abandon the reserve they have maintained up to the present moment. I cannot therefore do otherwise than make a pressing appeal to your Lordship's prudence and firmness, and *hope you may consider this a fitting occasion for the public reprobation of such profanation.*

"I remain, &c.

"The Minister of Instruction and

"Public Worship,

"ROULAND."

This missive arrived precisely at the time when Mgr. Laurence had issued the order, of which the reader is aware, to constitute a Commission of Inquiry into the extraordinary events that the All-Powerful Hand of God had created.

The following is the Bishop's reply.

"Monsieur le Ministre,

"Great has been my astonishment in reading your dispatch. I also have been informed as to what has happened at Lourdes; I also as Bishop am highly interested in reproving all that is of a nature calculated to injure religion, and afflict the faithful. I can assure you that the scenes of which you write, are not such as have been described to you. And if there have existed some things to be regretted, they were of so passing a nature that no traces of them now remain.

"The facts to which your Excellency alludes have occurred since the closing of the Grotto on the first week in July. Two or three children of Lourdes pretended to play the visionary, and made extravagant exhibitions in the streets. The Grotto having been at that time closed, as I have said, they found means of introducing themselves, and of offering their services to persons outside at the barricades, to cause their chaplets to touch the Grotto, and receive their offerings in order to appropriate them. One of these children, who made himself remarkable by his eccentricities, had been attached to the service of the church at Lourdes, as chorister. The Curé severely reprimanded him, drove him from the catechism, and excluded him from serving in the church. This disorder has been merely ephemeral in its character, and the public see in it simply a child's frolic, that a few menaces soon put a stop to. Such are the facts that certain *over zealous* persons have travestied in their reports, as being scenes of continual recurrence.

"I should be glad, Monsieur the Minister, if you would ascertain from the many honourable persons who have visited the town of Lourdes, for the purpose of seeing themselves the places, and of obtaining evidence of the facts, from the inhabitants, and from the girl to whom the Vision is said to have appeared—their sentiments regarding the recent occurrences at Lourdes. Such for instance as Monseigneurs the Bishops of Montpellier and Soissons, the Archbishop of Auch, M. Vène, inspector of mineral baths, Madame Bruat, M. Louis Veuillot, &c.

"The clergy, Monsieur the Minister, have not maintained up to the present moment a complete reserve as regards the events at the Grotto. The clergy of the town have acted with prudence in abstaining from appearing at the Grotto, thereby not accrediting the pilgrimage, but, on the contrary, sustaining the measures taken by the authorities. Yet it has been pointed out to you that they have connived at superstition. I do not accuse the First Magistrate of the Department, whose intentions have always been upright, but he has displayed in this affair an exclusive confidence in his own subordinates.

"By my letter, in reply to the Prefect, dated 11th of April last, a letter that has been placed before you, I offered my honest assistance to that magistrate, in order to bring the matter to a happy termination. But it was not in my power to act as he wished, and from the Episcopal chair to brand without examination, without inquiry, and without any avowed reason, those persons who went to pray at the Grotto, and to forbid their approach to it, more especially as no disorders whatever had been pointed out, although on certain days the visitors might be counted by thousands. The Church always gives a reason when she forbids anything; besides, I was not sufficiently informed, and felt sure, that at the moment of excitement, my voice would not have been attended to.

"The Prefect having been in council on the occasion of the revision at Lourdes, on the 4th of May, issued an order that the Commissary of Police at that place, should carry off the objects and religious emblems then in the Grotto, and, in an address to the Mayor of the Canton, said, that he had taken this measure in accordance with the wishes of the Bishop of the Diocese, an assertion that was repeated, some days later, by the journal of the Prefecture. I was informed of this measure by the journals, and by the Parish Priest of Lourdes, and hastened to write to the latter, desiring him to respect the orders of the Prefect. I did not complain, either then or since, of having been represented as connected with a measure of which I was ignorant. And although I have received numerous letters urging me to investigate the circumstances, yet I have abstained, up to the last moment, not wishing to add to the embarrassment of the situation.

"The religious objects having been carried off from the Grotto, we had hoped that these visits would diminish by degrees, and that the pilgrimage which had so unexpectedly and suddenly started up, would have been brought to an end. However, it has not been so. The public assumes, whether rightly or wrongly, that the water running in the Grotto operates in a miraculous manner. The concourse is increasing, and crowds are concentrating from the neighbouring departments.

"On the 8th of June the Mayor of Lourdes issued an order forbidding all access to the Grotto. Giving for his reasons that the measure was adopted in the interests of religion, and of the public health. Religion was put in the foreground, yet the Bishop had not been consulted. I made no complaint, but preserved a strict silence, for the reasons above given.

"You see, Monsieur le Ministre, from some of these details, that the reserve of the clergy has not been complete in this case. It has only been, in my opinion, prudent. Whenever I could, I lent my aid to the measures taken by the civil authorities; if they have not always been successful the Bishop is not to blame.

"Lately, yielding to the pressure that has been put upon me on all sides, I have considered that the time had arrived when I could act usefully in this affair. I have nominated a Commission, charging it to search for and collect all the evidence it can procure, in order to form a decision touching the question, which, considering all that has been brought before me, appears to concern,

not this neighbourhood only, but France itself.
I feel confident that the faithful will receive the
decision with submission, because they know that
I shall omit nothing that may be necessary in
order to arrive at the truth. This Commission
has been at work some days. I have determined
to publish my order by means of the press, with
the hope that it will contribute to cause tranquillity to exist in minds while they are waiting in
expectation till the decision becomes known, and
I shall have the honour of sending your Excellency, in a short time, a copy of their proceedings.
"I am, &c.,
"B. S., BISHOP OF TARBES."

Such was the letter of Mgr. Laurence to M.
Rouland. It was clear and conclusive, and he
had nothing to reply. The Minister of Worship
did not reply.

At the same time that these letters were passing, M. Filhol, the celebrated chemist, of the
Faculty of Toulouse, gave in his definite verdict
on the waters of the Grotto of Lourdes. This
great chemist, by his conscientious and very complete labours, reduced to nothing the official
analysis of M. Latour de Trie, of which M. Massy
had made such a parade.

"The undersigned Professor of Chemistry,"
&c., &c., writes M. Filhol, in transmitting to the
Mayor of Lourdes his analysis, adds as follows:
"The undersigned, &c. certifies that the above
water is from a spring in the environs of Lourdes,"
situated so and so. "The result of this analysis

shows that the water of the Grotto of Lourdes is potable in its character, analogous to the greater part of those found in the mountains where the soil is rich in calcareous matter.

"*The extraordinary effects which, we are assured, have been obtained from the use of this water, could not, according to the present state of science, be explained as owing to the salts found in its composition. This water contains no active ingredient capable of giving to it distinct medicinal properties.* It may be drunk without inconvenience.

"Signed,

"FILHOL.

"Toulouse, 7th August, 1858."

Thus, under the examination of that celebrated chemist, the hopes of the free thinking party vanished. Science had proved that the water of the Grotto possessed no mineral or curative properties. So that the audacious exponents of these fictitious examinations were caught in their own net.

EIGHTH BOOK.

I.

The order of the Bishop constituting a commission of enquiry, and the analysis of M. Filhol, took away from Baron Massy, M. Rouland, and M. Jacomet, all pretext for maintaining at the Grotto their rigorous prohibitions, the barriers and the Guards.

To justify the interdict of the communal land, it was said, "Considering that it is of importance, *in the interest of religion,* to put an end to painful scenes that have occurred at the Grotto of Massabielle." Now, in declaring things sufficiently grave for interfering, and taking in hand an enquiry into all that was important "to the interest of religion," the Bishop disarmed the civil power of a motive so loudly invoked.

To justify the interdict for going to drink at the Fountain that sprang forth under the hands of Bernadette in an ecstasy, it had been said, "Considering that the duty of the mayor is to watch over the public health; considering that there are serious reasons for thinking that this water contains mineral principles, and that it is prudent, before permitting its use, to wait until a scientific analysis has caused to be known the applications to which it can be put by medicine." Now, in declaring that the water has no mineral principle, and in establishing that it might be drunk without inconvenience, M. Filhol annihilated, in the name of science and medicine, the pretended reason of "public health."

Therefore, if these motives had been alleged in a spirit of sincerity, and not under specious pretexts; if it had acted "in the interest of religion and of public health," and not under the influence of evil passions and intolerance; if, in a word, it had been candid, and not hypocritical, the civil power would have had but to recall all its orders, its barriers, and prohibitions; it would have had but to leave the people free to drink at that Fountain, the perfect innocence of which was proclaimed by science; it would have had but to acknowledge their right to go and kneel at the foot of those mysterious rocks, where hereafter the Church would watch. It was not so.

There was an obstacle to this solution, so clearly indicated by the forces of logic and conscience—pride. Pride reigned from the bottom to the top of the ladder, from Jacomet to Rouland, including Baron Massy and all their philosophical sect. It seemed hard to them to have to give way and surrender their arms. Pride never submits. It prefers rather boldly to intrench itself in what is illogical, than to bend to the authority of reason. Furious, out of itself, absurd, it lifts itself up against evidence. It says, "I will not serve," as Satan in the Scripture. It resists, it refuses to fold itself up, it becomes stiff, until all at once a blow comes upon it and crushes it with violence, not without disdain.

II.

One resource, however, remained for the enemies
of superstition, one supreme effort more to attempt
in the struggle. If the battle seemed to be irre-
trievably lost in the Pyrenees, they might, perhaps,
reconquer the position at Paris, and seize hold of
public opinion, in France and in Europe, before
the cosmopolite band of tourists and bathers, on
returning to their firesides, should have spread
everywhere its offensive impressions and severe
judgments. The effort was made. A formidable
campaign was organized by the irreligious press of
Paris, in the provinces, and in foreign countries,
in opposition to the events of Lourdes and the order
of the Bishop.

Le Siecle, la Presse, l'Indépendance Belge, and
many foreign publications, with several smaller
provincial journals, rushed at once to the
rescue, and ranged themselves against the supernatural. Several lengthy quotations are given by
the author from these prints, redundant in falsehood.

Some, as *La Presse,* from the pen of Monsieur
Guéroult, or *Le Siecle,* from that of Messieurs
Bénard and Jourdan, attacked the miracle on principle, declaring that its day had passed, that
discussion upon it was out of the question, and on
a subject already judged *a priori* by the lights of
philosophy, any examination was beneath the
dignity of free enquiry. "The miracle," said M.
Guéroult, "belonged to a series of civilization that
is in course of disappearing. If God changes not,

the idea that men form of Him changes, from period to period, according to the degree of their moral feeling and light. Ignorant people, who do not suspect the important harmony of the laws of the universe, see everywhere the overthrow of those laws. Every day, God appears to them, speaks to them, converses with them, sends them His angels. In proportion as society becomes enlightened, as men are more instructed, as experimental sciences arise to form a counterpoise to the flights of the imagination, all this mythology vanishes. Man is not less religious; he is more so; he is so otherwise. He no longer sees face to face gods and goddesses, angels or devils. He seeks to decipher the Divine will written in the laws of the world. The miracle, which at certain epochs, may have been the condition of faith, and served to contain certain truths, has become, in our days, a bugbear to every one holding serious convictions."*

M. Gueroult declared that if he was informed that a supernatural fact, were it one of a very remarkable kind, was accomplished, at that very hour, by his side close to him, in la Place de la Concorde, "he would not turn out of his way to go and see it. If such events," added he, "could take place for a moment among the superstitious baggage of the ignorant masses, they provoked among enlightened men, among those whose opinion becomes, with time, that of the whole world, nothing but the repulse of defiance and the smile of scorn."†

* "La Presse," 31st August, 1858.   † Ibid.

As to the miraculous cures, they got rid of them by a single word. "The Hydropathists also pretend to effect the most brilliant cures by means of pure water, but they have not as yet cried out, on the tops of houses, that they worked any miracles."*

But the most curious specimen of good faith of free thought, or its sagacity for enquiring into the matter, may be found in the Dutch journal, which was called *Amsterdaamsche Courant.* "A new manifestation, destined to awaken and to feed the ardour of believers in the worship of the Holy Virgin, is now impending. The deliberation of the bishops, on this point, has had for its object the invention of the famous miracle of Lourdes. We know that the Bishop of Tarbes has issued a commission of enquiry, composed of ecclesiastics, and persons in the pay of the clergy, of course tending to the confirmation. *The pretended shepherdess, Bernadette, is not a simple peasant, but a young bourgeoise, very clever and highly cultivated, having passed several months in a convent of cloistered nuns, where she has been taught the rôle, that she now performs.* There, before a small number of compeers, representations by way of rehearsal, were held, long before appearing on the public stage. As we may see it, nothing was wanting for this comedy, not even the rehearsals. If some day there is a want of dramatists at Paris, we shall be able to find in the higher order of the clergy persons who will be able to fill up this gap to perfection. For the rest, the liberal press has quite

* The Siecle.

ridiculed the whole affair, and it is not impossible but that the clergy, in their own interest, may recognize the necessity of prudence."

Apart from the events themselves, the force of this attack was centered against the order of the Bishop of Tarbes. Philosophy, accordingly, in the name of its dogmatic infallibility, was indignant at the notion of an examination. "When any one connected with the Academy of Science, seized by hallucination, suggests that he has discovered perpetual motion, or the quadrature of the circle, the academy passes to the order of the day without loss of time, controlling such lucubrations. The same thing should be done with regard to miracles, in the name of reason and philosophy, let the same order be given. To examine supernatural facts, would be to admit their possibility, and to deny their own principles. In such cases, proofs and witnesses go for nothing. No one dreams of discussing impossibilities, they merely shrug their shoulders, and there is an end to it."

The irritated polemics of the irreligious press harped upon this theme, in a thousand different ways, vainly endeavouring to deny, or misrepresent, but fearing to examine. False theory lulled itself into fancied security, by remaining in the midst of the mists and troubled waters of pure speculation. Their actions betrayed their fear of light, and they felt that a defeat awaited them.

In this struggle against the evidence of facts, and common sense, the thin film of liberalism, with which the *Journal des Debats* covered its intolerance, dissolved away, exhibiting the furious bigotry which it had hitherto concealed, under the parade of philosophy. This journal, in an article by M. Prévost Paradol, made an appeal to the secular arm, and conjured Cæsar to crush the whole proceeding.

"We have conclusively established," continues the writer in the *Debats*, "the importance that should be attached, in various points of view, to the decision of the episcopal commission of Tarbes. Now, we shall here recall to mind that which M. de Morny, with great justice, laid before the *conseil général* of the Puy-de-Dôme, namely, that nothing of importance can be done in France without the previous sanction of the administration. If one cannot, as M. de Morny has well said, remove a stone, or sink a well, without the permission of the administration, all the more reason is there that its consent should be obtained to found a Church, or establish a miracle. Whoever is conversant in religious matters, and particularly as regards the opening of churches, or communal schools, knows perfectly well that the administrative authority has not only one means, but twenty or thirty, of giving the fullest powers in such matters. The meeting of the Commission in the diocese of Tarbes, can be anticipated, prevented, or dissolved, in a hundred ways, by the Concordat, by the Penal Code, by the law of 1834, by the decree of February 1852, by the central authority, by the municipal authority, and by *all imaginable authorities*. And further, the decision of this Commission once taken can be annulled, by legal prohibition, which would place a bar against the erection of a chapel, and would withdraw any license to use this so-called marvellous water.

The same authority can interdict, and disperse all assemblages, and prosecute the authors," &c., &c.

Having thus warned Cæsar, and cried aloud, *caveant consules*, (let the consuls beware), this astute writer assuming the mantle of liberalism, enquires, " whither would you lead us, in thus insisting on the preventive right of the administration? Is it to exhort us to make use of it? God forbid." And in this way he retreats by a side door, and joins the ranks of the friends of liberty.

The journals of the departments echoed the tone of the Parisian publications. But, on the other hand, the *Univers*, the *Union*, and other journals, well sustained the Catholic side. Powerful talents were brought to bear in the service of truth. The Christian press established the validity of the history, and dissipated the miserable arguments of philosophic fanaticism.

In the presence of unexplained facts, to which the faith or the credulity of the multitude attributes a supernatural character, "The civil authority," said M. Louis Veuillot, "has endeavoured to cut the question short, without seeking information, but also without success. The spiritual authority intervened in its turn, as was its right and duty. Before judging, it made diligent enquiry, and instituted a Commission to search into the facts, study, and determine their character. If they turn out to be true, the Commission will say so. If they are false, or of a natural character, it will say the same. What more can our opponents desire? would they have the Bishop abstain altogether, at the risk of disregarding a grace, which peradventure God has deigned to accord to his diocese, or, on the other hand, permit a superstition to take root ?

" The bishop, on the other hand, has observed upon the singular faith so strongly fixed in the minds of the whole people, on the word of a little indigent and uneducated girl. And it was due to himself to enquire into the cause of these cures, which are said to have been effected by means of a few drops of *pure* water, employed sometimes as a lotion, sometimes as a beverage. And if there has been no cure, we must know why people believe there has been any. Now, if the water be pure, its effect cannot be medicinal ; if it be a mineral water, it would be well to enquire how it came to pass that Bernadette, who is not a chemist, discovered it ; and, instead of shutting her up in an hospital for lunatics, it would only be simple justice to give her a recompense, for she has discovered a treasure. Again, if cures have actually taken place, it will be necessary to investigate the circumstances. And now let us suppose that the water is pure, as the chemists affirm, and that, nevertheless, the cures are certain, as is reported at present by many persons cured of their maladies, and by physicians themselves ; we have, then, no further difficulty in recognizing the supernatural and the miraculous, unless, be it well understood, we are prepared to accept the explanations of the *Siecle.*"

Thus did this vigorous polemic confront all his opponents at once. With one stroke of his pen he could easily overturn this absurd determination to deny the miracle, and to refuse examination to striking facts which a multitude beheld with their eyes, and acclaimed by falling on their knees.

"If M. Gueroult was told, that in the name of Christ a great miracle was accomplished on the place de la Concorde, he would not go and see it. He would do well, since he holds he must be incredulous; before such a spectacle he would be sure of finding a physical explanation to dispense him from going to confession. But it would be better still to see and believe, submitting to the testimony which God, in His mercy, would be willing thus to give him. At all events, he must understand that the crowd would care very little for his absence, would give itself very little trouble to hear him declare that they had seen one of the most natural things in the world, and that the crowd was altogether simply under an hallucination. Things might happen at Paris as at Lourdes. Men would cry out, a Miracle, and if it was, in fact, a Miracle, the Miracle would produce its effect, that is to say, that many men who had not hitherto *sought to decypher the Divine will,* or who had not succeeded in doing so, would know it and put it into practice; they would love God with all their heart, with all their soul, with all their mind, and their neighbour as themselves. Such is the object which God wishes to attain by Miracles. So much the worse for those who refuse to profit by them. This sort of men, says an ancient, crushes all philosophy that rejects the supernatural. They crush it, in effect, and, above all, since the introduction of Christianity, because, by endeavouring to withdraw God from the world, they have no longer any explanation of the world,

nor of humanity. That God whom they ex-
clude, some deny, to free themselves of Him altogether, others banish Him into a void, which is
inert and indifferent, having nothing to exact, and
exacting nothing from men whom He abandons to
chance, after having created them by a trick of
His disdainful power. Some, denying Him, and
affirming Him all at once, as if they wanted to
glut their ingratitude by offering Him a double
injury; they pretend to find him everywhere, and
thus dispensing themselves from acknowledging
and adoring Him anywhere. Nevertheless, around
them, in the midst of them, humanity cries out
and confesses God. They answer by sophisms that
satisfy them but little, by sarcasms the measure of
which they are ill able to dissimulate, and, in fine,
their science and their reason, driven to a corner
by their absurdity, shut up their eyes and ears.
They crush all philosophy......Taking pity on the
faith of the weak, whom these false doctors would
abuse, does God show Himself by one of those
unaccustomed marks of His power, which ceases
not, however, to be *one of the laws of the world?*
They deny it. Look! We do not wish to see!
David has said of the sinner: 'The unjust hath
said within himself, that he would sin; he would
not understand that he might do well.' (Ps. xxxv.)
'Ah! without doubt,' exclaimed the logician mentioned, 'there exists an unhappy crowd at whom
one can cast boldly, all platitudes; but there
exists, even at Lourdes, readers, whose good sense
is their guide, and demands, in such cases, where
such parties have adopted the plan of refusing
all enquiry, and denying everything a *priori;*

what becomes of history, palpable facts, and of upright and simple reason ? We doubt if the laws of France give power to the state to crush episcopal commissions, but if they do, it would be wise in the state not to exercise it. On the one side, nothing could be more in favour of superstition. Popular credulity would go astray as it might, for there is no law which can oblige a bishop to pronounce on a fact which he is unable to know, and is forbidden to know. The enemies of superstition have but one course to pursue in their difficulty, namely, to institute a commission themselves, in opposition, and publish the result; but this should only be done in the event of the episcopal enquiry concluding for the miracle. For if it should find the facts to be illusive, there would be an end to the controversy."

With a reserve truly admirable, in the midst of the strong public feeling, the Catholic press abstained from pronouncing on the character of the events. It did not prejudge in any way the opinion of the Commission. It confined itself to refuting calumnies, gross fables, sophisms, and maintaining the great historic theory of the supernatural, and vindicating in the name of reason, the rights and liberty of enlightened enquiry. "The fact of Lourdes," said the *Univers*, "is not as yet verified nor characterized. There may be a miracle there, or only an illusion. It is the decision of the bishop that shall settle the debate."

In the vast struggle caused by the question of miracles relating to the events at Lourdes, were seen two entrenched camps. On the one side, the Catholics appealed to a honest examination; on the other, the *pseudo-philosophers* trembled before the light. The first said, "Let an enquiry be made;" the latter cried, "Let us cut short all debate." The one had for its device liberty of conscience, the other conjured Cæsar to crush this religious movement, and strangle it in the cradle, not by the power of argument, but by brute force. All impartial minds viewing the position, could not fail to see that justice, truth, and reason, were on the side of the Catholics. For this purpose it was only necessary to be free and unprejudiced.

Although, in the person of a Commissary, a Prefect and a Minister, the administration had unhappily adopted in this grave affair a most intemperate line of conduct, there existed a powerful man, who had taken no part, and who stood, whatever his religious, philosophical, and political ideas may have been, in a position of perfect impartiality. Whether the Supernatural had manifested itself at the gates of Lourdes or not, it was quite indifferent to the plans of his mind and to the progress of his government. Neither his ambition, nor his self-love, nor his doctrines, nor his antecedents, were involved in that question. What intelligence is there that would not, under such conditions, be equitable, and act towards justice and truth in a reasonable manner? We do not violate justice, nor do we outrage truth, save when we think it useful to trample them under our feet, with a view to some powerful interest of fortune, ambition, or pride.

The man of whom we are speaking was called Napoleon III., and Emperor of the French.

Impassible, according to his custom, silent as the sphinxes of granite that watch at the gates of Thebes, he followed the dispute, beholding the battle rage to and fro, and awaiting till the public conscience should dictate to, so to speak, his decision.

IV.

The Almighty, at the same time He thus yielded up His work to the dispute of men, employed His enemies themselves to spread and increase its renown; whilst He continued to bestow visible graces on the humble and believing souls who came to implore the sovereign protection of the Virgin Mother at the miraculous source. At St. Justin, in the department of Ger, a boy named Jean-Marie Tambourné, had been infirm for some months. In consequence of extreme pain in the right leg, the muscles had become distorted, and the foot turned completely outwards, so as to form a straight angle with the other. The child's health soon gave way under constant suffering that deprived him of appetite and sleep. His parents, who were in tolerably easy circumstances, had tried every remedy suggested by the physicians of the locality, but nothing could conquer the disease; the waters of Blouscon, and the medicinal baths, were almost equally unsuccessful. Slight momentary ameliorations were invariably succeeded by disastrous relapses.

Despairing, at length, of effecting a cure by scientific means, the parents turned to the Mother of Mercy, who, it was said, had appeared at the Massabielle Rocks. On the 23rd of September, 1858, the woman, Tambourné, took Jean-Marie to Lourdes, by the public conveyance. The distance was long. It was about thirty miles. When they had arrived at the town, the mother took her son to the Grotto, and bathed him in the miraculous water, and, as she fervently prayed to her who in the Rosary is named "Health of the Sick," the child appeared to fall into an ecstasy, his eyes opening to their fullest extent, and his mouth half gasping; he seemed as though he was contemplating some unusual sight. "What is the matter with you?" asked his mother. "I see God and the Holy Virgin!" exclaimed he, in reply.

The poor woman, at these words, felt a profound emotion in her heart. A strange sweat came over his face. The child returned to himself.

"Mother!" exclaimed he, "I am healed. I have no longer any pain, and shall now be able to walk as well as ever."

Jean-Marie was right, he was cured, and walked back on foot to Lourdes, where he eat and slept. At the same time that the pain and infirmity went away, the appetite and sleep returned. The following day the woman, Tambourné, returned to bathe her son again at the Grotto, and, after causing a mass of thanksgiving to be said for them at the church of Lourdes, they departed, no longer in a conveyance, but on foot, towards their home. On approaching St. Justin, the boy perceived his father at a distance on the road, watching, probably, for the return of the pilgrims by some vehicle; and, letting go his mother's hand, he set off running to meet him, then rushed into the arms of his astonished father, crying out, "The Holy Virgin has cured me!" People flocked from all sides to see Jean-Marie, as he was well known to the inhabitants of the place, and as the report of the miracle had soon spread.

The sister of a notary at Tarbes, Mdlle. Marie Massot-Bordenave, was almost completely deprived of the use of her feet and hands, at the end of a serious and protracted illness. She only walked with extreme difficulty. As to her hands, being habitually swollen, purple in colour, and continually painful, they were almost incapable of use. She was returning to Arras, from a visit to her brother at Tarbes, and was alone inside the diligence, and, a bottle of wine happening to get uncorked and upset, she was powerless to raise or recork it. Lourdes was on her way; she stopped there, and went to the Grotto. On plunging her hands into the water, they were cured instantaneously; the same rapid cure took place with regard to her feet, when the water was applied to them. She falls on her knees. What does she say to the Blessed Virgin? How did she thank her? Such prayers may be guessed, but not expressed. Returning from the Grotto, she overtook a poor peasant girl with a large faggot of sticks, which she had laid down, overpowered by her burden and the heat of the day. She was sitting on a stone, alongside the road, laying down at her feet her bundle that was too much for her strength. Marie Massot addressed her at this moment. "My

child," said she, "God has just conferred a great
blessing on me, and has cured me, and taken
away my burden, permit me to assist you in my
turn." Saying this, she took up the heavy bundle
from the ground, placed it on her head, and thus
entered Lourdes, which she had left infirm and
paralytic, only an hour before. The first-fruits
of her newly-recovered strength were nobly employed in being consecrated to charity. "Whatever God gives you gratuitously, give to others
gratuitously," says the sacred Scripture.

A woman, already in years, Marie Capdevielle,
of the Bourg of Livron, in the environs of Lourdes,
was in like manner cured of a very serious deaf-
ness, that had threatened to be inveterate. "It
seems to me," said she, "that I am in another
world, when I hear the bells of the church which
I have not heard for three years."

These and many other cures continually attested
the direct intervention of Heaven. God manifested His power in restoring health to the sick,
and it was evident if He permitted persecution, it
was necessary for the fulfilment of His designs.
It depended on Him to arrest it, and to dispose the
hearts of the great ones of the earth, according to
His will.

V.

Discussion in the press on the subject of the
Grotto was worn out. In France and abroad the
public had been sufficiently well-informed to judge,
not of the reality of the Apparitions, but of the
violent oppression that liberty of conscience to;

examine, had undergone in a corner of the empire. The innumerable sophisms of unchristian fanaticism, and intolerance and pretended philosophy, had given way before the powerful logic of the Catholic journals; the "Debats," the "Siècle," the "Presse," and the other irreligious papers, were now silent, and probably regretted they had stirred up this unfortunate controversy. By so doing the renown of the miracles had extended; and from Italy, Germany, and still more distant countries, people wrote to Lourdes to procure some drops of the sacred water.

Meanwhile, the minister of Public Worship, M. Rouland, persisted in thwarting the liberty of the population, Jacomet and his guards watched day and night at the Grotto, arresting and bringing those to trial who dared to approach for the purpose of prayer. The Judge Duprat was passing sentence every day.

Sustained by such a minister, and with such agents to execute his commands, Baron Massy held out courageously in his illogical position, pluming himself on his all-powerful position and arbitrary will. More and more exasperated at the overthrow by the episcopal enquiry, and M. Filhol's analysis, of his pretexts for shutting up the Grotto on the ground of religion and public order, he felt a bitter satisfaction in acting the part of a tyrant. To the most undeniable evidence he opposed his will; it was gratifying to him to be himself alone stronger than the multitude, than the bishop, than common sense, or miracles, or than God Himself. "Etiamsi omnes, ego non." Though all, not I.

While this was passing at Lourdes, two eminent personages, Monseigneur de Salinis, Archbishop of Auch, and M. de Rességuier, formerly a deputy, sought an interview with the Emperor, who was at that time at Biarritz. Napoleon III. at the same time received urgent petitions from various quarters protesting, in virtue of the most sacred rights, against the violent and arbitrary measures of Baron Massy.

"Sire," said one of these petitions, "we do not pretend to decide the question of the Apparitions, although the majority of persons in these parts believe in their reality, on the faith of most striking miracles which they say they have seen. What is certain, and beyond all doubt, is, that the Source that suddenly sprung up, and from which we have been excluded, notwithstanding the scientific analysis that declared it innocuous, has done harm to no one; on the contrary, many people assert they have recovered their health by it. In the name, then, of liberty of conscience, which is independent of all human power, allow believers to pray there if such is their wish; in the name of the simplest humanity, let the sick seek a cure from the waters, if such is their hope. And, in the name of liberty of opinion, permit those who desire to study the question, to go there and discover the error, or substantiate truth."

The Emperor, as we have already said, was disinterested in the question, or, rather, it was his interest not to employ his power in uselessly opposing the progress of events. It was his interest to be equitable, and to avoid wounding by evident injustice those who believed after they had seen, and those who before believing claimed the right of publicly examining the mysterious facts that pre-occupied the whole of France. Napoleon III. was reserved in manner, his thoughts rarely expressed themselves in words ; they were known by his acts. On learning how the minister, the prefect, and their agents, had thrown discredit on authority by their absurd violence, his eye lighted up, it is said, with a flash of cold anger ; he shrugged his shoulders convulsively, while a cloud of deep displeasure passed over his features. He rang the bell violently.

"Take this to the telegraph office," said he.

It was a laconic dispatch for the Prefect of Tarbes, ordering him, on the part of the Emperor, instantly to take away the barricades from the Grotto, and to leave the population free.

VI.

It is known that the marvellous electric spark, which is transported from pole to pole by the iron wires that span the globe, is thought by scientific men to be nothing else than lightning. That day Baron Massy was of the same opinion, for the imperial telegram fell upon him like a sudden and stunning clap of thunder. The more he thought over it, the more impossible did it appear for him thus publicly to retract his steps. He would be obliged, however, either to swallow this bitter dose, or resign his office as Prefect.

When an unexpected catastrophe befalls us, we are slow to believe in its reality, and we still de-

bate even when all is lost. Baron Massy did not
escape this illusion. He had a vague hope that
the Emperor would change his determination, and
thereupon took upon himself not to obey, and keep
the despatch secret for some days. He wrote to
the Emperor, and also to M. Rouland, begging
him to use his influence with the former, to alter
his decision. Napoleon, however, was equally insensible to the remonstrances of the minister, and
the Prefect's supplication; the judgment he had
formed was based upon the evidence, and these
attempts had no other results than to show him
that the Prefect had dared to defer the execution
of his orders. A second dispatch left Biarritz,
and conceived in terms that left no room for observation or delay.

Baron Massy had only to choose between his
pride and his prefecture. He preferred the latter
alternative, and was humble enough to remain
Prefect. The chief of the department resigned
himself therefore to obey; but, in spite of the
imperative dispatches of his master, he still endeavoured not to resist, for that was evidently impossible, but to mask his retreat, and save the
disgrace of publicly laying down his arms.

In some way or other, a vague report had spread
concerning the orders that had come from Biarritz,
and was now the object of general conversation.
The Prefect neither confirmed nor denied these
rumours. He enjoined Jacomet and his agents to
cease their surveillance, thinking that the withdrawal of the police, following so closely upon the
rumours that were in circulation, was sufficient to
let things take their usual course, as it were of

themselves, and, that the people being freed from restraint, would immediately tear down the barricades and posts that bore the prohibition to enter the grounds approaching the Grotto.

Baron Massy was mistaken in his calculations, plausible though they were. The people feared a snare, and continued to go, for the purpose of prayer, to the opposite side of the Gave, while the infractions that took place had generally, as before, an isolated character. No one touched either the posts or the barriers, and the *statu quo* was obstinately maintained. Considering the character of Napoleon, and the precision of the orders from Biarritz, such a situation was perilous for the Prefect, and he was too intelligent not to perceive it. He must have been in momentary fear lest the Emperor should be informed of his manœuvre, and send him some terrible announcement, such as might crush him for ever, and banish him from the luminous functionary sphere, into the exterior darkness of the unofficial world. In the midst of this perplexity, M. Fould had occasion to visit Tarbes, and also Lourdes. He may have made some alarming communication, or another telegram may have been received, but, at all events, a few days after, on the 4th of October, M. Massy gave orders to the Mayor, in the name of the Emperor, publicly to remove the obstructions from the Grotto.

VII.

M. Lacadé was relieved, by this solution, from the hard task of endeavouring to conciliate the Prefect and the people. By an illusion common to undecided characters, the mayor imagined he had always been on the popular side, and therefore issued a proclamation, of which, unfortunately, the text is wanting, but the following was the tone and sense of it.* "Inhabitants of the town of Lourdes, the day so much desired by us is at length arrived; we have attained it by our wisdom, our perseverance, our faith, and courage."

The proclamation was read throughout the town to the sound of drums and trumpets. At the same time the following placard was fixed upon all the walls :

"The Mayor of the town of Lourdes—seen the instructions that have been addressed to him :

"DECREED.

"The decree made by him, the 8th of June, 1858, is withdrawn.

"Done at Lourdes, at the Hotel of the Mayoralty, the 5th October, 1858.

"The Mayor,
"A. LACADE."

* Many of the papers relating to the Grotto of Lourdes were retained by the family of M. Lacadé, instead of being left at the Archives of the Mayoralty. M. Lasserre says that all his efforts to see these papers were futile, and it was said that they were burned.

The police during this time proceeded to remove the posts and barriers. A crowd had already assembled when Jacomet arrived. Although a certain degree of embarrassment was perceptible in his manner, and one could divine from the pallor of his countenance his deep interior humiliation, still, contrary to general expectation, he had not the dejected air of one who had been vanquished. He wore his dress uniform for great occasions, which appeared singular. Escorted by his agents, who were armed with hatchets and pick-axes, he passed through the crowd and took up his position near the barriers, when a kind of vague tumult, or suppressed murmur, arose from the multitude. The Commissary mounted a fragment of rock, and motioned that he wished to speak. All listened with attention. "My friends," said Jacomet, "the barriers, that to my great regret the municipality had received orders to raise, are now about to fall. Who has suffered more than myself from this obstacle to your piety? I, too, am religious, my friends, and partake of your belief. But the functionary, like the soldier, has one duty only, often a cruel one, to perform, it is to obey. The responsibility does not lie with him. Well, then, my friends, upon witnessing your admirable order, your respect for authority, your persevering faith, I informed my superior, and pleaded your cause. I said, 'the people are inoffensive, why prevent them from praying at the Grotto, and drinking at the Fountain?' And thus it is, my friends, that the order has been withdrawn; thus it is that *M. le Préfet* and I have resolved, henceforth and for ever, to overthrow these barriers, so annoying to yourselves, and still more so to me."

There was a cold silence after this speech. Some young men whispered together and laughed, and Jacomet was visibly disconcerted at his ill-success. He gave the order to his agents to remove the barriers. This was speedily accomplished. They made a heap of the planks and the debris, leaving them at the side of the Grotto, and at night-fall the police came and carried them off.

The town of Lourdes was greatly excited. During the whole of this evening crowds passed to and fro along the roads leading to the Grotto. Before the Massabielle rocks innumerable persons were on their knees; they chanted canticles, they recited litanies of the Blessed Virgin, "Virgo potens, ora pro nobis." Virgin most powerful pray for us. They drank of the Fountain. The believers were free. God had conquered.

NINTH BOOK.

I.

In consequence of the events we have related, M. Massy could no longer remain at Tarbes, and the Emperor lost no time in sending him to the first prefecture that was vacant in the empire. It is worthy of remark, as a singular circumstance, that this prefecture was that of Grenoble; Baron Massy only left Notre Dame de 'Lourdes to encounter Notre Dame de la Salette.

Jacomet also left the country, being named Commissary of Police in another deparment. Placed on his true ground, he contributed in discovering, with rare sagacity, the artifices of some dangerous knaves who had foiled the efforts of his predecessor, and the most active researches of the magistracy. A considerable theft to the amount of two or three hundred thousand francs, had been committed, to the prejudice of a railway company. Here was his true vocation, and this made his fortune. His remarkable talents, justly appreciated by his chiefs, obtained for him an elevated post.

The Procureur Imperial, M. Dutour, was also soon called to other functions. M. Lacadé remained mayor, and his vague " silhoeutte " will appear again once or twice in the last pages of this history.

II.

Although he had instituted a tribunal of enquiry, towards the end of July, Mgr. Laurence,
before permitting it to enter on its functions,
wished first that a certain degree of calm should
be established in the public mind. To wait, he
thought, can never compromise anything, where
the works of God are concerned, who holds time
in His hands. The event proved he was right.
After the tumultuous debates in the French journals, and the violent measures of Baron Massy,
the Grotto had become free, and the scandal was
no longer to be feared of seeing a police agent
arrest the episcopal commission on the road to the
Massabielle Rocks, going to accomplish its work,
and study, at the place of the Apparition, the traces
of the hand of God.

On the 17th of November the Commission
arrived at Lourdes. Bernadette was examined.
" She presented herself before us," writes the
secretary in the procès-verbal, " with remarkable
self-possession. She was calm and unembar-
rassed in the midst of the numerous assembly of
venerable ecclesiastics whom she had not before
seen, but of whose mission she had been ap-
prized."

The young girl related the Apparitions, the
words of the Virgin, the order given by her to
construct on that spot a chapel to her honour, the
sudden bursting out of the fountain, the name,
" Immaculate Conception," that the Vision had
given herself. She exposed, with the grave cer-

tainty of a witness, who was sure of herself, and the humble candour of a child, all that was personal to her in this supernatural drama, the vicissitudes of which had exhibited themselves nearly for a year. She replied to every question, leaving no obscurity in the minds of those who interrogated her, not now in the name of men like Jacomet, the Procureur, and many others, but in the name of the Catholic Church, the eternal spouse of God. All that to which she gave testimony, our readers know. We have explained ourselves the events, according to their date, in the different pages of this narrative.

The Commission visited the rocks of Massabielle, and beheld the great volume of water that gushed from the supernatural source; it ascertained, by the unanimous assertion of those living in the vicinity, that no such spring of water had existed previous to that which surged up miraculously before the eyes of the multitude under the hand of Bernadette in ecstasy. It then made a searching enquiry, at Lourdes and its outskirts, into the extraordinary cures accompanying the use of the water of the Grotto. In this delicate investigation there were two very distinct parts, the facts themselves, and their circumstances, taken from human testimony; their natural, or supernatural character, requiring for their solution, to a great extent, at least, the aid of medical science. The method followed by the tribunal of enquiry inspired this twofold thought. The Commission, during its progress through the dioceses of Tarbes, Auch, and Bayonne, summoned before it those who were spoken of as having been the objects of these singular cures, it questioned them with careful minuteness on all the details of their malady, and of their sudden, or gradual, return to health, causing technical questions such as would probably not occur to the minds of mere theologians, to be put to them by men of human science. It also summoned the parents, friends, and neighbours who had seen the sick person, or had assisted their cure, &c., in order to substantiate the evidence. Once arrived, in this way, at the certain knowledge of all the facts of the case, they were submitted to the consideration of two eminent physicians, Dr. Vergèz, of Barèges, a professor of the faculty at Mountpellier, and Dr. Dozous, who had already studied, on his own account, many of these curious incidents. Each physician consigned his opinion on the nature of the case, to a separate report ; sometimes denying the miracle, and attributing the recovery to health to natural causes; at other times, declaring it quite inexplicable unless by the supernatural action of divine power; sometimes, again, not coming to any decision, but inclining slightly either to one or the other solution. The Commission then deliberated, having full knowledge of the facts on one side, and the conclusions of science on the other, and proposed its judgment to the Bishop, together with the facts and documents connected with the process. The Commission had not, nor could have any, preconceived opinion. Believing in the supernatural, so frequently met with in the history of the world, it knew at the same time that nothing so much tends to the discredit of true miracles coming from God as the

false prodigies of men. Equally averse to affirm
beforehand, or prematurely to deny, its task was
limited to the search for truth alone ; it acted
openly in summoning for its enlightenment all
who were in a position to give testimony or information, those who disbelieved, as well as those
who believed. Resolutely determined to cast aside
what was vague and uncertain, and to accept
nothing but what was sure and incontestable, it
refused every assertion based on mere report ;
upon each witness it imposed two conditions, the
first was to depose only to what he personally
knew, and had seen ; the second, to engage, by a
solemn oath, to tell the whole truth and the truth
alone.

With precautions such as these, and with so
wise and prudent an organization, it was impossible that false miracles could succeed, even for a
moment, in deceiving the judgment of the Commission. It was especially impossible, in presence
of so many hostile spirits arrayed against the supernatural, and interested in combating and over-
throwing every error and exaggeration, every
doubtful assertion, or ill-attested miracle. If,
then, true miracles incompletely verified, escaped
the sanction of the Commission of inquiry, it was,
at least, quite certain that no lying wonder could
stand before the strictness of the examination, or
maintain its ground in connection with supernatural events.

If there was any one who wished to contest such
or such a miracle, not by vague general theories,
but by proofs from personal knowledge of the
facts, they were publicly invited to present them-

selves at the enquiry.   Not to do so was, in point
of fact, to acknowledge that they had nothing
tangible to allege, and no counter-proof to furnish.
To refuse the combat, was to accept defeat.

III.

For several months the attention of the Episcopal Commission was engaged investigating miracles in the localities which public rumour had
signalised as being remarkable. A great number
were verified, several of which have been mentioned already in this history.   Two were of
recent date, and had taken place a short time after
the re-opening of the Grotto.   One had occurred
at Nay, the other at Tartas.   Though the two
Christians who were the objects of the benedictions
of Heaven, were unknown to each other, a mysterious link seemed to unite these two events.
Let us relate them successively, such as we have
studied them, and written them down under the
impression of the living testimonies which we
have heard.

IV.

In the same town of Nay, where, some months
previously, a young man, Henry Busquet, had been
miraculously cured, lay a poor woman of the name
of Madame Madeleine Rizan, a widow, apparently
at the point of death.   Her life for the last twenty-
four or twenty-five years had been one continued
state of suffering.   Struck down in 1832 by

cholera, she remained from that time nearly
paralysed on the left side. She was lame, and
could only go about the house by supporting herself against the walls and furniture. Not more
frequently, perhaps, than two or three times a
year in summer, and assisted by others, could she
go to the church, though it was close to her
house, in order to hear mass there. It was impossible for her, without the aid of others, to kneel
or rise from her knees. One of her hands was
entirely affected with atrophy. Her general
temperament was not much less than her limbs
under the influence of this disease. She was
afflicted with constant vomitings of blood. No
solid food could rest on her stomach. The
feeble spark of life left in her was sustained by
soup and coffee. The poor woman was always
cold, even during the months of July and August,
constantly asking to be placed by the fire in her
arm chair. For the last sixteen or eighteen
months, at the time we speak of, her condition
had become worse, the paralysis of the left side
was complete, and the same infirmity had commenced to attack the right leg ; her limbs, under
the effects of atrophy, had swelled, and she appeared to be dropsical.

Madam Rizan was at length obliged to leave her
arm-chair for her bed, where she lay unable to
move of herself, so that persons were obliged, from
time to time, to change her position. She had
lost all sensibility of feeling, as well as power of
movement. " Where are my limbs ?" she would
sometimes say to those who came to move her.

Her body and limbs were doubled up, and she lay on her side in the form of a Z.

Two physicians had successively attended her. Dr. Tolamon had for a long time declared that she was incurable, he, however, frequently visited her, but only as a friend, and refused to order her any remedies, saying that medical treatment would simply add to the weakness of the patient, whose strength was already nearly exhausted. Dr. Subervielle, by the express desire of Madame Rizan, had ordered some remedies, which proved useless, and he likewise had given up all hope. If the paralysed limbs had become insensible, the sufferings that this unfortunate person felt in other parts of the body, sometimes in the stomach, sometimes in the head, were extreme. In consequence of being always in a recumbent posture, the skin broke, and bed-sores appeared in various parts of her body. Death was apparently at hand.

Madam Rizan had two children. Her daughter Lubine lived with her, and watched her at all hours with devoted attention. Her son, M. Romain Rizan, was connected with a commercial house at Bordeaux. When Dr. Subervielle had given up all hope, and declared that the patient had but a few hours to live, M. Rizan was sent for in all haste. He came only to embrace his mother, receive her blessing and last adieu; for, by the imperative desire of his employer, he was obliged at once to tear himself away from the bed of death by the cruel tyranny of business: he left his mother with the sad certainty that he should see her no more.

The dying woman received extreme unction.

Her agony was prolonged in the midst of intolerable suffering. "My God!" she cried frequently, "put an end to so many sufferings. Grant me, Lord, either that I may recover or die!" She begged the Sisters of the Cross at Igon, of which her sister-in-law was superior, to make a novena to the Blessed Virgin to ask her powerful aid in obtaining for her either a cure, or that she might be taken from this world. At the same time the sick woman likewise expressed a desire to obtain some of the water from the Grotto, and a neighbour, Madam Nessans, who was going to Lourdes, promised to bring her some of it.

Latterly she was obliged to be attended night and day. On Saturday, the 16th of October, a violent crisis announced the definitive approach of her last hour. The spittings of blood were continual. A livid tint spread itself over her emaciated countenance. The eyes became glassy. She scarcely spoke, save to moan over her acute suffering. She repeatedly asked of God to take her, and Dr. Subervielle, who had been to see her, on leaving, said to those around the sick woman, "Her prayer will soon be heard; she will die to-night, or before morning. There is no more oil in the lamp." Her friends and neighbours, the priests, Abbé Dupont, and the Abbé Sanarens, the Vicar of Nay, came silently and softly from time to time to enquire if the dying woman still lived. In the evening, on quitting her, M. L. Abbé André Dupont, her consoler and friend, could not restrain his tears. Night came, by degrees there was a solitude in the house, her daughter, Lubine, knelt and prayed before a statue of the Blessed Virgin, and nothing was heard but the painful breathing of the mother. At midnight she called to her mother. "Go," said she, in a dying voice, as if starting from a dream, "go, my dear child, to our neighbour, Madam Nessans, who ought by this time to have returned from Lourdes, and ask her for a glass of the water of the Grotto. This water will cure me. The Holy Virgin desires it." "My dear mother," replied Lubine, "it is now too late. I cannot leave you alone, every one is in bed at Madam Nessans. But, to-morrow morning, I will go to her by the first light." "We will wait, then." And the sick woman lay silent. The joyous bells of Sunday announced day-break. The morning Angelus bore to the Blessed Virgin Mary the prayers of the faithful. Lubine ran to Madam Nessans, and returned quickly with a bottle of Lourdes water. "Here, drink mother, and may the Holy Virgin come to your succour." Madam Rizan drank a little of the water. "O, my child, it is life that I drink. There is life in this water! Bathe my face, bathe my arm with it, bathe my whole body with it!" Trembling and astonished, Lubine steeped a piece of linen in the miraculous water, and washed her mother's face. "I feel that I am cured!" she cried, in a voice clear and strong. "I am cured!" Then Lubine bathed, with the help of some wet linen, the paralysed and swelled limbs of the sick woman. With mingled joy, alarm, and fright, the girl saw the swellings reduce, and quickly disappear under the rapid movement of her hands, the extended and shining skin return to its natural state, quickly and completely,

health and life returned to her hands. "It seems
to me," said the mother, "that things like burning pimples are leaving all my body." It was,
without doubt, the interior principle of the disorder
which was escaping from her body hitherto afflicted
with pain, and which left her for ever, under the
action of a superhuman will. All this was accomplished in a moment. In a minute or two the
agonised body of Madam Rizan, washed by her
daughter, regained its full strength. "I am
cured, altogether cured!" cried out the overjoyed woman. "How good is the Holy Virgin,
and how powerful! Lubine, my dear child, I am
hungry, bring me something to eat." "Will you
have coffee, or wine, or milk?" stammered the
young girl, troubled, and, in a manner thunder-
struck by the sudden effects of the miracle. "I
wish for meat and bread, my child," said the
mother, who had not eaten solid food for twenty-
four years. There was some cold meat in the
house. Madam Rizan eat and drank. "And
now," said she, "I wish to rise." "That is not
possible, mother," said Lubine, hesitating.
Madam Rizan insisted, and called for her clothes.
They had been folded up and put aside for some
months past in a chest of drawers, in an adjoining
room, doubtless supposing she would never wear
them again. Lubine went for the clothes, and
returned quickly. When arriving at the door, she
uttered a cry, and let the clothes fall from her
hands. Her mother, during her short absence,
had left her bed and was kneeling before a statue
of the Blessed Virgin. Lubine, terrified, as if before the resurrection of a dead person, was incapa-

ble of giving assistance, the mother lifted the clothes from the ground, and quickly dressed herself, and again fell upon her knees before the sacred image.

It was about seven in the morning. First mass was over. The cry of Lubine was heard by persons in the street. "Poor girl," said they, "her mother has just expired. It was impossible she could live out the night." Several friends and neighbours went to the house to console Lubine in her grief. Amongst others, two Sisters of the Holy Cross. "Well, my poor child, your good mother is dead, but you will see her again in heaven." The young girl was leaning against the half-opened door, her countenance agitated. Lubine could barely reply to them. "My mother has risen again," said she, in a voice filled with emotion, and scarcely able to stand. "She is delirious," thought the Sisters, as they entered the room, followed by some persons who mounted the stairs with them. Lubine had spoken the truth. Madam Rizan had left her bed. She was dressed and at prayer before an image of the Blessed Virgin Mary. She arose, and said, "I am cured! Let us all thank the Holy Virgin on our knees!"

The fame of this extraordinary event spread like lightning through the town of Nay. All that day and the next the house was beset by persons wishing to see Madam Rizan, and to convince themselves with their own eyes, that they might engrave in their memory the details of this supernatural drama.

M. the Doctor Subervielle, unhesitatingly acknowledged the supernatural and divine character of this extraordinary cure. The Abbé Dupont wrote to Bordeaux to M. Romain Rizan, who thought, on opening the letter, that it was to inform him of the death of his mother. The first words that struck his eye were these, "Deo gratias! Alleluia!" "Yes, rejoice my dear friend, your mother is cured, *completely* cured. It is the Holy Virgin that has miraculously restored her to health." And he related in the letter all the circumstances.

The young man was not alone on this occasion. A friend was with him, and partook of his emotion. The friend was employed in a printing establishment at Bordeaux, where was published the "Messager Catholique." "Give me this letter," said he, to M. Rizan; "the works of God must be known, and our Lady of Lourdes glorified." Half willingly, and half by force, he obtained the letter. The "Messager Catholique," published it a few days later."

As for the happy son, he left instantly for Nay. Upon the arrival of the diligence, a woman was seen waiting at the spot. She ran to him, as he was alighting from the carriage. It was his mother.

Ten years later the author of this History went to see Madam Rizan, and found her in the enjoyment of perfect health. She was in her seventy-first year, and free from the infirmities that age brings with it. No trace remained of her former severe sufferings. Those who had previously known her, some of whom we questioned on the circumstances, were still in astonishment at f great a prodigy.

24

We wished to see Dr. Subervielle, but learned that he had been dead some years. "But," we said to an ecclesiastic of Nay, who served as our guide, "was not the sick person visited by another physician of the country, Dr. Talamon?" "He is a very distinguished man," replied our companion. "He went frequently to Madam Rizan, not as a physician, but as a neighbour and friend. But, from the time of the miraculous cure, he ceased to visit her until eight or ten months after the occurrence." "Perhaps he did not wish to be questioned on the extraordinary fact, which, doubtless, was little in accord with his philosophic ideas?" "I cannot say," replied the priest. I determined to see this gentleman. We knocked at his door.

Dr. Talamon is a fine, handsome, old man. He had a remarkable forehead, a crown of white hair, a firm look, which indicated a decided mind, a mouth constantly in motion, upon which a smile of scepticism was often playing. Such were the principal traits we observed in him as we approached him. We informed him of the object of our visit.

"It is a long time since this circumstance happened," said he to us. "Ten or twelve years ago, and my memory is not clear enough to speak positively on the subject, and, besides, I was not a direct witness. I did not see Madam Rizan for some months afterwards, and I am ignorant under what conditions, by what agents, by what progressive means, whether slow or rapid, her cure was effected."

"What, Doctor, you had not the curiosity to

verify a fact so extraordinary, and which you must
have known from its having been so generally
spread throughout the country?" "Faith, sir,"
he replied to me, "I am an old physician, and I
know that the laws of nature are never upset;
and, to speak freely to you, I am no believer in all
these miracles." "Ah! Doctor, you sin against
faith," cried the Abbé, who had introduced me.
"And I, Doctor, I do not accuse you of having
sinned against faith, but I accuse you of having
sinned against the particular science that you
profess, medicine." "How so, and in what way?"
he said.

"Medicine is not a speculative science, it is an
experimental one. Experience is its law. Observation of facts its first and fundamental principle.
If any one had told you that Madam Rizan had
been cured in some way by rubbing herself with
an infusion of such or such a plant recently discovered in the mountains, you would certainly not
have failed to go and make yourself acquainted
with the cure, examine the plant, and note a discovery which would have appeared to you equal in
importance to that of quinine in the last century.
You would have done the same had this cure been
suddenly produced by some new spring, sulphur-
eous or alcaline. But here, when you are told of
a water miraculously gushing forth, you have no
wish to go and see it. Forgetting that you are a
physician, that is to say, an humble enquirer into
facts, you have refused to look, as the academy of
science denied the powers of steam, refused to
condescend to examine into it, and who proscribed
the use of quinine upon the pretext of, I know not

what, pretended medical principles. In medicine, when a fact presents itself that contradicts an accepted principle, it is a proof that the principle is false. Experience is the supreme judge. And now, sir, permit me to make this observation, —if you had not a vague belief, and fear of the truth of the miracle, you would not have hesitated to examine it, and it would have given you pleasure to have been able to expose the imposture that had put all the country in commotion. But examination would have exposed you to the danger of having to render up your arms. And you have been like those party men who do not wish to hear the reasons of their adversaries. You have listened to philosophic prejudices, and you have been wanting in your duty to the law of medicine, which should oblige you to study facts, no matter from what quarter they may come, in order to learn. I tell you these things, Doctor, with all the more freedom, that I am aware of your high merit, and I am not ignorant that your great mind is capable of understanding truth. Many physicians refuse to certify facts of this nature from human respect, not daring to face either the displeasure of the faculty, or the railleries of their brethren. As for yourself, Doctor, if your philosophy has deceived you, the fear of man has not been altogether dispelled from your mind."

" No, certainly," said he; " and, perhaps considering the matter in your point of view, I should have done better had I examined the case."

V.

A long time before the events at Lourdes, at a period when Bernadette was not even living, in 1843, in the month of April, a highly respectable family of Tartas, in the Landes, experienced the most serious disquiets. About a year previously, Mademoiselle Adele de Charton, had married Monsieur Moreau de Sazenay, and she had approached the term of her confinement.

The crisis of first becoming a mother is always alarming. The physicians, who were called in with all haste at the appearance of the premonitory symptoms, declared that the delivery would be painful, and did not dissemble the possibility of some danger.

There is nobody but what knows or understands the cruel anxieties of such situations. The most poignant is not always felt by the poor woman who groans on her bed of pangs, and who is almost wholly absorbed by her state of physical suffering. It is felt by the husband, whose heart is at this moment a prey to unspeakable torture. They are at an age of strong impressions; they have but just entered upon a new state of existence, a state pleasing to both; they have tasted the first joys of a union which God has seemed to bless; they have passed some months in mutually forming hopes for the future; they have, in a certain manner, sat down together in felicity, as people sit down side by side, in a quiet little vessel. The river of life lulls you, and carries you gently along amidst flowery banks. And, behold, all at once,

in the fulness of happiness, the threatening shadow
of death presents itself. The heart of a husband,
which is elevated at the hope of seeing a child that
is going to be born, finds itself suddenly under
the effects of alarm that a wife may perish. He
hears heart-rending cries. How will the crisis
terminate? Is it joy that is in prospect, or is it
misfortune? What is it that will leave that
chamber? Will it be life, or death? What must
he go and seek? Is it a cradle or a coffin? Is it,
alas! horrible contrast, one or the other? Is it
even two coffins, one for the mother, and the other
for the infant?

Human science is silent, and does not pronounce.

These anguishes are frightful; they must be so,
above all, for those who derive not from God their
strength and consolation.

But M. Moreau was a Christian. He knew
that the thread of our lives is in the hands of a
Supreme Master, before whom we may always
make an appeal from the decision of the doctors of
science. When man has condemned, the King
of Heaven, as the sovereigns of the earth, has
reserved to Himself the right of pardon.

The Holy Virgin, thought the unhappy husband,
will perhaps deign to hear my prayer. And he
addressed himself with confidence to the Mother of
Christ.

The peril which had appeared at first so menacing, disappeared by degrees like a black cloud,
which, in the height of the atmosphere, clear and
scatter the breezes of the air. The horizon
brightens up again, resumes its calmness, and

delays not in becoming radiant. A little girl is born.

Assuredly this happy delivery had nothing extraordinary in it. The malady, however alarming it might have appeared to M. Moreau, had nothing in it of a character such as the doctors had absolutely despaired of overcoming. The favourable issue of the crisis might then have been altogether in conformity with the rules of nature.

The heart of the husband and father felt itself, however, penetrated with gratitude towards the Holy Virgin. His was not a soul that was insensible to the duty of gratitude, that preferred to doubt of the benefit in order to dispense itself from being grateful.

"What name are you going to give your daughter?" people said to him.

"Mary? But it is the most common name we have here. All the women among the people, all the servants are called Mary. And then Mary Moreau, is a little euphonic. The two M's and the two R's cannot go well together."

A thousand reasons of the same description were likewise alleged. It was a general *toll*. M. Moreau de Suzenay was a man who was very easy, very accessible, and habitually very inclined to the advice given to him; but, in the present case, he was unbending to every one, he resisted every petition and counsel; he braved all their churlishness, and his tenacity was extraordinary. He remembered that, in his recent alarm, he had invoked a sacred name, and that it was the name of the Queen of Heaven.

"She shall be called Mary; I will that she shall

have the Holy Virgin as her patroness. I tell you sincerely, this name will bring her happiness."

Every one around him was astonished at his obstinacy, but it did not give way no more than that of Zachary, when he willed, as the Gospel relates, that his son should be called John.

Vainly did they beset him on all sides; they had to submit to his inflexible will. The first-born of that family received then the name of Mary. The father willed, besides, that during three years, she should be vowed in white, the colour of the Blessed Virgin. And such, accordingly, took place.

More than sixteen years had elapsed since these occurrences. A second child was born, which was called Martha. Mademoiselle Marie Moreau received her education with the Dames of the Sacred Heart at Bordeaux.

Towards the commencement of January, 1858, she was attacked by a disorder in her eyes that forced her rapidly to interrupt all her studies. She supposed it was caused by a little draft of air, and would go away as it came; but her hopes were deceived, and her state of health finally assumed a character quite disquieting. The ordinary physician of the house judged it necessary that an eminent oculist from Bordeaux, M. Bermont, should be called in and consulted.

It was not a draft of air, it was an amaurosis.

" The disorder is very grave," said M. Bermont, " One of the two eyes is quite gone, and the other is in a bad state."

The parents were immediately informed. The mother quickly rushed to Bordeaux and took away her child in order to make her follow in the bosom of her family, and with attentive solicitude, the treatment which the oculist had prescribed, if not to cure the eye which was lost, at least to save that which still remained, and which·was already so much affected, as only to be able to perceive objects in a confused and misty manner.

Medicaments, sea-baths, all that science suggested, was useless. Spring and autumn were passed in these vain efforts.

This deplorable complaint resisted everything, and slowly became worse. Total blindness seemed imminent. M. and Madame Moreau decided to take their daughter to Paris to consult our medical celebrities.

Whilst preparations were being made for their journey, fearing lest they were already too late to arrest the malady that threatened their child, the letter carrier brought them a weekly number of a little journal of Bordeaux, for which they were subscribers, called the "Messager Catholique." It was in the early part of November.

Now, it was precisely this number of the "Messager Catholique" which contained the letter of Abbé Dupont, and the narrative of the miraculous cure of Madame, the widow Rizan, of Nay, by the employment of the water of the Grotto.

M. Moreau opened it mechanically, and his eyes fell upon this divine history. He became pale in reading it.

Hope began to waken up in the soul of the desolate father, and his mind, or rather his heart, had received a flash of light.

"Behold," said he, "the door at which we must knock. It is evident," added he, with a marvellous simplicity, of which we are bound to preserve the textual expression, "it is evident that if the Blessed Virgin has appeared at Lourdes, she has an interest in working miraculous cures there, to attest and prove the reality of such Apparitions. And this is, above all, true in the beginnings, so long as the event is not universally credited......Let us hasten there. There, as everywhere else, it will be the first come the first served. My wife! my daughter! it is to our Lady of Lourdes we must address ourselves."

The sixteen years that had elapsed since the birth of his daughter, had not cooled, as we may see, the faith of M. Moreau.

A novena was determined upon, in which the companions and friends in the neighbourhood of the sick young lady, united. By a providential circumstance, a priest in the town had at this moment with him a bottle of water from the Grotto, so that the novena was begun almost immediately.

The parents, in case of cure, made a vow of going on pilgrimage to Lourdes, and vowing for a year their young daughter in white and blue, the colours of the Blessed Virgin, which she had already worn during three years, when she was quite a little infant, just on her entering into existence.

The novena began on the evening of the 8th of November.

Must we say it? The sick young lady had but little faith in the cure. The mother dared not to

hope. The father alone had that tranquil faith
which the beneficent powers of heaven never
resist.

All prayed together, in the chamber of M.
Moreau, before an image of the Blessed Virgin.
The mother, the young sick lady, and her little
sister, got up one after the other to retire to rest,
but the father remained on his knees. He thought
himself alone, and his voice arose with a fervour,
the accent of which kept behind him his family
who were ready to depart, his family, who have
given us this account, and who cannot recal to
their memory this solemn moment without shiver-
ing with emotion.

"Holy Virgin," said the father; "most Holy
Virgin Mary, you must cure my daughter! Yes,
indeed you must. It is for you an obligation, and
you cannot refuse it. Remember then, O Mary,
remember, that it is in spite of all, that it is in spite
of all that I have willed to choose you to be her
patron. You must remember what contests I have
had to sustain to give her your sacred name.
Well, Holy Virgin, can you forget all this? Can
you forget that then I defended your name, your
power, your glory, against all the pressing and
vain reasons of those who surrounded me? Can
you forget that I publicly placed this child under
your protection, saying and repeating to all that
this name, your name, Holy Virgin Mary, would
bring her happiness? She was my child, I have
made her yours. Can you then forget it? Is it,
then, that you are not bound in honour, now that
I am unhappy, now that we are praying to you
for our daughter, for yours—to come to our assist-

ance and to cure her malady? Will you allow
her to become blind after the faith I have showed
in you? No, no, it is impossible; you will cure
her!"

Such were the sentiments that the unhappy
father allowed to burst aloud from him, making an
appeal to the heart of the Holy Virgin, putting her,
in some manner, in arrears, and summoning her
to pay the debt of gratitude.

It was ten o'clock at night.

The young lady, at the moment of going to bed,
dipped a silk veil in some of the water from
Lourdes, and placed it on her eyes, while fastening
it behind her head.

Her mind was agitated. Without having the
faith of M. Moreau, she said to herself, that, after
all, the holy Virgin might really cure her; that soon,
perhaps, at the end of the novena, she would have
recovered her sight. Then a doubt came over her,
and it seemed to her that a miracle was not a
thing for her. While revolving these thoughts in
her mind, she had a great difficulty in getting to
sleep, and it was only very late she at length succeeded in doing so.

The following morning, on awaking, her first
movement, which was one of vague hope and
uneasy curiosity, was to take off the veil which
covered her eyes. She uttered a great scream.

All around her, the light of the early morning
inundated the room, and she saw clearly and distinctly. The distempered eye had recovered its
healthy state; the eye which was dead, was restored
to life.

"Martha, Martha!" cried she to her sister; "I see! I see! I am cured!"

The young Martha, who was in bed in the same room, cast herself down to the foot of the bed, and hastened to her. She beholds the eyes of Mary entirely disencumbered of their bloody veil, her eyes black and brilliant, in which strength and life were conspicuous. The heart of the little girl turned towards her father and mother, who were not participating in their joy.

"Papa! mamma!" cried she.

Mary made her a sign to be quiet.

"Wait, wait," said she, "I wish to know beforehand if I can read. Give me a book."

The child took up one which was upon the table in the room.

"Take this," said she.

Mary opens the book, and immediately read in it, straightforward, without effort, as the rest of the world. Her cure was complete, radical, absolute, and the Holy Virgin had not done things by halves. The father and mother had hastened to appear.

"Papa, mamma, I see, I see! I am cured."

How could we paint this indescribable scene? Every one may understand it, every one may see it by descending into his own heart.

The door of the house was not yet opened. The windows were still closed, and their transparent glass did not allow to pass through them any but the first glimmerings of the morning. Who then could have been able to enter and mix in the joy of this family recovering their happiness all at once?

And, nevertheless, those Christians who had been favourably listened to, understood that they were not alone, and that a being, powerful and invisible, was at that moment in the midst of them.

The father and mother, and the little Martha, fell on their knees. Mary, still in bed, joined her hands, and, from these four breasts, overwhelmed with emotion and gratitude, burst forth as an act of thanksgiving, the name of the Mother of God.

"O, Holy Virgin Mary! O, our Lady of Lourdes!" What were their other words, we know not. As to their sentiments, who does not fathom them, while assisting in thought at that wondrous event, at that manifestation of the power of God, traversing all at once, the destiny of a sorrowful family, and changing their mourning into felicity.

Is there any need for adding that, a short time afterwards, Mademoiselle Marie Moreau went with her parents to thank our Lady of Lourdes, at the Grotto of the Apparition? She deposited her garments upon the altar and resumed, all happy and proud to wear them, the colours of the Queen of Virgins.

M. Moreau, whose faith had been before so great, was in a stupor. "I believed," said he, "that these graces were only granted to saints. How has it happened that such favours descend also upon such miserable sinners as we are?"

These facts have had for witnesses the whole population of Tartas, who had a sympathy for the affliction of this family, which was one of the most respected in the country. Every one in the town has seen, and can attest, that the malady, hitherto of a desperate nature, had been suddenly cured at the commencement of the novena. The superioress of the Sacred Heart at Bordeaux, one hundred and fifty pupils, who were the companions of Mademoiselle Marie Moreau, the physicians of that establishment, have attested both the gravity of her illness before the event we have described, and then her complete cure. She returned, in fact, to Bordeaux, where she passed two more years in order to terminate her studies.

The oculist, before named, M. Bermont, gave a written declaration, to the effect that the sudden and instantaneous nature of the cure showed it to be entirely beyond the power of medical science.

This declaration, dated February 8, 1859, is among the Bishop's papers at Tarbes, together with a number of letters on the subject, from the inhabitants of Tartas, where the family resided, and, amongst others, one from the Mayor of that town, M. Desbord, all testifying to the miracle.

Mademoiselle Marie wore the colours of the Holy Virgin until the day of her marriage, which took place at the end of her studies, and when she left the convent of the Sacred Heart. On that day, too, she went to Lourdes and put off her dress as a young girl, and put on that of a wife. She wished to make a present of this dress in white and blue to Bernadette. Having the same mother, were they not in some degree sisters? It is the sole present that Bernadette ever accepted. She has worn it several years, until it was quite worn out. Ten years have passed by since this cure.

The sight of Mademoiselle Moreau has remained quite perfect. Never has she had a relapse, nor a slight indisposition. Upon leaving the convent of the Sacred Heart, Mademoiselle Moreau became the wife of M. d'Jzarn de Villefort, and has three children, boys, all remarkable for the beauty of their eyes.

VI.

Miraculous cures continued to multiply. They might be counted by hundreds. It was impossible to verify all. The Episcopal Commission submitted thirty to the strictest enquiry; never admitting the supernatural, but when it was impossible to do otherwise.

In their report to the bishop, the Commission, with the concurrence of the physicians, divided the cases into three categories. Having carefully studied them, they recorded all the details in the official report, which was signed in each case by the persons cured, together with the witnesses' signatures.

The first category comprised cures that were striking, but, nevertheless, susceptible of a natural explanation. They were six in number, viz., Jean Marie Arqué, the Widow Crozat, of Blaise Maumus, the child Laffitte, these three being inhabitants of Lourdes; the child Lasbareilles, of Gez, of Jean Crassus, of Arcizan-Avant; and Jeanne Pomiès, of Loubajac.

The second category was composed of cures that the commission were inclined to admit as supernatural. They were as follows, Jean Pierre

Malon, Jeanne Marie Daube, Bernarde Soubies, and Pauline Bordeaux, of Lourdes. Jean Marie Amaré, of Baucens. Marcel Peyregne, of Agose. Jeanne Marie Massot Bordenave, of Arras. Jeanne Gezma, and Auguste Bordes, of Poutacq.

"In these last cases, the greater part," said the medical enquiry, "presented nearly all the conditions required to be admitted as supernatural. In excluding them, we acted, perhaps, with too great reserve. Still we are satisfied that we were right in so doing, severity in such a matter being the prudent course."

The third class comprised those cases that presented themselves in a form clearly and undeniably supernatural. They were fifteen in number. Blaisette Soupène, of Benoîte Cazeaux; Jeanne Crassus; the wife, Crozat; of Louis Bourriette; of the infant, Justin Bouhohorts; of Fabian and Suzanne, Baron of Lourdes. Those of the widow Madame Rizan, and Henri Busquet, of Nay; of Catherine Latapie, of Soubajac; the widow Lauon, of Bordères; Marianne Garrot, and Denys Bouchet, of Lamarque; Jean Marie Tambourné, of Saint-Justin; Mdlle. Marie Moreau de Sazenay, of Tartas; and Paschaline Abbadie, of Rabasteins. All these were recognized as being incontestably miraculous.

In the face of such marvellous facts, so carefully and so publicly examined, in presence of an enquiry so conscientious, so complete, and deeply entered into, as was that of the Commission, taking into consideration the formal declarations and conclusions of chemistry and medicine united, the bishop could not fail to be convinced. And he

25

was completely convinced. At the same time, such was the extreme prudence with which he was endowed, that before pronouncing a solemn episcopal verdict on this momentous question, Mgr. Laurence required an additional proof of these supernatural cures, namely, that of time. He allowed three years to pass over, and then a second enquiry was instituted. The cures that had been acknowledged as miraculous, stood the test of time, none came forward to retract his former evidence, none to contest the facts. Lapse of time affects not the work of the Being who reigns in eternity. It was after this superabundant series of proofs that Mgr. Laurence at length gave his judgment, which was as follows.

VII.

MANDATE OF MGR. THE BISHOP OF TARBES,

Giving judgment on the Apparition that had taken place at the Grotto of Lourdes.

"Bertrand - Sévère - Laurence, by the Divine Mercy, and favour of the Holy Apostolic See, Bishop of Tarbes, Assistant to the Pontifical throne, &c. To the Clergy and Faithful of our diocese, health and benediction in the Lord Jesus Christ.

"In all the epochs of the human race, Dearly Beloved Co-operators, and our ever Dear Brethren, marvellous communications have been established between heaven and earth. At the beginning of the world the Lord appeared to our first parents

to reproach them for their crime of disobedience.
In the ages following we see Him conversing with
the patriarchs and prophets. And in the Old
Testament mention is often made of celestial
apparitions with which the Children of Israel were
favoured. These divine manifestations were not
to cease with the Mosaic law. On the contrary, it
was to be under the law of grace more frequent and
more astonishing. From the earliest infancy of
the Church, in the times of bloody persecution the
Christians received visits from Jesus Christ or
His angels, who came sometimes to reveal future
events, sometimes to deliver them from their
chains, sometimes to fortify them in their com-
bats. It is in this manner, according to the
belief of a judicious writer, that God encouraged
these illustrious confessors of the faith, when the
powerful of the earth united all their efforts to
strangle in the bud the doctrine that should save
the world. These supernatural manifestations
were not confined to the first ages of Christianity.
History attests that they have been perpetuated
from age to age for the advancement of religion
and the edification of the faithful.

"Amongst the celestial Apparitions, those of
the Blessed Virgin occupy a large place, and they
have been for the world a source of abundant
blessings. In passing through the Catholic world,
the traveller meets from place to place, temples
consecrated to the Mother of God, and many of
these monuments owe their origin to the Apparition of the Queen of Heaven. We possess already
one of these blest sanctuaries, founded four centuries ago, in consequence of a revelation made to

a young shepherdess, and where thousands of
pilgrims go every year to kneel before the throne
of the glorious Virgin Mary to implore her good
offices. Praise be rendered to the Most High !
in the infinite treasures of His bounty He has
reserved for us a new favour. He has decreed
that in the diocese of Tarbes a new sanctuary
should be raised to the glory of Mary. And what
is the instrument He employs to communicate to
us His designs of mercy ? *It is the very thing
which, according to the world, is thought the most
feeble.* A child fourteen years of age, Bernadette
Soubirous, born at Lourdes, of poor parents. (Here
the bishop recounts the history of the Apparitions
that appeared to Bernadette of the ever Blessed
Virgin. The reader is acquainted with them.
Mgr. Laurence continues.)

"Such is in substance the recital that we have
collected from the lips of Bernadette, in presence
of the Commission met together to consider the
matter for the last time.

" The young girl, therefore, had seen and heard
a being calling herself the Immaculate Conception,
and who, although clothed in a human form, had
neither been seen nor heard by any of the numerous spectators present at the scenes. It was consequently a supernatural being. What must be
thought of this event ?

" You are not ignorant, Our very dear Brethren,
that the Church guards a wise slowness, and
caution in matters relating to the supernatural.
She demands sure proofs before admitting and pro-
claiming them divine. Since the fall of man,
especially in such matters, human reason is sub-

ject to much error. Who does not know that sometimes the evil one transforms himself into an angel of light, in order to cause us to fall more easily into his snares? And so the beloved disciple tells us not to believe every spirit, but to prove if the spirits come from God. This proof we have made, ever Dear Brethren. The occurrence we relate to you has been for four years the object of our solicitude. We have watched it in its different phases, and we have called together a Commission composed of pious and intelligent priests, who have interrogated the girl, studied the facts, examined everything, and weighed everything. We have likewise called to our aid the assistance of science, and we have arrived at the conviction that the Apparition is supernatural and divine, and, consequently, that which Bernadette has seen, is the Ever-Blessed-Virgin. Our conviction is formed on the testimony of Bernadette, but more especially on the results, that can only be explained by Divine intervention.

"The testimony of the young girl presents all the guarantees that we could desire. And, in the first place, her sincerity has never been questioned. Who is there that does not admire, in approaching her, the modesty of this child? Whilst every one conversed on the marvels that had been revealed, she alone was silent. She never spoke of them unless interrogated, and then she recounted everything without affectation, and with a touching simplicity. To the numerous questions that were addressed to her, she gave, without hesitation, answers short, precise, and to the purpose, evidence of a strong conviction. Sub-

jected to severe trials, she has never been shaken
by menace, and to the most generous she has
replied by a noble disinterestedness. Always true
to herself, she has, in the different interrogatories
that has been put to her, constantly maintained
all that she had before stated, without adding or
retracting anything. The sincerity, then, of Bernadette, is incontestible. We may add, incon-
tested ; her contradictors, when she had any, have
themselves rendered her this homage.

   " But if Bernadette has not wished to deceive,
has she not been deceived herself? Might she
not have thought she saw and heard that which
she neither did see or hear ? Might she not have
been the victim of hallucination ? How can we
believe this ? The sagacity of her replies reveal
in this child a right spirit, a calm imagination, a
good sense beyond her years. The sentiment of
religion has never in her been pushed to extremes.
No one has ventured to state that there was in
the young girl either intellectual disorder, or
aberration of mind, or wildness of character, or
morbid affection, which might have disposed her
mind to imaginary creations. She saw not once
only, but eighteen times. She saw at first suddenly, when she could not have been prepared for
what occurred. And, during the fifteen days when
she expected to have seen the Vision each of those
days, she saw nothing during two of those days,
although she was placed in precisely identical
circumstances. And then what passed during the
Apparitions ? A transformation came over Bernadette, her physiognomy took a new expression,
her eyes revealed to the spectators that she saw

objects she had never before seen, she heard a language that she had never heard before, that she could not altogether comprehend, but of which, however, she preserved the recollection. These circumstances, united, will not permit the belief in hallucination. The young girl, then, really saw and heard a being calling herself The Immaculate Conception, and this phenomenon could not be explained naturally. We are, therefore, bound to believe that the Apparition is Supernatural.

"The evidence of Bernadette, important by itself, borrows additional force, we might say certainty, from the marvellous facts that were accomplished from the first moment. If one may judge the tree from its fruits, we can say that the apparition recounted by the young girl is supernatural and divine. What has passed, very dear Brothers? The Apparition was scarcely known, when the news spread with a rapidity of lightning: it was known that Bernadette was to go for fifteen consecutive days to the Grotto, and behold the whole country was afoot. Crowds rushed to the place of the Apparition, and awaited with religious impatience the solemn hour. And during the time that the young girl was in ecstasy, and absorbed by the object she contemplated, the witnesses of this prodigy, moved and softened, partook themselves of the same sentiment of admiration and prayer.

"The Apparitions ceased, nevertheless the concourse continued. Pilgrims came from distant countries, as well as from the neighbourhood, all hastening to the Grotto. There were seen press-

ing around it, persons of all ages, all ranks, all
conditions. And what was the sentiment that
animated these numerous and various visitors?
Ah! they came to the Grotto to pray, and ask
some favour from Immaculate Mary. They proved
by their collected attitude that they felt as if a
divine breath animated this rock that would
become for ever celebrated. Souls newly awakened were strengthened in virtue; men, cold
from indifference, have been led to the practice of
religion; obstinate sinners reconciled to God
after they had invoked in their favour our Lady of
Lourdes. These marvels of grace, that bear a
character of universality and duration, can have
God alone for its author. Does not this consequently confirm the truth of the Apparition?

"If, from the effects produced on the souls of
men, we pass to those relating to the body, what
fresh prodigies have we not to recount! Our
readers will call to mind the gushing forth of the
source where Bernadette drank and washed in
presence of the multitude. The sick, prompted
by an inward feeling, tried the waters of the
Grotto, and not without success. Many whose
infirmities had resisted treatment the most energetic, suddenly recovered their health. These
wonderful cures were circulated widely, the noise
spread far and wide.

"The sick of all countries sent for the waters of
Massabielle, when they could not be transported
themselves to the Grotto. How many infirm
have been healed! how many families consoled!
If we were to invoke their testimony, innumerable voices would arise to proclaim with accents

of thanksgiving the sovereign efficacy of the
waters of the Grotto. We cannot here enumerate
all the favours obtained; but what we are able to
say with certainty is, that the waters of Massabielle have cured the sick when abandoned and
declared incurable. And these cases have been
accomplished by the use of a water deprived of
all medicinal properties, as has been proved by
the reports of skilful chymists, who have made
the most rigorous analysis. Some have been cured
instantaneously, others after two or three applications of the water, either as a drink or a lotion.
And, moreover, the cures have been permanent.
What is the power that has produced these effects?
Is it the power of the organical structure?
Science consulted on the subject has answered in
the negative. These cures are then the work of
God. But it is through the Apparition that they
come; it is she who is the agent; it is she who
has inspired the confidence of the sick and
infirm: there is then a close affinity between the
cures and the Apparition. The Apparition is
divine, since the cures bear a divine seal. But
that which comes from God is true, consequently
the Apparition calling herself the Immaculate
Conception, that which Bernadette saw and heard,
is the Ever Holy Virgin. We declare then, the
finger of God is here! *Digitus Dei est hic!*

"Who is there that will not admire, ever dear
Brothers, the economy of Divine Providence?
At the close of 1854 the immortal Pius IX. pro-
claimed the dogma of the Immaculate Conception.
The sound went forth to the utmost extremities
of the earth, bearing the words of the Pontiff.

The hearts of Catholics beat with joy, and everywhere was celebrated the glorious privilege of Mary by the fêtes of which the remembrance remain for ever graven in our memories. And behold, about three years afterwards, the Holy Virgin appears to a child, and says to her, *I am the Immaculate Conception......I wish men to raise here a chapel to my honour.* Does it not seem that she wished to consecrate by a monument the infallible words of the successor of St. Peter?

"And where was it that she wished that this monument should be erected? It was at the foot of our Pyrenean mountains, a country where numerous strangers meet together, coming from all parts of the world to seek health at our thermal waters. Might it not be said that she invited the faithful of all nations to meet and honour her in the new temple that will be built to her?

"Inhabitants of the town of Lourdes, rejoice! The august Mary deigns to cast upon you her eyes of mercy. She desires that close to your town may be raised a sanctuary where she will pour out upon you her benefits. Thank her for this proof of predilection that she has manifested for you. And since she has showered upon you the tenderness of a mother, prove yourselves worthy to be her devoted children by imitating her virtues, and by your unalterable attachment to our holy religion.

"And, moreover, let us rejoice in seeing that the Apparition has already borne amongst you abundant fruits of salvation. You are eye-witnesses to the occurrences at the Grotto, and their happy results. Your confidence has been great, and your conviction has been strong We have admired your prudence, your docility in following our counsel by submission to the civil authority, when for some weeks you were obliged to cease your visits to the Grotto, and allow to ebb in your hearts the sentiments with which you have been inspired at the spectacle that had so vividly struck your eyes during the fifteen days of the Apparition.

"And to you all, much-loved inhabitants of our diocese, I say, open your hearts to hope. A new era of graces commences for you. You are all called to collect your part of the benedictions that are promised to us. In your supplications, and in your canticles, you will mingle henceforth the name of our Lady of Lourdes with the blessed names of our Lady of Guraison, of Poeylaün, of Héas, and of Piétat. From the heights of these sacred sanctuaries the Immaculate Virgin will watch over you, and cover you with her tutelary protection. Yes, ever dear fellow-labourers, and our very dear brothers, if, with hearts full of confidence, we keep our eyes fixed on this 'Star of the Sea,' we shall traverse without fear of shipwreck the tempests of life, and we shall arrive, safe and secure, in the haven of eternal bliss.

"*For these reasons*

"After having conferred with our Venerable Brothers, the Dignitaries, Canons, and Chapter of our Cathedral:

" Invoking the Holy Name of God :

"We establish, according to the rules wisely laid down by Benedict XIV. in his work on the Beatification and Canonization of Saints, for the discerning of Apparitions, true or false, as follows :—

"Considering the favourable report that has been presented to us by the Commission charged to examine into the Apparition at the Grotto of Lourdes, and the facts they had to try :

" Considering the written evidence of the doctors of medicine whom we have consulted on the subject of the numerous cures obtained in consequence of the use of the water of the Grotto :

" Considering, in the first place, that in looking at the fact of the Apparition, whether as regards the young girl, or in the extraordinary effects produced, they cannot be explained in any other way than by the supernatural :

" Considering, in the second place, that this occurrence cannot be other than divine, since, on the one hand, its effects have been such as to produce the sensible signs of grace, such as the conversion of sinners, and on the other, a change in the laws of nature, by miraculous cures that cannot be attributed to any other than the Author of Grace, and to the Master of the Universe :

" Considering, lastly, that our conviction is fortified by the immense and spontaneous concourse of the faithful to the Grotto, a concourse that has not ceased from the first Apparition, and whose end and object is to ask favours, or offer thanks for graces already obtained :

"In reply to the legitimate and urgent pressure of our Venerable Chapter, the clergy and laity of our diocese, and so many pious souls, who have for a long time asked the decision of ecclesiastical authority, which has been delayed solely from motives of prudence :

"Desirous, also, of satisfying the wishes of many of our colleagues in the episcopate, and a great number of distinguished personages unconnected with our diocese ;

"After having invoked the light of the Holy Spirit, and the assistance of the most Holy Virgin ;

"We have declared, and do declare as follows :—

"Art. I. It is our judgment that the Immaculate Mary, Mother of God, did really appear to Bernadette Soubirous, the 11th of February, 1858, and on eighteen other occasions, at the Grotto of Massabielle, near the town of Lourdes. That this Apparition was invested with all the characters of truth, and that the faithful may believe in the certainty of it.

"We humbly submit our judgment to that of the Sovereign Pontiff, who is charged with ruling over the Universal Church.

"Art. II. We authorize in our diocese the *culte* of our Lady of the Grotto of Lourdes ; but we forbid the publication of any particular formulary of prayers, any canticles, any book of devotion, relative to this event, without our approbation given in writing.

"Art. III. In order to conform to the will of the Holy Virgin, several times expressed by the

Apparition, we propose building a sanctuary on the spot, those lands having become the property of the Bishops of Tarbes.

"This construction, in consequence of the abrupt and difficult position of the site, will require a long period in erection, and the necessary funds will be considerable. Therefore, in order to realize our pious project, we require the assistance of the priests and faithful throughout France and other countries.

"We appeal to the generosity of their hearts, and particularly to all pious persons throughout the country, who are devoted to the *culte* of the Immaculate Conception of the Virgin Mary.

"Art. IV. We address ourselves with confidence to the Religious Orders, men and women, consecrated to the instruction of youth, to the congregations of the Children of Mary, to the Confraternities of the Holy Virgin, and to the different pious associations within our diocese, or throughout France.

"This our Mandate shall be read and published in all the churches, chapels, and oratories of seminaries, colleges, and hospitals, in our diocese, on the Sunday following the receipt thereof.

"Given at Tarbes, under our sign manual, with our seal, and counter-seal of our secretary, the 18th of January, 1862, Fête of the Chair of St. Peter at Rome.

✠ BERTRAND SRE.
BISHOP OF TARBES.

[By Order]
FOURCADE, *Canon-Secretary*."

VIII.

In the name of the bishopric, that is, in the name of the Church, Mgr. Laurence purchased from the town of Lourdes, the Grotto and the lands surrounding the entire group of the Massabielle Rocks. M. Lacadé was still the mayor. It was he who proposed to the municipal council ceding to the Church these precincts, to be for ever sacred, where had appeared the Mother of God. It was he who signed the deed of sale. M. Rouland authorized this sale, and also the construction of a church to the eternal memory of the Apparition of the Most Holy Virgin to Bernadette Soubirous, the gushing forth of the Fountain, and the innumerable miracles that were accomplished at it, attesting the reality of these divine visions.

Whilst the vast temple dedicated to the Immaculate Conception on the abrupt rocks of Massabielle was being raised stone by stone, our Lady of Lourdes continued to reply to the prayers of men by miracles and benefits. At Paris, Bordeaux, in Perigord, in Bretagne, Anjou, in the midst of solitary countries, in the bosom of populous towns, many invoked our Lady of Lourdes, and everywhere our Lady of Lourdes answered by unexceptionable signs of her power and goodness.

We shall give, before the close of this recital, some of these divine histories—one of which forms, in the life of the author of this book, an episode which, he says, he will never forget, and which he relates as follows.

In the preface to this work, M. Lasserre tells his readers that he undertook it in consequence of having himself received a signal favour from the Almighty. The following is his description of the circumstances, nearly seven years ago.

TENTH BOOK.

—

I.

Throughout the whole of my life I had excellent sight. I distinguished objects at an immense distance, and I could also read distinctly the smallest print. Nights passed in study never caused the least fatigue to my eyes. I was consequently greatly surprised and disappointed when, in the months of June and July, 1862, I felt my vision gradually becoming weak, and at length I was obliged completely to give up reading and writing in the evenings. If I attempted to take up a book, at the end of three or four lines, and sometimes even at the first glance, I experienced such pain that I was forced to lay it down. I consulted several physicians, and more especially two eminent oculists, M. Desmares, and M. Giraud-Teulon. The remedies they ordered were of very little use. One day I could read and write for some length of time in the afternoon, but on the following I fell back into the same state as before; in short, my infirmity assumed a chronic character, and threatened to be incurable. By the advice of my physicians I was condemned to absolute idleness. Not content with the precaution of wearing blue glasses, I left Paris for the country, and retired to my mother's residence,

25

accompanied by a young lad, who acted as my secretary. Three months had passed in this state, and in September I began to be seriously uneasy, as also were my friends, but we concealed our mutual alarm.

I have habitually confided my troubles and my joys to a very intimate friend whom I have known from childhood. I dictated a letter to him through my secretary, in which I informed him of my unhappy condition, and the great alarm I felt for the future.

The friend of whom I speak, and his wife, are both Protestants. I cannot give his name, but I shall call him M. de ——. In his answer to my letter, he said: "I have lately returned from Canterets, and passing through Lourdes (near Tarbes) visited the celebrated Grotto, and there I learned such astonishing things relating to cures effected by the use of these waters, principally for maladies of the eyes, that I would most seriously advise you to try them. If I were a Catholic, believing as you do, and were so afflicted, I should not hesitate to run the chance. If it be true that maladies have been suddenly cured, you may hope to increase the number; and if it be not true, what do you risk by the attempt? I may add that I have some little personal interest in this trial; and if it should be successful, what an important fact for me to register! I should have before me a miraculous fact, all the more striking, as the principal witness would be beyond suspicion. It appears," added my friend, in a postscript, "that it is not necessary to go to Lourdes to take this water; you have only to

apply to the parish priest, and he will forward a
bottle of it to you. It will be necessary previously
to perform certain formalities, of what nature I
am unable to inform you, but this you will learn
from the Curé of Lourdes. Beg of him also to
send a little pamphlet, by the Vicar General of
Tarbes, relating to the miraculous cures which
have been well attested."

My friend's letter greatly surprised me. He
has a clear, practical, mathematical mind, not
much inclined to be carried away by enthusiasm.
He, moreover, is a Protestant, as I have said ; so
such counsel coming from him astonished me all
the more. I resolved, however, upon not following it, and in my reply said I felt somewhat
better, and that if I continued to improve there
would be no necessity to have recourse to the
extraordinary remedy he advised, and that perhaps
I had not the necessary faith.

The secret motive of my resistance was, I am
ashamed to say, that I should be under the necessity of going to confession. At the same time, I
was not wanting in faith. And though knowing
nothing of the miraculous water, save what was
said of it in some evil-minded journals, I had the
moral certainty that there, as in many other
places, the power of God could manifest itself by
cures. Nay, more : I had an assured presentiment that if I tried this water that had burst
forth, as was said, in consequence of an Apparition of the Holy Virgin, I should be cured. But
I acknowledge I feared the responsibility of so
great a favour. " If an ordinary physician were
to cure me," I said to myself, " I should be quits

at once upon paying him; but if God did so by a miracle, that would be altogether another affair, and I should then be obliged to amend my life in good earnest. If God gave my eyes to me as it were a second time, how could I allow them to wander as formerly? After a miracle operated in my favour, God would exact His salary, and it would be more troublesome to pay Him than the doctor." So, fearing my weakness, I refused the grace of God, and the counsel that Providence, always so hidden and inscrutable in its ways, had sent me by one outside the Church. Vainly, however, I resisted; an inward voice told me that man was powerless to effect a cure, and that the Master whom I had offended wished Himself to restore my sight, and by so doing give me a new life, and a fresh opportunity to lead a better. Meanwhile, my condition remained stationary, or rather somewhat more aggravated.

In the early part of October I was obliged to go to Paris, and by a fortuitous circumstance, M. de —— and his wife were there. My first visit was to them. My friend was staying with his sister, who lived in Paris with her husband, M. P——.

"And what about your eyes?" enquired Madam de M. upon my entering the room.

"They are in the same state, and I begin to fear I have lost my sight for ever," I replied.

"But why not try the remedy we recommended?" said my friend. "Something tells me that, were you to do so, you would be cured."

"Bah!" I replied, "I confess that, without denying positively, or being hostile, I have no

great faith in all these waters and pretended apparitions. I am not reluctant to believe them possible, but never having examined the matter, I
neither affirm nor contest it; it is beyond me.
In short, I have no great inclination to have recourse to the means you advise."

"But you have no valid objection," he said to
me, "and according to your religious principles
you ought to believe in these things. Why not
then make a trial? What will it cost you to do
so? I tell you that it can do you no harm, as it
is natural water; its chemical composition shows
it to be such, and since you believe in miracles,
and have faith in your religion, are you not struck
by advice given you by Protestants to have recourse to the Virgin? I declare beforehand that
if you are cured it will be a terrible argument
against me."

Madam de —— joined her entreaties to those
of her husband; M. and Madam P———, who
are Catholics, insisted not less strongly. I was
driven into my last entrenchment. "Well!" I
said at last, "I will tell you the whole truth. I
am not a disbeliever, but I have failings, and
many miseries. Now, such a miracle would impose upon me the obligation of sacrificing all in
order to become a saint, that would be a terrible
responsibility, and I am coward enough to fear
it. If God were to cure me, what would He not
exact of me? In the case of an ordinary physician I should be quits with him for a little money.
You suppose my faith wavering, and that I fear
the miracle should not take place. You are
wrong, my fear is that it may succeed!" My

friend tried to convince me that I exaggerated the responsibility in one way, and diminished it in another.

"Should you be cured by a physician," said he, "you would receive a gift from heaven which would oblige you just as much to lead a virtuous life." This did not appear to me quite clear; however, at length I gave up the battle to my friends, and said I should write to Lourdes as soon as I could provide myself with a secretary.

"I will be your secretary on this occasion," said M. de ———.

"Well, be it so; to-morrow we shall breakfast together at the *Café de Foy*, afterwards we can see about the letter."

"Why not at once ?" said he, "we shall save a day." I consented, and dictated a letter to the parish priest at Lourdes, which was posted the same evening.

The following day M. de ——— came to me. "My dear friend," he said, "since the lot is cast, and you are about to try this water, you should do the thing seriously, and follow the requisite conditions, without which the trial would be useless. Go to confession and put your soul into a proper state, in short, perform whatever your religion requires. You understand that this is of primary importance."

"You are perfectly right," I said, "and I will do as you direct. But it must be confessed that you are a singular Protestant; the last few days you have been preaching faith to me, and now you preach the practice of religion. The tables are strangely turned, for who would not wonder at hearing us speak in this way, you a Protestant and I a Catholic. I must confess, alas! the impression would not be to my advantage."

"I am a scientific man," replied he, "and it is but natural I should wish, since the experiment is to be made, that the necessary conditions should be fulfilled. I reason in the same way as if it was a matter of physical science, or chymistry."

I acknowledged to myself the necessity of making my confession, but as I had not committed any gross sins, such as would cause sudden reaction, I deferred from day to day. Man is more averse to the sacrament of penance during temptation, than after sin has been committed, when he feels its humiliation. It is less easy to combat and resist, than to ask pardon after a fall. Who has not experienced this?

About a week passed thus. M. and Madam de ———— enquired each day if I had received an answer from the Curé of Lourdes. The latter replied at length, announcing that he had forwarded the water by mail, and that I should soon receive it. We awaited its arrival impatiently, but, strange to say, the impatience was less on my side than on that of my Protestant friend.

One morning, Friday, the 10th of October, 1862, I awaited M. de ———— in the Galerie d'Orleans, in the Palais Royal, as we were to breakfast together. I was at the rendezvous before him, and tried meanwhile to read two or three advertisements of new works in front of the library Dentu. Large as was the print, the

fatigue to my eyes was so great, that I was obliged
to desist. I felt much depressed by this circumstance, which was a fresh proof of the terrible extent of the malady.

That day, on returning home, the porter told
me that a little case, addressed to me, had arrived
from the railway station. I hurried into his
room, and found a little wooden box labelled,
Eau naturelle. I did not allow the great emotion I felt to appear, and saying that I should
return presently and take the case upstairs, went
out and walked about pensively for a few minutes.
The matter has now become serious, I thought,
De ——————— is right, and I must prepare forthwith in good earnest. In the present state of my
soul, I could not ask of God to perform a miracle
in my favour. I must strive to cure my soul
before I supplicate Him to heal my body. And,
reflecting thus, I directed my steps to the house of
my confessor, the Abbé Ferrand de Missol. He
was at home, but, as several persons were already
waiting in the ante-chamber, they would see him,
of course, before me. Some time after, his servant
asked me to return in the evening about seven
o'clock. I left, and, on going into the street,
hesitated as to whether I should not make a visit
that I had much at heart, or pursue my first intention of going home to pray. An inward voice
called me to recollection. I deliberated for a long
time, feeling strongly inclined towards the side of
the distraction, but at length my good angel prevailed, and I returned to my lodgings. I took the
little case from the porter, and, entering my apartment, knelt down and prayed, all unworthy as I

was to turn my eyes towards heaven and speak to God. Then I arose. I had placed the case and a pamphlet on the Apparitions of Lourdes, on the mantel-piece, and could not refrain from constantly turning my eyes towards the box containing the mysterious water, I felt tempted to open it, and not to wait till after my confession, as I had proposed. This struggle lasted some time, then I exclaimed, "My God, I am a miserable sinner, and unworthy to touch an object you have blessed, but the depth of my misery will excite your compassion." Invoking next the assistance of the Mother of Mercy, I ventured to open the case and uncork the bottle, then poured some of the water into a cup, and took a towel in my hand. To this day I retain a vivid recollection of the solemnity impressed on these preparations, common-place as they were. I felt assured that in this solitary chamber something extraordinary was about to happen. Again I knelt to pray, then bathed my eyes and forehead with the water of Lourdes. Scarcely had I done so when, to my surprise, I may almost say alarm, I was instantly cured, and with the speed of lightning.

Strange contradiction of human nature! A moment before my faith had promised me a cure, and now I could scarce believe my senses that assured me it was accomplished. I committed the fault of Moses, and struck the rock twice, that is to say, I continued to pray and bathe my eyes and forehead, not daring to rise and prove my cure. At the end of ten minutes, however, I could doubt no longer, and looked for some book on which I might try my sight. Then, making a

sudden stop, "No," thought I, "it is not any sort
of book that suits me at this moment;" and, taking
up the notice on the Apparitions, I read upwards
of one hundred pages without experiencing the
least fatigue.   Twenty minutes before I could not
have read three lines !   When I left off at the
one hundred and fourth page, it was just half
past five o'clock, p. m., and the 10th of October,
when it is almost night in Paris.   That evening
I made my confession, and informed the Abbé
Ferrand of the great mercy I had received from
Heaven.   Although, as I have already said, I was
unprepared, he allowed me to communicate on the
following morning, to return thanks to God for
so special and extraordinary a favour, and to
strengthen the good resolutions that such an event
ought to call forth in my heart.

M. and Madam ——, as may be well supposed,
were singularly affected by an occurrence in which,
through Providence, they had taken so prominent
a part.   What passed in their hearts is their own
secret and that of God.   What I do know I am
not at liberty to divulge.   God knows His hour
and the mode He chooses to attain His ends.
His action was too apparent in what had happened,
for me not to avoid interference on my own side,
notwithstanding the desire I felt, and which my
friends were aware of, that they should enter the
Catholic Church.

Seven years have passed since my miraculous
cure.   My sight is excellent, and neither reading,
nor long evenings passed in arduous toil, affect it
in the least.   May God grant me the grace never
to employ them other than in His service.

II.

ANOTHER EPISODE.

We sometimes meet among civilians persons whose air and manner resemble that of a soldier; although never having lived in camps, all who pass mistake them for military men, they have a carriage somewhat stiff, a firm walk, regimental aspect, and good nature, concealed under this appearance. Such men are often met with amongst those connected with public offices; though purely civil their employment, they adopt much of their system from the army. On the one hand they have, as men of private life, a family, a home, and domestic existence; on the other, they are moulded in a thousand ways into a rule altogether military. Hence result those singular physiognomies of which we speak.

Again, if you have ever seen a brave cavalry officer in the dress of a citizen, his hair and moustache closely trimmed, the latter commencing to turn grey, if you have remarked in addition to his energetic features, those lines in the face, peculiar, as it were, to the soldier; if you have cast your eyes on the forehead, evidently disdaining the hat, but which appears made expressly for the military cap, or the three-cornered silver-laced hat covering those eyes, firm, yet soft, that by day are accustomed to brave danger, and at night love to be assuaged by the attractions of his own hearth and caress his children; if you can bring such a type to your imagination, you have before you M. Roger Lacassagne, employé in the custom-house at Bordeaux.

"When I first called on him, about two years since," says M. Lasserre, "at the Rue du Chai des Farines, No. 6, at Bordeaux, I was struck at once by his severe aspect and rude exterior. He asked me, with that politeness, somewhat sudden, of men in office, the object of my visit. 'Sir,' I said, 'I have heard the history of your journey to Lourdes, and am engaged at present in the study of this subject; I came to learn the history from your own lips.' "

At the words, "Grotto of Lourdes," the rough countenance expanded with emotion, and the austere lines in his face softened. "Be seated," said the honest man, "and pardon my having to receive you in this disordered apartment. My family have gone to Arcachon, and so our house is disarranged."

"It is of no consequence," said I; "relate to me the occurrence of which I have been imperfectly informed."

"For myself," said he, in a voice filled with emotion, "for myself, I shall never forget, during my life, any of the details. Sir," said he, after a moment's silence, "I have but two sons, the younger of whom I am about to speak, is named Julius. You will see him presently, and you will remark how gentle he is; he is good and pure.

M. Lacassagne did not tell me how great was his affection for his little boy, but the accent of his voice became so tender and caressing when speaking of the child, as to reveal at once the depth of his paternal affection, and I understood the feeling that concentrated itself in the manly heart that was opening his mind to me.

"His health," continued he, "had been excellent up to his tenth year, when there came upon him unexpectedly, and without any apparent cause, a malady, the gravity of which I could not at that time have conceived. On the 25th of January, 1865, just as we were about to sit down to supper, Julius complained of a stoppage in his throat that prevented him from swallowing solid food, and consequently, he could only take a little soup. This state continuing the following day, I called in one of the most distinguished physicians of Toulouse, M. Noguès."

"It is a nervous complaint," said the doctor to me, giving me, at the same time, hopes of a speedy cure. And, in fact, a few days after the boy could eat, and I believed that all would have been right, when the malady again seized him and took an intermittent form more or less regularly up to the end of the month of April. And from this time his state became stationary. The poor child had to be nourished exclusively with liquids, milk, gravy and soup, and it was necessary even to strain the latter, for such was the extreme minuteness of the orifice in his throat that it was absolutely impossible for him to swallow even so fine a substance as tapioca. The poor little fellow, reduced to this miserable diet, became daily thinner and thinner.

The physicians, for there were two, as from the commencement, I had begged a well-known medical man, M. Roques, to consult with M. Noguès. —The physicians were astonished at the singu-

larity and persistence of the malady, and endeavoured in vain to discover a remedy. One day,
the 10th of May, (for I retain all the dates in my
mind, so much had I thought and suffered from
this sad affair,) one day, being in my garden, I
saw Julius running with unusual precipitation,
and in a strange manner. I was apprehensive of
the least agitation, and calling to him to stop, I
took him by the hand. He instantly escaped
from me. "Papa," said he, "I cannot, I must
run, whether I like it or not." I placed him on
my knees, his limbs shook convulsively, and soon
after, his face became distorted. The true character of the malady now declared itself. My unfortunate son was seized with the dreadful complaint
known by the name of St. Vitus's dance. The
principal seat of the malady was in the gullet.
The doubts of physicians were now settled. Still,
though recognizing the form of the disease, they
were powerless in their endeavours to conquer it.
All they were able to effect after fifteen months
treatment, was to appease the agitation of the
limbs and head, or rather, as I am disposed to
think, these disappeared of their own accord, by
an effort of nature—and as for the extreme contraction of the throat, it became chronic and
resisted remedies of all kinds; the country, and
the baths of Luchon were successively and uselessly
tried for a period of nearly two years. These
various treatments seemed only to annoy the suf-
ferer. Our last attempt was a season at the
sea-side—my wife took our child to Saint Jean de
Luz. It is needless to tell you that his condition
of health absorbed all our means. Our great

desire was to keep him alive. All work and study was interdicted, we treated him as a hot-house plant.

Now, he was endowed with an active and serious mind, and this privation of all intellectual exercise plunged him into the deepest gloom. The poor little fellow was moreover ashamed of his malady ; he saw other children running about in the enjoyment of health, and he felt himself disgraced, and as it were, an outcast, and so he avoided society.

The father, at this part of his story, moved at the recollection of these events, stopped for an instant, endeavouring to master his tears. He avoided society, he repeated, and necessarily was sad. When a book fell in his way, he would take it up to pass away the time. And it so happened that at Saint-Jean-de Luz he one day saw on the table of a lady who lived in the neighbourhood, a little pamphlet on the Apparition at Lourdes. He read it, and was, it appears, deeply struck by its contents, and told his mother the same evening, that he was sure the Holy Virgin could cure him ; but she paid no attention to these, as she thought, childish words.

Upon returning to Bordeaux, (for a short time previously, I had been ordered to the place at which I now reside)—Upon returning to Bordeaux, the boy was in precisely the same condition. It was in August last. After such vain efforts, so much spent upon physicians, all to no purpose, you can well conceive how greatly we were dejected. Discouraged by the uselessness of all these different trials, we ceased to use remedies, allowing nature to act, and resigning ourselves to the inevitable evil it pleased the Almighty to send us. It seemed as if so much suffering had in some manner redoubled our love for this child. Our poor Julius was nursed by his mother and by myself with an equal tenderness and solicitude at all times. This trouble has added many years to both our lives. Old as I appear to be, I am but forty-six years of age.

I looked at the poor father; upon the manly visage where grief had left his mark, my heart felt moved, and I seized his hand in cordial sympathy and commiseration.

However, he went on to say, the child's strength visibly diminished. During two years he had never taken solid food. It was only by great cost, and using all our ingenuity to make the liquid nourishment as substantial as possible, that we had been able to prolong his life. He had become frightfully emaciated. His pallor was extreme, he appeared to have no blood in his body, so that one would have said he was a statue made in wax. It was visible that death was fast approaching. It was certain, and imminent. In truth, sir, notwithstanding the failure of medical skill, such was my grief that I could not prevent myself from again having recourse to medicine. Nothing else presented itself to my mind. And I called in the most eminent physician in Bordeaux, M. Gintrac. He examined the child's throat by probing, and stated that in addition to its extreme contraction, (the alimentary canal being almost closed,) it presented rugosities which was a very bad symptom—shook his head, and gave me but little hope. Seeing my great anxiety, he added,

" I do not say that a cure is impossible, *but he is very ill.*" These were his words. He employed local remedies, first injections, afterwards, ether applied to the part affected. But this treatment so upset my son, that it was thought prudent to abandon it.

In one of my visits to Dr. Gintrac, I spoke to him of an idea that had occurred to my mind. "It appears to me," I said, "that if Julius *determined to do so,* he could swallow, and perhaps this difficulty may be the effect of fear, a malady of the mind, and can only be cured by moral power."

The doctor dispelled this illusion. "You deceive yourself," said he. "The malady is in the organ, that is too surely and seriously attacked. The eye may be deceived, but I have probed the part with an instrument, and have felt it likewise with my finger. The gullet is covered with wrinkles, and the passage so much closed, that it is impossible for the child to take other nourishment than liquids, the orifice is such as a needle only could pass. Should the slightest swelling in the throat occur, he would be suffocated.

" The commencement of the malady was characterized by alternatives, well one day, and ill the next. These slight interruptions corroborate my observations. Had your son been once cured, he would have continued so, if the malady were on the mind. Unhappily, the complaint is in the organs."

The same observations had already been made to me at Toulouse, but I did not like to accept

26

them. I was, however, now convinced. I returned home completely cast down.

What was now to be done? We had tried the
most skilful physicians at Toulouse and Bordeaux,
all to no purpose. The fatal evidence was before
my eyes. Our poor son could not survive.

It was while we were in this sad and despairing
state that Julius said to my wife, with an accent
of confidence and certainty that struck her forcibly,
the following words :—"You see, mother, that
neither M. Gintrac nor any other physician can
do anything for me. It is the Holy Virgin that
will cure me. Send me to the Grotto of Lourdes,
and you will see that I shall be cured. I am sure
of it." Upon my wife informing me of this, I
said that we should not hesitate, that he must be
taken to Lourdes, and the sooner the better.

It was not, sir, that I had faith. I did not
believe in miracles, I did not think these extraordinary interventions of the Deity possible. But
I was a father, and any chance, however small,
was not in my mind to be neglected. I hoped,
moreover, independent of supernatural occurrences,
that this might produce on the child a salutary
moral effect. But as a complete cure, you can
understand, sir, that such an idea did not even
enter my mind.

We were then in winter, at the beginning of
February. The weather was bad, and I was
apprehensive lest Julius should suffer in travelling
at such a time, and wished him to wait for fairer.
From the day he had read, eight months previously at Saint-Jean-de-Luz, the little notice before
mentioned, this feeling never left him. Having

expressed his belief as related, and no notice having been taken, he spoke no more about it; but the idea remained and increased during the time that he submitted, with what patience we have seen, sir, to the treatment of the physicians.

This faith, so full and so complete, was all the more wonderful as the child had not been brought up in a very devotional manner. My wife fulfilled her religious duties, but that was all, and as for myself, as I have already told you, my philosophical ideas led me to a very different way of thinking.

On the 12th of February the weather became fine. We took the train to Tarbes. During the entire way the child was gay, and full of faith in being cured,—a faith overwhelming. "I shall be cured," he would say to me every moment. "You will see it. Many others have been cured, and why not I? The Holy Virgin will cure me."

And I, sir, continued to talk to him, but without partaking in this confidence so great, this confidence that I may characterize so *astounding*, if I may so say, without disrespect to that God who had inspired it.

At Tarbes, we alighted at the Hotel Dupont. The people remarked this poor child, so pale, so ailing, and at the same time, with an aspect so gentle and charming, that one liked to look upon him. A good omen might have been drawn from the interest and desire shown by these people, and when we left, I could see that they awaited our return with anxiety.

However, in spite of my doubts, I took with me a box of biscuits. Upon arriving at the Crypt, which is over the Grotto, Mass was going on. Julius prayed with a faith apparent on his countenance, a celestial ardour. The poor child seemed transfigured.

The priest had remarked his fervour, and on leaving the altar, he returned almost immediately from the sacristy and advanced towards us. A happy thought came into his mind on seeing the poor boy. He went to Julius still on his knees.

"My child," said he, "would you wish that I should consecrate you to the Holy Virgin ?"

"Oh! yes," replied Julius.

The priest proceeded at once with this simple ceremony, and recited over my son the formularies. "And now," cried the child, with an accent of perfect confidence which struck me, "and now, father, I am going to be cured." We descended to the Grotto. The child knelt before the statue of the Blessed Virgin, and prayed. I watched the expression on his countenance, his attitude, and his hands joined. He arose, and we went to the fountain. It was a terrible moment. He washed his neck and breast. Then he took the glass and drank a few mouthfuls of the miraculous water. He was calm, happy, gay, radiant with confidence. As for me, I trembled at what was going on. It was with difficulty that I contained my emotion. I did not wish him to perceive my doubts.

"Try now to eat," I said, offering him a biscuit. He took it, and I turned aside my head, not having sufficient strength to look at him. It was, in fact, life or death that was about to be decided. In this position, so terribly anxious to a father's heart, I played, as it were, my last card. If I failed, I had the certainty before me that my well-beloved son was doomed to an early grave. This last effort would have been decisive, and I could not have endured the sight.

My agony was of short duration. Julius, in a voice at once joyous and soft, said, "Papa! I can swallow, I can eat, I was sure of it, I had the faith that it would be so!"

Sir! judge of my situation. My child about to fall into the grave, was saved, and so suddenly. And I, his father, a witness to this astonishing resurrection! However, lest my son should be agitated, I had the presence of mind not to appear surprised. "Yes, Julius, it was certain, and could not have been otherwise," I said to him, in a voice as calm as I could assume. And nevertheless, sir, a tempest was raging within me. If anyone could have seen into my breast, they would have found it burning as if it had been on fire.

We renewed the trial. He eat some more biscuits, not only without difficulty, but with an increased appetite. I was obliged to caution moderation.

I now felt a desire to give thanks to God, and saying to Julius, "Wait here for me and pray to the Blessed Virgin," I ascended the hill to the chapel, and leaving him on his knees at the Grotto, I ran to announce the happy news to the priest. My mind was in a state of disorder. A happiness so sudden and unexpected completely upset me. And added to this, a revolution had come over me, causing agitation, tumult and confusion in my breast. All my former philosophi-

cal ideas fell to the ground and crumbled into
pieces.

The priest hastily descended, and found Julius
finishing his last biscuit. The Bishop of Tarbes
happening to be that day at the Grotto, expressed
a wish to see my son. I recounted to him the
deplorable state in which the child had been for so
long a period.

I now thought of his mother, and the happiness
that awaited her. I ran to the telegraph office,
my despatch contained but one word, "cured."
Scarcely had it been sent when I felt a desire to recall it. Perhaps, thought I, my haste has been too
great. Who knows but that he may have a
relapse! I dared not believe in the happiness
that had come to me; when I thought of it, I
feared lest it should escape me. As for the child,
he was happy without the least mixture of uneasiness, glowing with joy and confidence.

"You see, papa," he repeated frequently, "that
none but the Holy Virgin could cure me. When
I told you so, I was sure of it."

At the hotel, he eat with an excellent appetite.
I could not take my eyes off him. He was anxious
to return to the Grotto, and again express his
thankfulness; he did so on foot. The priest
found him there, and said, "You will be ever
thankful to the Holy Virgin." He pointed to
her image, and then towards heaven. "Ah! I
shall never forget her," cried he.

At Tarbes, on our return to the same hotel, we
found the people on the watch for us. They had
a certain degree of presentiment as to how the
event would turn out, and showed an extraordinary

joy. They grouped themselves around us in order to see the child eat, and he partook of everything before him. The previous evening he could only swallow a few spoonfulls of liquid. This malady, that had baffled the skill of the most eminent physicians, and of which he was miraculously cured, had lasted two years and nineteen days.

We were anxious to return to his mother, and took the express train to Bordeaux. The child, overcome by the fatigue of the journey, probably increased by the excitement occasioned by the sudden cure, wished to go to bed on our arrival, and, overcome by sleep, eat no supper. When his mother saw him in this state, and refusing food, though filled with joy before our arrival, was now seized with doubt and anxiety, said I was under a delusion. What then was her happiness, when, the next morning, our Julius sat down to breakfast with a better appetite than ourselves! Then only did she become tranquillized and reassured.

"And from this time," I asked, "has he had any return of the malady?" "None, sir, none whatever," was the reply. "And the physicians," I said, "have they acknowledged by any written declaration the former state of Julius? It would have been only fair to have done so."

I think with you, sir, and I pressed the doctor at Bordeaux upon this point, as he was the last who had the care of my son, but he preserved such a reserve on the subject that I could not urge him further. However, Dr. Roques of Toulouse, to whom I at once wrote, did not hesitate to acknowledge the miraculous character of the fact which was accomplished, so far beyond the power of

medicine. "In presence of this cure, so long
desired, and so promptly obtained," he said to me,
"we must quit the narrow horizon of scientific
explanation, and open the mind to the avowal, in
this strange event, that Providence seemed to
yield to the faith of a child." He repudiated
energetically, as a physician, the theories that
were put forward in like cases, such as, "moral
stimulus," "effects of imagination," &c.; and he
acknowledged freely in this case, "a precise action,
positive, of a superior existence, revealing itself,
and imposing on the conscience."

Such was, sir, he said, the appreciation of M.
Roques, physician at Toulouse, who knew as well
as myself the former condition and malady of my
son. Here is his letter, dated February 24.

Moreover, the facts that I have related were so
notorious, that no one attempted to contest them.
It was superabundantly established that science had
been utterly powerless against the strange malady
by which Julius had been attacked. As to the
cause of the cure, each person is at liberty to think
for himself. As for me, who, before these extraordinary facts, believed only in purely natural
action, I now see that I must seek explanation
from a higher order of things. And every day I
live I return thanks to God who, in putting so
unexpected an end to this long and severe trial,
wished, at the same time, to use it in drawing me
more to Himself.

I understand, I said, your thoughts and sentiments, and it appears to me in the same light as
it does to you, that such were the Divine plans.
Having said these words, I remained a long time

silent, absorbed in my reflections. Afterwards the conversation reverted to the child so miraculously cured. The father's heart ever turned to that point, as the needle to the North Pole.

From this period, said he, he has been endued with the piety of an angel. You will see him immediately. High-mindedness is visible in his countenance; his nature is upright and elevated. He is incapable of falsehood or deceit. And, moreover, his piety has developed to a still higher degree his natural qualities. He goes to the school of M. Conagle, close at hand, Rue du Mirail. The poor boy has very quickly made up by attention for his loss of time. He is fond of study, and the first in his class. At the last distribution of prizes he received the highest. But what is of still more consequence, he is sensible, gentle, and good, and he is beloved by his masters and school-fellows, and is our joy and consolation.

At this moment the door opened, and Julius entered with his mother, the apartment in which we were sitting. I arose and kissed him. A glow of health was spread over his face. His forehead was open, his attitude had a modest and gentle firmness that inspired secret respect. His eyes, large and very bright, reflected a rare intelligence, purity, and a well-ordered mind.

You are a happy father, said I, to M. Lacassagne. Yes, sir, very happy, but my wife and I have suffered much.

I took him a little aside from Julius. Do not complain, I said, the thorny path of grief was the road that conducted you from darkness to light, from death to life, and yourself to God. At Lourdes the Holy Virgin showed herself doubly as the mother of the living. She gave to your son a temporal life, and to yourself an eternal.

I quitted this family blest of God, and, impressed with a strong feeling at what I had seen and heard, and with my heart moved, I wrote that which I now recount.

ELEVENTH BOOK.

I.

Let us return to Lourdes. Time had passed, and human activity was at work. The vicinity of the Grotto where the Virgin appeared had changed its aspect. Without losing anything of its grandeur, this wild and rugged place had assumed a lively and pleasant appearance. A superb church, as yet unfinished, was proudly rising on the summit of the Rocks of Massabielle. This steep eminence, hitherto uncultivated, where the foot of the mountaineer could with difficulty traverse, was now covered with a verdant turf; among dahlias, roses, and acacias, a broad winding path, neatly kept, and gravelled, led from the church to the Grotto. The latter was enclosed by a gate and iron rails, so as to form a sanctuary. From the vault was suspended a gilt lamp. Under those sylvan rocks, where the Holy Virgin had placed her feet, a number of wax candles burned night and day. Outside this enclosure, a portion of the miraculous stream flowed from three bronze tubes into a stone reservoir, the remainder being conducted by a channel cut in the rock, to baths so constructed as to allow the infirm to bathe un-

observed in the blessed water. The course of the
mill-stream, and that of the Gave itself, had been
removed to some distance in order to allow the
construction of a convenient road conducting to
these rocks, formerly so completely unknown, and
now so famous. Along the banks of the river the
ground had been levelled, and formed a long
green sward planted in lines of elm and poplar.

All these changes were accomplished in the
midst of an incessant concourse of believers.
Copper money thrown daily in quantities by the
people into the Grotto, and votive offerings acknowledging favours received in the cure of maladies either of soul or body; these were the means
by which a gigantic work was being carried on,
the general estimate approximating two millions
of francs. When God, in His goodness, deigns to
call upon man to co-operate directly in His works,
He employs neither soldiers nor tax-gatherers,
nor *gens darmes*, to raise the impost, accepting
nought from the creature of His hands but what
is offered willingly. The Master of the universe repudiates compulsion. Thus the church
was raised, the course of the river altered, the
ground levelled, trees planted, and roads formed
around these celebrated rocks where the Mother of
Christ had manifested herself in her glory to the
eyes of a mortal.

Encouraging the workmen, surveying all that
went on, suggesting ideas, putting sometimes his
own hands to the work, to raise a stone wrongly
placed, or a tree ill-planted, was a man of lofty
stature, reminding the beholder by his indefatigable ardour and enthusiasm of the grand form of

Esdras or Nehemias, occupied by God's command in constructing the walls of Jerusalem. Conspicuous by his height and long black robe, the Abbé Peyramale, for it was he, seemed to be at all points at once. The message sent to him by the Most Holy Virgin, was unceasingly present to his mind, the miraculous cures that were performed each day before his eye, stimulated his zeal to devote his life in executing the commands of the Queen of Heaven. The least delay or time lost seemed to him ingratitude on the part of man, and frequently excited his indignation. His faith was unbounded, and soared high above the miserable narrownesses of human prudence, which he trod under foot with the disdain of one accustomed to view things from the height of that mountain whence the Son of God proclaimed the nothingness of this world and the greatness of heaven. "Be not afraid......Seek ye first My kingdom, and all the rest shall be added unto you."

One day the architect approached M. l'Abbé Peyramale, who was standing with a group of ecclesiastics and laymen before the miraculous fountain, and presented to him the design for a church over the Grotto. It was pretty, but small, and the Curé had no sooner cast his eyes on the plan, than the blood mounted to his face, and, tearing it to pieces, he cast the shreds into the Gave. "What are you doing?" exclaimed the amazed architect.

"You see," replied the priest, "I blush at the meanness of such an offering to the Mother of my God. What ought to be erected here in memory of the great events that have been accomplished, is not a little village church, but a marble temple, as extensive as the space will admit on the summit of the Rocks of Massabielle, and as magnificent as your imagination can conceive. Sir, let nothing arrest your genius, and let us have a *chef-d'œuvre*. Know, moreover, that were you even a Michael Angelo, your plan would still be utterly unworthy of the Virgin that appeared here."

"But, M. Peyramale," observed those around, "it would cost millions to realize your idea."

"She who called forth the fountain from the sterile rock, can also excite generosity in the hearts of the faithful. Go," he added, "and doubt not. Why are ye afraid, Christians of little faith?"

A temple was raised in accordance with the wish expressed by the man of God. Often did he exclaim, as he viewed the works: "When shall it be granted to me to assist with the priests and faithful, at the first procession, that inaugurates in this hallowed spot the public worship of the Catholic Church? Ought I not then to sing my *Nunc dimittis?*" And at this thought his eyes filled with tears.

Occasionally, at the time when there were fewest people at the rocks of Massabielle, a little girl came humbly to kneel there and drink at the Fountain. She was a child of the people, and poorly clothed. Nothing distinguished her from others, and unless she happened to be known to one of the pilgrims, who might point her out to the rest, none could divine that this was Berna-

dette. The privileged of the Lord had retired
into shade and silence. She continued to attend
the Sister's school, where she was the simplest of
all, and would willingly have been ignored. The
numberless visits she received did not disturb her
peace of mind, before which she had ever present
the thought of heaven, and the remembrance of
the incomparable Virgin. Bernadette preserved
these things in her heart. Like the saintly
priest of Lourdes, she too looked forward, as to
the happiest of days, that on which she should
see the priests of God themselves lead the faithful, with the cross in front and banners unfolded,
to the Rock of the Apparition.

On the 4th of April, 1864, the Church took
solemn possession of this spot, for ever sacred, by
the inauguration of a statue of the Holy Virgin,
in fine Carrara marble, placed, with all the usual
pomp in such cases, in a rustic niche, above the
Grotto where the Mother of God had appeared to
a daughter of men. The concourse of people
that came to witness this grand fete of earth and
heaven was immense. A procession, such as was
never known in the memory of man, set out from
the church at Lourdes to the Grotto. At its
head marched the troops, decked in all the éclat
of military splendour; following these came the
confraternities of Lourdes, and corporations from
neighbouring departments, carrying their cross
and banners; next were the Congregation of the
Children of Mary, dressed in white; the Sisters
of Nevers in their long black veils; the Sisters of
Charity; the Sisters of St. Joseph; the Religious
Orders of men, the Carmes, Christian Brothers,

&c.; a prodigious multitude of pilgrims, men, women, and children, to the number of from fifty to sixty thousand, ranged in two interminable files, and extending along the flowery road that led to the illustrious rocks of Massabielle. From time to time the popular enthusiasm burst forth in a chorus of voices and musical instruments. Closing the procession, and surrounded by four hundred priests, with the dignitaries and chapter of his cathedral church, came Monseigneur Bertrand Sévère Laurence, Bishop of Tarbes, in his mitre and pontifical robes, with one hand blessing the people, the other resting on his crosier.

On this day of solemn triumph, the venerated Cure of Lourdes lay on his bed of suffering, attacked by, it was thought, a mortal illness. As the procession went by, he attempted to rise, but his strength failed, and he had not even a passing view of this longed-for spectacle. Bernadette was also absent from illness. In sending her this trial, God gave her a proof of His predilection; and, fearing perhaps the temptation of vain-glory, Providence withdrew her from the scene where her name was repeated amidst the acclamations of thousands, and where she would have heard her eulogy from the lips of preachers in ardent addresses from the pulpit. As her parents were too indigent to have her properly tended at home, Bernadette had been transported to the hospital, where she lay on a humble pallet at the charity of the public, amidst those poor that this passing world would term unfortunate, but that Jesus Christ has blessed, declaring them to be the inheritors of His eternal kingdom.

Eleven years have elapsed since the Apparitions of the Most Holy Virgin. The vast temple is nearly completed, and for a long time the Holy Sacrifice has been celebrated at all the altars of the subterranean crypt. Close by, there is a house for the missionary priests, who have been appointed by the bishop to preach the Word of God, and to dispense the sacraments to the pilgrims. These last have increased in numbers to an extent perhaps hitherto unexampled, for never, until our epoch, have these vast movements had at their disposition the means of transport invented by modern science. The railroad of the Pyrenees, that originally was marked out in a more direct and less costly line from Tarbes to Pau, has taken a *detour* in order to pass by Lourdes, where it brings an incessant crowd of travellers, not only from the various provinces of France, but also from England, Belgium, Spain, Russia and Germany. From America in the far west, pious Christians have traversed the ocean to kneel before these celebrated Rocks that the Mother of God has sanctified by her presence.

Nearly all the personages named in the course of this history are living, with the exception of the Prefect, Baron Massy, the Judge Duprat, the Mayor Lacadé, and M. Fould, who are dead. Several have made a step in advance on the road to fortune. M. Rouland has ceased to be Minister of Public Worship, for which office it appears he was little suited; he now administers ingots of gold at the Bank of France. M. Dutour, *Procureur Impérial*, has become *Conseiller à la Cour.* M. Jacomet is chief Commissary in one of the

27

principal towns of the empire. Bourriette, Croisine Bouhohorts and her son, Madam Rizan, Henri Busquet, Mademoiselle de Lezenay, the widow Crozat, Jules Lacassagne, all whose cures have been recounted by M. Lasserre, are alive and well. Dr. Dozous is still the most eminent physician of Lourdes. Dr. Vergez is the physician at Baréges, and can attest to the visitors of those celebrated baths the miracles he has witnessed. M. Estrade, the impartial observer, whose impressions have been more than once related, is at Bordeaux, Rue Ducau 14. Monseigneur Laurence is still Bishop of Tarbes. The Prelate's faculties are not diminished by age. His lordship possesses a house near the Grotto, where he retires occasionally to meditate upon the great duties and responsibilities of a Christian bishop, whose diocese had received a grace so marvellous. The Abbé Peyramale has recovered from the dangerous malady already mentioned. He is ever the venerated pastor of this Christian town of Lourdes, where his power for good is marked in indelible traces.

Louise Soubirous, mother of Bernadette, died the 8th of December, 1866, the feast of the Immaculate Conception. While millions of francs are being given to complete the Church above the Grotto, the miller Soubirous is still a poor and hard-working man. His daughter Marie, who was with Bernadette when the first Apparition appeared, has married a good peasant, a miller, who works with his father-in-law. The other companion of the child, Jeanne Abadie, is a servant at Bordeaux.

Bernadette is no longer at Lourdes. She has

taken the veil of the Sisters of Charity and Christian Instruction at Nevers, and devotes herself to tending the sick in the hospitals. Her name in religion is Sister Mary-Bernard. Although she is now twenty-five years of age, her face preserves her child-like character and expression; there is about her a fragrance of peaceful innocence, an indescribable charm that belongs not to this earth. Beyond this there is nothing extraordinary to distinguish her, nothing that could make one suppose she had received so great a mission from on high. The enthusiasm of the multitude has not had more effect in troubling her soul than would the waters of a torrent to tarnish during an hour or a century the imperishable purity of the diamond.

Visited no longer by radiant Apparitions, she has instead the visitation of frequent and severe suffering, which she endures with a gentle patience and almost with joy. She never alludes to the divine favours of which she has been the object, unless questioned on the subject. She was the Virgin's witness. Now that she has fulfilled her message, she has retreated into the obscurity of religious life; retired in her cell or absorbed in the care of the sick, she has closed her ear to the tumult of earth, and avoids all that could recall to her mind the celebrity of her name. This history that we have written, and that speaks so much of Bernadette, Sister Mary-Bernard will never read.